Tolley's
Capital Gains Tax
Workbook
2002/03

by

David Smailes FCA
Kevin Walton BA(Hons)

Members of the LexisNexis Group worldwide

United Kingdom	LexisNexis Butterworths Tolley, a Division of Reed Elsevier (UK) Ltd, Halsbury House, 35 Chancery Lane, LONDON, WC2A 1EL, and 4 Hill Street, EDINBURGH EH2 3JZ
Argentina	LexisNexis Argentina, BUENOS AIRES
Australia	LexisNexis Butterworths, CHATSWOOD, New South Wales
Austria	LexisNexis Verlag ARD Orac GmbH & Co KG, VIENNA
Canada	LexisNexis Butterworths, MARKHAM, Ontario
Chile	LexisNexis Chile Ltda, SANTIAGO DE CHILE
Czech Republic	NakladatelstviOrac sro, PRAGUE
France	Editions du Juris-Classeur SA, PARIS
Hong Kong	LexisNexis Butterworths, HONG KONG
Hungary	HVG-Orac, BUDAPEST
India	LexisNexis Butterworths, NEW DELHI
Ireland	Butterworths (Ireland) Ltd, DUBLIN
Italy	Giuffré Editore, MILAN
Malaysia	Malayan Law Journal Sdn Bhd, KUALA LUMPUR
New Zealand	LexisNexis Butterworths, WELLINGTON
Poland	Wydawnictwa Prawnicze LexisNexis, WARSAW
Singapore	LexisNexis Butterworths, SINGAPORE
South Africa	LexisNexis Butterworths, DURBAN
Switzerland	Stämpfli Verlag AG, BERNE
USA	LexisNexis, DAYTON, Ohio

© Reed Elsevier (UK) Ltd 2002

All rights reserved. No part of this publication may be reproduced in any material form (including photocopying or storing it in any medium by electronic means and whether or not transiently or incidentally to some other use of this publication) without the written permission of the copyright owner except in accordance with the provisions of the Copyright, Designs and Patents Act 1988 or under the terms of a licence issued by the Copyright Licensing Agency Ltd, 90 Tottenham Court Road, London, England W1T 4LP. Applications for the copyright owner's written permission to reproduce any part of this publication should be addressed to the publisher.

Warning: The doing of an unauthorised act in relation to a copyright work may result in both a civil claim for damages and criminal prosecution.

Any Crown copyright material is reproduced with the permission of the Controller of Her Majesty's Stationery Office. Any European material in this work which has been reproduced from EUR-lex, the official European Communities legislation website, is European Communities copyright.

A CIP Catalogue record for this book is available from the British Library.

ISBN 0 7545 1731 4

Typeset by Interactive Sciences Ltd, Gloucester
Printed by Antony Rowe Ltd, Chippenham, Wilts

Visit Butterworths LexisNexis *direct* at www.butterworths.com

About This Book

Tolley's Capital Gains Tax Workbook illustrates the practical application of UK capital gains tax and corporation tax on chargeable gains legislation through worked examples. The computations aid understanding of complex areas of the law and provide guidance on layout. Detailed explanatory notes and statutory references are provided wherever appropriate. The comprehensive index and table of statutes make it easy to find a particular computation quickly.

The Workbook is designed to be used on its own or in conjunction with Tolley's Capital Gains Tax, and so the chapters follow the order of the commentary in that volume.

This 2002/03 edition is fully up to date and includes the provisions of Finance Act 2002. Cross-references prefixed 'IT' and 'CT' refer to the companion volumes Tolley's Income Tax Workbook 2002/03 and Tolley's Corporation Tax Workbook 2002/03.

Comments and suggestions for improvements are always welcome.

LEXISNEXIS BUTTERWORTHS TOLLEY

Abbreviations and References

ABBREVIATIONS

ACT	=	Advance Corporation Tax
Art	=	Article
b/f	=	brought forward
C/A	=	Court of Appeal
CCAB	=	Consultative Committee of Accountancy Bodies
C/D	=	Chancery Division
c/f	=	carried forward
CGT	=	Capital Gains Tax
CGTA	=	Capitals Gains Tax Act 1979
CT	=	Corporation Tax
DTR	=	Double Tax Relief
EIS	=	Enterprise Investment Scheme
ESC	=	Extra-Statutory Concession
FA	=	Finance Act
F(No 2)A	=	Finance (No 2) Act
FIFO	=	First In, First Out
FYA	=	First-Year Allowance
H/L	=	House of Lords
HMIT	=	Her Majesty's Inspector of Taxes
ICTA	=	Income and Corporation Taxes Act 1988
IRPR	=	Inland Revenue Press Release
IT	=	Income Tax
LIFO	=	Last In, First Out
NBV	=	Net Book Value
para	=	paragraph
PAYE	=	Pay As You Earn
P/e	=	Period ended
Reg	=	Regulation
s	=	section
SC/S	=	Scottish Court of Session
Sch	=	Schedule
Sec	=	Section
SI	=	Statutory Instrument
SSAP	=	Statement of Standard Accounting Practice
TCGA	=	Taxation of Chargeable Gains Act 1992
TMA	=	Taxes Management Act 1970
Y/e	=	Year ended

REFERENCES

STC	=	Simon's Tax Cases, (Butterworth & Co (Publishers) Ltd, Halsbury House, 35 Chancery Lane, London, WC2A 1EL)
TC	=	Official Tax Cases, (H.M. Stationery Office, P.O. Box 276, SW8 5DT)

Contents

CHAPTER		PAGE
201	Annual Rates and Exemptions	2
202	Anti-Avoidance	5
203	Assets held on 6 April 1965	10
204	Assets held on 31 March 1982	26
205	Companies	32
206	Disposal	34
207	Enterprise Investment Scheme	48
208	Exemptions and Reliefs	53
209	Hold-Over Reliefs	56
210	Indexation	66
211	Interest on Overpaid Tax	74
212	Interest and Surcharges on Unpaid Tax	75
213	Land	76
214	Losses	90
215	Married Persons	94
216	Mineral Royalties	97
217	Offshore Settlements	99
218	Overseas Matters	104
219	Partnerships	109
220	Private Residences	116
221	Qualifying Corporate Bonds	121
222	Retirement Relief	124
223	Rollover Relief — Replacement of Business Assets	140
224	Settlements	149
225	Shares and Securities	157
226	Shares and Securities — Identification Rules	180
227	Taper Relief	189
228	Wasting Assets	197
	Table of Statutes	201
	Index	207

201.1 Annual Rates and Exemptions

201 Annual Rates and Exemptions

201.1 **GAINS CHARGEABLE AT INCOME TAX RATES** [*TCGA 1992, s 4; F(No 2)A 1997, s 34, Sch 4 para 24; FA 1998, s 120, Sch 27 Pt III(29); FA 1999, s 26; FA 2000, s 37*]

M, a single person and established sole trader, had trading income of £15,000 for the year ended 30 April 2002, but made a trading loss of £11,000 for the year ended 30 April 2003. He had no other source of income, but realised a capital gain (after taper relief) of £38,600 in 2002/03 from the sale of a country cottage. He claims relief for the trading loss under *ICTA 1988, s 380(1)(b)* against his income for 2002/03.

M's income tax position for 2002/03 is as follows

	£
Schedule D, Case I	15,000
Less: Loss relief	11,000
	4,000
Less: Personal allowance (maximum £4,615)	4,000
Taxable income	Nil

His capital gains tax computation is as follows

	£
Gain	38,600
Annual exemption	7,700
Gain chargeable to tax	£30,900

Capital gains tax payable	£
1,920 at 10%	192.00
27,980 at 20%	5,596.00
1,000 at 40%	400.00
£30,900	£6,188.00

Notes

(a) For 1999/2000 and subsequent years, an individual's gains are chargeable at a rate equivalent to the lower rate of income tax (20%). However, to the extent if any that gains, if treated as the top slice of income, exceed the basic rate limit (£29,900 for 2002/03), they are chargeable at 40%. For 2000/01 and subsequent years, the 10% starting rate of income tax also applies to gains to the extent that, again if treated as though they were the top slice of taxable income, they fall within the starting rate band (£1,920 for 2002/03).

(b) The unused personal allowance of £615 is not available to reduce the chargeable gain. If M's trading losses had exceeded his total income, he could have claimed, under *FA 1991, s 72*, to have the gain reduced by the unused losses (see IT 10.2 LOSSES).

Annual Rates and Exemptions 201.2

201.2 **ANNUAL EXEMPTION** [*TCGA 1992, s 2(2)(4)–(8), s 3; FA 1998, s 121(3)(4), Sch 21 paras 2, 3; FA 2002, s 51, Sch 11 paras 2, 7, 8*]

(A) Interaction with losses

For 2002/03, R has chargeable gains (after indexation but before taper relief) of £14,900 and allowable losses of £4,000. He also has allowable losses of £11,000 brought forward.

	£
Adjusted net gains (£14,900 − £4,000)	10,900
Losses brought forward (part)	3,200
	7,700
Annual exempt amount	7,700
Taxable gains	Nil
Losses brought forward	11,000
Less utilised in 2002/03	3,200
Losses carried forward	£7,800

Note

(*a*) TAPER RELIEF (227), if otherwise available in respect of the 2002/03 chargeable gains, is effectively lost as the taxable gains are reduced to nil in any case.

(B) Interaction with losses and settlement gains attributed under *TCGA 1992, s 87*

(i)

For 2002/03, P has the same gains and losses (including brought-forward losses) as R above, but is also a beneficiary of an offshore trust. Trust gains of £8,300 are attributed to her for 2002/03 under *TCGA 1992, s 87*.

	£
Adjusted net gains (£14,900 − £4,000 + £7,700 (note (*a*))	18,600
Losses brought forward (part)	10,900
	7,700
Annual exempt amount	7,700
	Nil
Add: section 87 gains not brought in above	600
Taxable gains	£600
Losses brought forward	11,000
Less utilised in 2002/03	10,900
Losses carried forward	£100

201.2 Annual Rates and Exemptions

(ii)
Q is in the same position as P except that his attributed gains are only £6,300.

	£
Adjusted net gains (£14,900 − £4,000 + £6,300)	17,200
Losses brought forward (part)	9,500
	7,700
Annual exempt amount	7,700
Taxable gains	Nil
Losses brought forward	11,000
Less utilised in 2002/03	9,500
Losses carried forward	£1,500

Notes

(a) Attributed gains (as in (b) below) are included in adjusted net gains *only* to the extent that they do not exceed the annual exempt amount. Such gains cannot be covered by personal losses and will already have been reduced by any taper relief available to the trustees. The exempt amount is effectively allocated to attributed gains in priority to personal gains.

(b) For the purposes of (a) above, 'attributed gains' include non-resident settlement gains attributed to a beneficiary under *TCGA 1992, s 87* (as in this example) and those similarly attributed under *TCGA 1992, s 89(2)*. For years before 2003/04, unless, in relation to gains accruing in any one or more of the years 2000/01 to 2002/03 inclusive, an election is made under *FA 2002, Sch 11 para 8* to enable the set-off of personal losses against them (see 214.2 LOSSES), 'attributed gains' also include gains charged on a settlor under *TCGA 1992, s 77* (UK settlement) or *s 86* (non-resident settlement).

202 Anti-Avoidance

202.1 VALUE SHIFTING [TCGA 1992, s 29]

Jak owns all the 1,000 £1 ordinary shares of K Ltd. The shares were acquired on subscription in 1978 for £1,000 and had a value of £65,250 on 31 March 1982. In December 2002, the trustees of Jak's family settlement subscribed at par for 250 £1 ordinary shares in K Ltd, thereby acquiring 20% of the voting power in the company.

It is agreed that the value per share of Jak's holding immediately before the December 2002 share issue was £175 and immediately afterwards was £150. The value per share of the trust's holding, on issue, was £97 per share.

The proceeds of the deemed disposal are computed as follows

Value passing out of Jak's 1,000 shares is £25,000 (1,000 × £25 per share (£175 − £150)).

Value passing into the trust's 250 shares is £24,250 (250 × £97 per share) *less* the subscription price paid of £250 (250 × £1 per share) = £24,000.

The proceeds of the deemed disposal are equal to the value passing into the new shares, i.e. £24,000. (The trust's acquisition cost is £24,250, i.e. actual plus deemed consideration given.)

The disposal is a part disposal (see 206.2 DISPOSAL), the value of the part retained being £150,000 (1,000 × £150 per share).

Jak will have a capital gain for 2002/03 as follows (subject to indexation allowance to April 1998 and TAPER RELIEF (227))

	£
Proceeds of deemed disposal	24,000
Allowable cost $\dfrac{24,000}{24,000 + 150,000} \times £65,250$	9,000
Unindexed gain	£15,000

Note

(a) The legislation taxes the amount of value passing *into* the transferee holdings, not (if different) the amount passing from the transferor. The deemed proceeds are thus equal to the value received by the transferee(s). See Revenue Capital Gains Manual CG 58855.

202.2 VALUE-SHIFTING TO GIVE TAX-FREE BENEFIT [TCGA 1992, s 30, Sch 11 para 10(1); FA 1996, Sch 20 paras 46, 47(a)]

M owns the whole of the issued share capital in C Ltd, an unquoted company. He is also a director of the company. M receives an offer from a public company for his shares. Prior to sale, C Ltd pays M £30,000 for loss of his office as director. M then sells the shares for £100,000.

On the sale of M's shares, the Revenue may seek to adjust the consideration in computing M's chargeable gain on the grounds that M has received a tax-free benefit and the value of his shares has thereby been materially reduced.

202.3 Anti-Avoidance

202.3 **VALUE SHIFTING: DISTRIBUTION WITHIN A GROUP FOLLOWED BY A DISPOSAL OF SHARES** [*TCGA 1992, ss 30, 31, Sch 11 para 10(2); FA 1996, Sch 20 paras 46, 47(a)*]
Topco Ltd owns 100% of A Ltd, which owns 100% of B Ltd. Both A and B were acquired for negligible amounts. A bought some land in 1991 for a relatively small sum. It is now worth £100,000. In an attempt to realise the proceeds of the land at a tax saving, Topco arranges for B to borrow £100,000. In June 2002, A sells the land to B for this amount, and A, which previously had no undistributed reserves, then pays a dividend of £100,000 to Topco. Topco then sells all of its shares in A Ltd to an unconnected person at their market value which is now a nominal sum.

On the sale of the A Ltd shares, the Revenue may seek to apply *TCGA 1992, ss 30, 31* to increase the consideration on the sale by Topco Ltd to £100,000.

202.4 **ASSETS DISPOSED OF IN A SERIES OF TRANSACTIONS** [*TCGA 1992, ss 19, 20*]
L purchased a set of 6 antique chairs in June 1990 at a cost of £12,000. He gave 2 chairs to his daughter in February 1997, another pair to his son in November 1999, and sold the final pair to his brother for their market value in August 2002.

The market value of the chairs at the relevant dates were

	2 chairs £	4 chairs £	6 chairs £
February 1997	6,000	14,000	26,000
November 1999	7,800	18,000	34,200
August 2002	10,400	24,000	46,200

Indexation factors are

June 1990 – February 1997	0.223
June 1990 – April 1998	0.283

The capital gains tax computations are as follows

February 1997
Disposal to daughter

Deemed consideration	£6,000

As the consideration does not exceed £6,000, the disposal is covered by the chattel exemption (see note (*a*)).

November 1999
(i) *1996/97 disposal to daughter recomputed*

Original market value (deemed disposal consideration at February 1997)	£6,000
Reasonable proportion of aggregate market value as at February 1997 of all assets disposed of to date £14,000 × $\frac{2}{4}$	£7,000

6

	£
Deemed consideration (greater of £6,000 and £7,000)	7,000
Cost $\dfrac{7,000}{7,000 + 14,000} \times £12,000$	4,000
Unindexed gain	3,000
Indexation allowance £4,000 × 0.223	892
Chargeable gain 1996/97	£2,108

(ii) *1999/2000 disposal to son*

Original market value (deemed disposal consideration)	£7,800
Reasonable proportion of aggregate market value as at November 1999 of all assets disposed of to date £18,000 × $\frac{2}{4}$	£9,000

	£
Deemed consideration (greater of £7,800 and £9,000)	9,000
Cost $\dfrac{9,000}{9,000 + 7,800} \times (£12,000 - £4,000)$	4,286
Unindexed gain	4,714
Indexation allowance £4,286 × 0.283	1,213
Chargeable gain 1999/2000	£3,501

August 2002

(i) *Gain on 1996/97 disposal to daughter recomputed*

Original market value (deemed consideration in recomputation at November 1999)	£7,000
Reasonable proportion of aggregate market value as at February 1997 of all assets disposed of to date £26,000 × $\frac{2}{6}$	£8,667

	£
Deemed consideration (greater of £7,000 and £8,667)	8,667
Cost $\dfrac{8,667}{8,667 + 14,000} \times £12,000$	4,588
Unindexed gain	4,079
Indexation allowance £4,588 × 0.223	1,023
Revised chargeable gain 1996/97	£3,056

202.4 Anti-Avoidance

(ii) *Gain on 1999/2000 disposal to son recomputed*

Original market value (deemed consideration in computation at November 1999)	£9,000
Reasonable proportion of aggregate market value as at November 1999 of all assets disposed of to date £34,200 × $\frac{2}{6}$	£11,400
	£
Deemed consideration (greater of £9,000 and £11,400)	11,400
Cost $\frac{11,400}{11,400 + 7,800}$ × (£12,000 − £4,588)	4,401
Unindexed gain	6,999
Indexation allowance £4,401 × 0.283	1,245
Revised chargeable gain 1999/2000	£5,754

(iii) *Gain on 2002/03 disposal to brother*

Original market value (actual consideration)	£10,400
Reasonable proportion of aggregate market value as at August 2002 of all assets disposed of to date £46,200 × $\frac{2}{6}$	£15,400
	£
Deemed consideration (greater of £10,400 and £15,400)	15,400
Cost (£12,000 − £4,588 − £4,401)	3,011
Unindexed gain	12,389
Indexation allowance £3,011 × 0.283 (note (*d*))	852
Chargeable gain 2001/02 (subject to TAPER RELIEF (227))	£11,537

Notes

(*a*) The disposal in February 1997 is at first covered by the chattel exemption of £6,000. As the second disposal in November 1999 is to a person connected with the recipient of the first disposal, the two must then be looked at together for the purposes of the chattel exemption, and, as the combined proceeds exceed the chattel exemption limit, the exemption is not available. [*TCGA 1992, s 262*]. See also 208.1(C) EXEMPTIONS AND RELIEFS.

(*b*) The three disposals are linked transactions within *TCGA 1992, s 19* as they are made by the same transferor to persons with whom he is connected, and take place within a six-year period.

(*c*) It is assumed in the above example that it is 'reasonable' to apportion the aggregate market value in proportion to the number of items. In other instances a different basis may be needed to give the 'reasonable' apportionment required by *TCGA 1992, s 20(4)*.

(*d*) Other than for the purposes of corporation tax on chargeable gains, indexation allowance is frozen at its April 1998 level. Therefore, the indexation factor for April 1998 is used in respect of disposals in a later month (and expenditure incurred in April 1998 or later does not attract indexation allowance at all). See 210 INDEXATION.

202.5 **DEPRECIATORY TRANSACTIONS: GROUPS OF COMPANIES** [*TCGA 1992, s 176; FA 1996, Sch 20 para 57*]

G Ltd owns 100% of the share capital of Q Ltd, which it acquired in June 1989 for £75,000. Q Ltd owns land which it purchased in 1985 for £50,000. In 1994, the land, then with a market value of £120,000, was transferred to G Ltd for £50,000. In April 2002, Q Ltd was put into liquidation, and G Ltd received liquidation distributions totalling £30,000.

The loss on the Q Ltd shares is £45,000 (£75,000 – £30,000). The Revenue are likely to disallow the whole or part of the loss on the grounds that it resulted from the depreciatory transaction involving the transfer of land at less than market value.

203.1 Assets held on 6 April 1965

203 Assets held on 6 April 1965

203.1 QUOTED SHARES AND SECURITIES [*TCGA 1992, s 109(4)(5), Sch 2 paras 1–8; FA 1996, Sch 21 para 42(1)(2)*]

(A) Basic computation of gain

H acquired 3,000 U plc ordinary shares in 1962 for £15,000. Their market value was £10 per share on 6 April 1965 and £12 per share on 31 March 1982. In September 2002, H sells 2,000 of the shares for £30 per share. The indexation factor for March 1982 to April 1998 is 1.047 (see note (*e*)).

	£	£	£
Sale proceeds	60,000	60,000	60,000
Cost	10,000		
6 April 1965 value		20,000	
31 March 1982 value			24,000
Unindexed gain	50,000	40,000	36,000
Indexation allowance:			
£24,000 × 1.047	25,128	25,128	25,128
Indexed gain	£24,872	£14,872	£10,872

Chargeable gain (subject to TAPER RELIEF (227)) £10,872

Notes

(*a*) The comparison is firstly between the gain arrived at by deducting cost and that arrived at by deducting 6 April 1965 value. The smaller of the two gains is taken. If, however, an election had been made under either *TCGA 1992, Sch 2 para 4* or *TCGA 1992, s 109(4)* for 6 April 1965 value to be used in computing all gains and losses on quoted shares held at that date, this comparison need not be made and the taxable gain, subject to (*b*) below, would be £14,872.

(*b*) The second comparison is between the figure arrived at in (*a*) above and the gain using 31 March 1982 value. As the latter is smaller, it is substituted for the figure in (*a*) above by virtue of *TCGA 1992, s 35(2)*. If, however, an election had been made under *TCGA 1992, s 35(5)* for 31 March 1982 value to be used in computing all gains and losses on assets held at that date, neither this comparison nor that in (*a*) above need be made and the taxable gain would still be £10,872.

(*c*) Indexation is based on 31 March 1982 value in all three calculations as this gives the greater allowance. [*TCGA 1992, s 55(1)(2)*].

(*d*) All comparisons are between gains *after* indexation and *before* taper relief.

(*e*) Other than for the purposes of corporation tax on chargeable gains, indexation allowance is frozen at its April 1998 level. Therefore, the indexation factor for April 1998 is used in respect of disposals in a later month (and expenditure incurred in April 1998 or later does not attract indexation allowance at all). See 210 INDEXATION.

(B) Basic computation—no gain/no loss disposals

J acquired a holding of quoted shares in 1956 for £1,000. The market value of the holding at 6 April 1965 and 31 March 1982 respectively was £19,000 and £20,000. J sells the holding in September 2002 for £18,000. The indexation factor for the period March 1982 to April 1998 is 1.047.

(i) Assuming no elections made to use 1965 value or 1982 value

	£	£
Sale proceeds	18,000	18,000
Cost	1,000	
6 April 1965 value		19,000
Unindexed gain/(loss)	17,000	(1,000)
Indexation allowance:		
£20,000 × 1.047 (see below) = £20,940 but restricted to	17,000	—
Indexed gain/(loss)	Nil	£(1,000)
Chargeable gain/allowable loss		Nil

As one computation shows no gain/no loss and the other a loss, the disposal is a no gain/no loss disposal. [*TCGA 1992, Sch 2 para 2(1)*]. There is no need to compute the gain or loss using 31 March 1982 value as re-basing cannot disturb a no gain/no loss position. [*TCGA 1992, s 35(3)(c)*]. Other than for the purposes of corporation tax on chargeable gains, indexation allowance is frozen at its April 1998 level. Therefore, the indexation factor for April 1998 is used in respect of disposals in a later month (and expenditure incurred in April 1998 or later does not attract indexation allowance at all). See 210 INDEXATION.

(ii) Election made to use 6 April 1965 value

	£	£
Sale proceeds	18,000	18,000
6 April 1965 value	19,000	
31 March 1982 value		20,000
(Loss)	(1,000)	(2,000)
Allowable loss	£1,000	

The allowable loss is £1,000 as re-basing cannot increase a loss. [*TCGA 1992, s 35(3)(b)*].

(iii) Election made to use 31 March 1982 value

There is an allowable loss of £2,000.

203.1 Assets held on 6 April 1965

(C) Parts of holding acquired at different times
L has the following transactions in shares of A plc, a quoted company

Date	Number of shares bought/(sold)	Cost/(proceeds) £
9.1.57	1,500	1,050
10.11.62	750	600
15.7.69	1,200	3,000
12.10.80	1,400	5,000
16.12.83	850	5,950
17.9.95	1,150	5,200
19.12.02	(6,000)	(63,000)
	850	

Market value of A shares at 6 April 1965 was £1.60
Market value of A shares at 31 March 1982 was £4.00

Indexation factors		
March 1982 to April 1998 (note (c))		1.047
December 1983 to April 1985		0.091
April 1985 to September 1995		0.589
September 1995 to April 1998 (note (c))		0.080

(i) No election made to substitute 1965 market value

Identify 6,000 shares sold on a LIFO basis as follows

Section 104 holding

	Shares	Qualifying Expenditure £	Indexed Pool £
16.12.83 acquisition	850	5,950	5,950
£5,950 × 0.091			541
6.4.85 pool	850	5,950	6,491
Indexed rise: April 1985 to September 1995			
£6,491 × 0.589			3,823
17.9.95 acquisition	1,150	5,200	5,200
	2,000	11,150	15,514
Indexed rise: September 1995 to April 1998			
£15,514 × 0.080			1,241
			16,755
19.12.02 disposal	(2,000)	(11,150)	(16,755)
Balance of pool	—	—	—

	£
Sale proceeds (2,000 × £10.50)	21,000
Cost (as above)	11,150
Unindexed gain	9,850
Indexation allowance (£16,755 − £11,150)	5,605
Chargeable gain (subject to TAPER RELIEF (227))	£4,245

Assets held on 6 April 1965   203.1

		£	£
1982 holding			
Sale proceeds (1,200 + 1,400) × £10.50		27,300	27,300
Cost (£3,000 + £5,000)		8,000	
Market value 31.3.82 (2,600 × £4)			10,400
Unindexed gain		19,300	16,900
Indexation allowance £10,400 × 1.047		10,889	10,889
Gain after indexation		£8,411	£6,011
Chargeable gain (subject to TAPER RELIEF (227))			£6,011

	£	£	£
10.11.62 acquisition			
Sale proceeds (750 × £10.50)	7,875	7,875	7,875
Cost	600		
Market value 6.4.65 (750 × £1.60)		1,200	
Market value 31.3.82 (750 × £4)			3,000
Unindexed gain	7,275	6,675	4,875
Indexation allowance £3,000 × 1.047	3,141	3,141	3,141
Gain after indexation	£4,134	£3,534	£1,734
Chargeable gain (subject to TAPER RELIEF (227))			£1,734

	£	£	£
9.1.57 acquisition (part)			
Sale proceeds (650 × £10.50)	6,825	6,825	6,825
Cost (650 × £0.70)	455		
Market value 6.4.65 (650 × £1.60)		1,040	
Market value 31.3.82 (650 × £4)			2,600
Unindexed gain	6,370	5,785	4,225
Indexation allowance £2,600 × 1.047	2,722	2,722	2,722
Gain after indexation	£3,648	£3,063	£1,503
Chargeable gain (subject to TAPER RELIEF (227))			£1,503

Summary of chargeable gains	Number of shares	Chargeable gain £
Section 104 holding	2,000	4,245
1982 holding	2,600	6,011
10.11.62 acquisition	750	1,734
9.1.57 acquisition (part)	650	1,503
	6,000	£13,493

Remaining shares
850 acquired on 9.1.57 for £595

203.1 Assets held on 6 April 1965

(ii) Election made to substitute 1965 market value

Identify 6,000 shares on a LIFO basis as follows

Section 104 holding
Disposal of 2,000 shares as in (i) above   £4,245

1982 holding	Shares		Pool cost
			£
9.1.57	1,500 × £1.60		2,400
10.11.62	750 × £1.60		1,200
15.7.69	1,200		3,000
12.10.80	1,400		5,000
	4,850		11,600
19.12.02 disposal	4,000	4,000/4,850 × £11,600	9,567
Remaining shares	850		£2,033

	£	£
Sale proceeds (4,000 × £10.50)	42,000	42,000
Cost (as above)	9,567	
Market value 31.3.82 (4,000 × £4)		16,000
Unindexed gain	32,433	26,000
Indexation allowance £16,000 × 1.047	16,752	16,752
Gain after indexation	£15,681	£9,248

Chargeable gain (subject to TAPER RELIEF (227))   £9,248

Summary of chargeable gains/allowable losses	Number of shares	Chargeable gain/(loss)
		£
Section 104 holding	2,000	4,245
1982 holding	4,000	9,248
	6,000	£13,493

Notes

(*a*)   Because re-basing to 31 March 1982 applies in this case, the result is the same whether or not the election to substitute 6 April 1965 value has been made, but with a lower 31 March 1982 value the computations could produce differing overall gains/losses.

(*b*)   Note that indexation is based on 31 March 1982 value whenever this gives the greater allowance, and that comparisons are made between gains *after* indexation and *before* taper relief.

(*c*)   Other than for the purposes of corporation tax on chargeable gains, indexation allowance is frozen at its April 1998 level. Therefore, the indexation factor for April 1998 is used in respect of disposals in a later month (and expenditure incurred in April 1998 or later does not attract indexation allowance at all). See 210 INDEXATION.

Assets held on 6 April 1965   203.2

(d) See 226.1 SHARES AND SECURITIES (IDENTIFICATION RULES) for rules for matching disposals after 5 April 1998 with acquisitions after that date (not illustrated in this example).

203.2 **LAND REFLECTING DEVELOPMENT VALUE** [*TCGA 1992, Sch 2 paras 9–15*]
K sells a building plot, on which planning permission has just been obtained, in November 2002 for £200,000. He acquired the plot by gift from his father in 1958 when its value was £2,000. The market value was £5,000 at 6 April 1965 and £10,000 at 31 March 1982, and the current use value in November 2002 is £15,000. The indexation factor for March 1982 to April 1998 is 1.047 (see note (d)).

	£	£	£
Sale proceeds	200,000	200,000	200,000
Cost	2,000		
Market value 6.4.65		5,000	
Market value 31.3.82			10,000
Unindexed gain	198,000	195,000	190,000
Indexation allowance £10,000 × 1.047	10,470	10,470	10,470
Gain after indexation	£187,530	£184,530	£179,530
Chargeable gain (subject to TAPER RELIEF (227))			£179,530

Notes

(a) Time apportionment would have substantially reduced the gain of £187,530, using cost, such that re-basing to 31 March 1982 would have given a greater gain than that based on cost and would not therefore have applied. However, as the plot has been sold for a price in excess of its current use value, no time apportionment can be claimed.

(b) Gains must be compared after applying the indexation allowance, which is based on 31 March 1982 value, this being greater than either cost or 6 April 1965 value.

(c) Other than for the purposes of corporation tax on chargeable gains, indexation allowance is frozen at its April 1998 level. Therefore, the indexation factor for April 1998 is used in respect of disposals in a later month (and expenditure incurred in April 1998 or later does not attract indexation allowance at all). See 210 INDEXATION.

(d) In this case, the gain is computed in accordance with the rules in 204 ASSETS HELD ON 31 MARCH 1982 as the gain by reference to 31 March 1982 value is lower than the gain by reference to 6 April 1965 value which in turn is lower than the gain by reference to cost.

203.3 Assets held on 6 April 1965

203.3 **OTHER ASSETS** [*TCGA 1992, Sch 2 paras 16–19; FA 1996, Sch 21 para 42(1)(3)*]

(A) Chattels
M inherited a painting on the death of his mother in 1940, when it was valued for probate at £5,000. On 5 October 2002 he sold the painting for £270,000 net. The painting's value was £130,000 at 6 April 1965, but only £125,000 at 31 March 1982. The indexation factor for March 1982 to April 1998 is 1.047 (see note (*e*)).

(i) Time apportionment

Period of ownership since 6 April 1945	(note (*a*))	57 years 6 months
Period of ownership since 6 April 1965		37 years 6 months

	£
Unindexed gain (£270,000 – £5,000)	265,000
Indexation allowance £125,000 × 1.047 (note (*b*))	130,875
	£134,125

Gain after indexation £134,125 × $\dfrac{37y\ 6m}{57y\ 6m}$ (note (*c*))   £87,473

(ii) Election for 6.4.65 value

	£
Sale proceeds	270,000
Market value 6.4.65	130,000
Unindexed gain	140,000
Indexation allowance £130,000 × 1.047 (note (*b*))	136,110
Gain after indexation	£3,890

Election for 6.4.65 value is beneficial, subject to re-basing.

(iii) Re-basing to 1982

	£
Sale proceeds	270,000
Market value 31.3.82	125,000
Unindexed gain	145,000
Indexation allowance £130,000 × 1.047 (note (*b*))	136,110
Gain after indexation	£8,890

Re-basing cannot increase a gain. [*TCGA 1992, s 35(3)(a)*]. **Therefore, the gain of £3,890 stands** (subject to TAPER RELIEF (227), and see note (*d*)) **and the election for 6.4.65 value is beneficial.**

Notes
(*a*) Under time apportionment, the period of ownership is limited to that after 5 April 1945.

(*b*) In (i) above, indexation is based on 31.3.82 value, being greater than cost — it cannot be based on 6 April 1965 value as this does not enter into the calculation. In (ii), indexation is on the higher of 31.3.82 value and 6.4.65 value. This is also the case in (iii) as one is comparing the position using 6.4.65 value and 31.3.82 value. See *TCGA 1992, s 55(1)(2)*.

Assets held on 6 April 1965   203.3

(c) The time apportionment calculation is applied to the gain *after* indexation (*Smith v Schofield* HL 1993, 65 TC 669, [1993] STC 268).

(d) Taper relief should be computed by reference to the *chargeable* gain. Therefore, if time apportionment had produced the lower gain (disregarding taper relief at this stage), it is the time-apportioned gain that would be tapered. This is because taper relief comes after all other reliefs apart from the annual exemption. [*TCGA 1992, s 2A(1)(2); FA 1998, s 121(1)(4)*].

(e) Other than for the purposes of corporation tax on chargeable gains, indexation allowance is frozen at its April 1998 level. Therefore, the indexation factor for April 1998 is used in respect of disposals in a later month (and expenditure incurred in April 1998 or later does not attract indexation allowance at all). See 210 INDEXATION.

(B) Land and buildings

X acquired land on 5 June 1960 as a distribution in specie on liquidation of his company. The value of the land was then £7,250. He acquired access land adjoining the property for £2,750 on 1 January 1961 and, having obtained planning consent, on 30 July 1963 incurred expenditure of £15,000 in building houses on the land, which were let. On 6 September 2002, X sells the houses with vacant possession for £300,000, net of expenses. The value of the houses and land is £20,000 at 6 April 1965 and £100,000 at 31 March 1982. The indexation factor for March 1982 to April 1998 is 1.047 (see note (*e*)).

The gain using time apportionment is

	£	£
Net proceeds of sale		300,000
Deduct Cost of land	7,250	
Cost of addition	2,750	
Cost of building	15,000	25,000
Unindexed gain		275,000
Indexation allowance £100,000 × 1.047		104,700
Gain after indexation		£170,300

Apportion to allowable expenditure   (note (*c*))

	£	£
(i) Land $\dfrac{7{,}250}{25{,}000} \times £170{,}300$	49,387	
Time apportion £49,387 × $\dfrac{37\text{y 5m}}{42\text{y 3m}}$		43,738
(ii) Addition $\dfrac{2{,}750}{25{,}000} \times £170{,}300$	18,733	
Time apportion £18,733 × $\dfrac{37\text{y 5m}}{41\text{y 8m}}$		16,822
		c/f £60,560

203.3 Assets held on 6 April 1965

	£	£
		b/f 60,560
(iii) Building $\dfrac{15,000}{25,000} \times £170,300$	102,180	
Time apportion $£102,180 \times \dfrac{3\text{/y }5\text{m}}{39\text{y }1\text{m}}$		97,824
Gain after indexation and time apportionment		£158,384

The gain using re-basing to 1982 is

	£
Net proceeds of sale	300,000
Market value at 31.3.82	100,000
Unindexed gain	200,000
Indexation allowance	
£100,000 × 1.047	104,700
Gain	£95,300

Chargeable gain (subject to TAPER RELIEF (227), and see note (*d*))	£95,300

Notes

(*a*) An election for 6 April 1965 valuation could not be favourable, even were it not for the effect of re-basing, as the value is less than historic costs.

(*b*) It is the gain/loss *after* time apportionment that is compared with the gain/loss produced by re-basing. [*TCGA 1992, Sch 3 para 6*].

(*c*) The time apportionment calculation is applied to the gain *after* indexation (*Smith v Schofield* HL 1993, 65 TC 669, [1993] STC 268).

(*d*) Taper relief should be computed by reference to the *chargeable* gain. Therefore, if time apportionment had produced the lower gain (disregarding taper relief at this stage), it is the time-apportioned gain that would be tapered. This is because taper relief comes after all other reliefs apart from the annual exemption. [*TCGA 1992, s 2A(1)(2); FA 1998, s 121(1)(4)*].

(*e*) Other than for the purposes of corporation tax on chargeable gains, indexation allowance is frozen at its April 1998 level. Therefore, the indexation factor for April 1998 is used in respect of disposals in a later month (and expenditure incurred in April 1998 or later does not attract indexation allowance at all). See 210 INDEXATION.

Assets held on 6 April 1965 203.3

(C) Unquoted shares

On 6 April 1952, A acquired 5,000 shares in C Ltd, an unquoted company, for £15,201. At 6 April 1965, the value of the holding was £15,000. A sells the shares (his entire holding in the company) on 6 April 2002 for £75,000. The indexation factor for the period March 1982 to April 1998 is 1.047 (note (b)). No election for universal 31 March 1982 re-basing is made but the market value of the holding at that date is agreed at £17,000.

The gain using time apportionment is as follows

Total period of ownership:	50 years	
Period after 6 April 1965:	37 years	
		£
Proceeds		75,000
Cost		15,201
Unindexed gain		59,799
Indexation allowance:		
31.3.82 value £17,000 × 1.047		17,799
Gain after indexation		£42,000
Gain after time apportionment: £42,000 × 37/50		£31,080

The gain with an election to use 6.4.65 value is as follows

	£
Proceeds	75,000
6.4.65 value	15,000
Unindexed gain	60,000
Indexation allowance:	
31.3.82 value £17,000 × 1.047	17,799
Gain after indexation	£42,201

The gain with re-basing to 1982 is as follows

	£
Proceeds	75,000
31.3.82 value	17,000
Unindexed gain	58,000
Indexation allowance:	
31.3.82 value £17,000 × 1.047	17,799
Gain after indexation	£40,201

Time apportionment is more beneficial than an election for 6 April 1965 value. Re-basing does not apply as it cannot increase a gain. The chargeable gain is therefore **£31,080** (subject to TAPER RELIEF (227), and see note (*a*)).

Notes
(*a*) Taper relief should be computed by reference to the *chargeable* gain. Therefore, if, as in this example, time apportionment produces the lower gain (disregarding taper relief in making the comparison), it is the time-apportioned gain that is tapered. This is because taper relief comes after all other reliefs apart from the annual exemption. [*TCGA 1992, s 2A(1)(2); FA 1998, s 121(1)(4)*]. See generally 227 TAPER RELIEF.

19

203.3 Assets held on 6 April 1965

(b) Other than for the purposes of corporation tax on chargeable gains, indexation allowance is frozen at its April 1998 level. See 210 INDEXATION.

(D) Unquoted shares — share exchange before 6 April 1965 [*TCGA 1992, Sch 2 para 19(1)(3)*]

N purchased 5,000 £1 ordinary shares in R Ltd, an unquoted company, on 1 January 1961. The purchase price was £3 per share, a total of £15,000. On 1 December 1964, R Ltd was acquired by D Ltd, an unquoted company, as a result of which N received 10,000 8% convertible preference shares in D Ltd in exchange for his holding of R shares. In November 2002, N sold the D Ltd shares for £4.45 per share. The market value of the D Ltd shares was £2.03 per share at 6 April 1965 but only £1.50 per share at 31 March 1982. The indexation factor for March 1982 to April 1998 is 1.047 (see note (*e*)).

The gain, disregarding re-basing, is

		£
Disposal consideration 10,000 at £4.45		44,500
Allowable cost	10,000 at £2.03	20,300
Unindexed gain		24,200
Indexation allowance £20,300 × 1.047		21,254
Gain after indexation		£2,946

The gain using re-basing to 1982 is

	£
Disposal consideration (as above)	44,500
Market value 31.3.82 10,000 at £1.50	15,000
Unindexed gain	29,500
Indexation allowance £20,300 × 1.047	21,254
Gain after indexation	£8,246

The overall result is

	£
Chargeable gain (subject to TAPER RELIEF (227))	£2,946

Notes

(a) Subject to re-basing, allowable cost *must* be taken as 6.4.65 value.

(b) Indexation is based on the greater of 31.3.82 value and 6.4.65 value. [*TCGA 1992, s 55(1)(2)*].

(c) Where the effect of re-basing would be to increase a gain, re-basing does not apply. [*TCGA 1992, s 35(3)(a)*].

(d) By concession (ESC D10), CGT is not charged on a disposal of the *entire* new shareholding on more than the actual gain realised, i.e. by reference to original cost but without time apportionment.

(e) Other than for the purposes of corporation tax on chargeable gains, indexation allowance is frozen at its April 1998 level. Therefore, the indexation factor for April 1998 is used in respect of disposals in a later month (and expenditure incurred in April 1998 or later does not attract indexation allowance at all). See 210 INDEXATION.

Assets held on 6 April 1965   203.3

(E) Unquoted shares — share exchange after 5 April 1965 [*TCGA 1992, Sch 2 para 19(2)(3)*]

S acquired 10,000 £1 ordinary shares in L Ltd at their probate value of £5,000 on 31 May 1959. The shares are not quoted, and their value at 6 April 1965 was £6,000. On 1 September 1989, the shares were acquired by R plc, in exchange for its own ordinary shares on the basis of 1 for 2. The offer valued L ordinary shares at £2.23 per share. In February 2003, S sells his 5,000 R shares for £8.60 per share. The agreed value of the L Ltd shares at 31 March 1982 was £2.05 per share.

Indexation factors	March 1982 to September 1989	0.468
	September 1989 to April 1998 (note (*c*))	0.395
	March 1982 to April 1998 ((note (*c*))	1.047

The gain without re-basing to 1982 is computed as follows

(i) Using time apportionment

Deemed disposal at 1.9.89:

	£
Proceeds (market value £2.23 × 10,000)	22,300
Cost	5,000
Unindexed gain	17,300
Indexation allowance	
MV 31.3.82 10,000 × £2.05 × 0.468	9,594
Gain after indexation	£7,706

Gain after time apportionment:

$£7,706 \times \dfrac{24y\ 5m}{30y\ 3m}$ £6,220

Actual disposal in February 2002:

	£
Proceeds 5,000 × £8.60	43,000
Deemed acquisition cost at 1.9.89	22,300
Unindexed gain	20,700
Indexation allowance £22,300 × 0.395	8,809
Gain after indexation	£11,891

Total gain 2001/02 £(6,220 + 11,891)	£18,111

(ii) With election for 6.4.65 value

	£
Disposal consideration	43,000
Allowable cost	6,000
Unindexed gain	37,000
Indexation allowance 10,000 × £2.05 × 1.047	21,463
Gain	£15,537

Subject to re-basing, the election is beneficial.

203.3 Assets held on 6 April 1965

The gain using re-basing to 1982 is

	£
Disposal consideration	43,000
Market value 31.3.82 10,000 × £2.05	20,500
Unindexed gain	22,500
Indexation allowance £20,500 × 1.047	21,463
Gain after indexation	£1,037

The overall result is

Chargeable gain (subject to TAPER RELIEF (227))	£1,037

Re-basing applies as it produces a smaller gain than that using 6 April 1965 value.

Notes

(a) The deemed disposal on 1 September 1989 is *only* for the purposes of *TCGA 1992, Sch 2 para 16* (time apportionment).

(b) If an election is made for 6 April 1965 value, no valuation is required at 1 September 1989.

(c) Other than for the purposes of corporation tax on chargeable gains, indexation allowance is frozen at its April 1998 level. Therefore, the indexation factor for April 1998 is used in respect of disposals in a later month (and expenditure incurred in April 1998 or later does not attract indexation allowance at all). See 210 INDEXATION.

Assets held on 6 April 1965 203.3

(F) Part disposals after 5 April 1965 [*TCGA 1992, s 42, Sch 2 para 16(8)*]
H bought land for £15,000 on 31 October 1960. Its value at 6 April 1965 was £17,200. On 1 February 1988, H sold part of the land for £50,000, the balance being then worth £200,000. On 9 April 2002, H gives the remaining land to his daughter. Its value is then £300,000. The agreed value of the total estate at 31 March 1982 was £150,000 and H made a claim on the February 1988 disposal for that value to be used for indexation purposes under the law then in force.

Indexation factors	March 1982 to February 1988	0.305
	March 1982 to April 1998 (note (*e*))	1.047

1988 disposal

	£
Proceeds of part disposal	50,000
Deduct allowable cost $\dfrac{50,000}{50,000 + 200,000} \times £15,000$	3,000
Unindexed gain	47,000
Indexation allowance £150,000 $\times \dfrac{50,000}{50,000 + 200,000} = £30,000$	
£30,000 × 0.305	9,150
Gain after indexation	£37,850

Time apportionment

Chargeable gain $\dfrac{22\text{y } 10\text{m}}{27\text{y } 3\text{m}} \times £37,850$ £31,715

If an election were made to substitute 6 April 1965 valuation, the computation would be

	£
Proceeds of part disposal	50,000
Deduct allowable cost $\dfrac{50,000}{50,000 + 200,000} \times £17,200$	3,440
Unindexed gain	46,560
Indexation allowance £150,000 $\times \dfrac{50,000}{50,000 + 200,000} = £30,000$	
£30,000 × 0.305	9,150
Chargeable gain	£37,410

An election would not be beneficial.

203.3 Assets held on 6 April 1965

2002 disposal

The gain without re-basing to 1982 is as follows

Computation of entire gain over period of ownership:

	£
Proceeds	300,000
Cost £(15,000 − 3,000)	12,000
Unindexed gain	288,000
Indexation allowance	
MV 31.3.82 £(150,000 − 30,000) × 1.047	125,640
Gain after indexation	£162,360(A)

Computation of gain for period 31.10.60 − 1.2.88:

	£
Market value at date of part disposal	200,000
Cost £(15,000 − 3,000)	12,000
Unindexed gain	188,000
Indexation allowance £(150,000 − 30,000) × 0.305	36,600
Gain after indexation	£151,400(B)

Time apportionment £151,400 × $\dfrac{22y\ 10m}{27y\ 3m}$	£126,861(C)
Balance of gain (1.2.88 to 9.4.02) ((A) − (B))	£10,960(D)
Chargeable gain (subject to re-basing) ((C) + (D))	£137,821

The gain using re-basing to 1982 is as follows

	£
Disposal proceeds	300,000
Market value 31.3.82 £150,000 × $\dfrac{12,000}{15,000}$ (note (*b*))	120,000
Unindexed gain	180,000
Indexation allowance £120,000 × 1.047	125,640
Gain after indexation	£54,360

The overall result is

Chargeable gain (subject to TAPER RELIEF (227))	£54,360

Re-basing applies as it produces neither a larger gain nor a loss.

Assets held on 6 April 1965   203.3

Notes

(*a*) The deemed disposal on 1 February 1988 is only for the purposes of *TCGA 1992, Sch 2 para 16(3)–(5)* (time apportionment). For re-basing purposes, the asset is still regarded as having been held at 31 March 1982.

(*b*) Where there has been a part disposal after 31 March 1982 and before 6 April 1988 of an asset held at 31 March 1982, the proportion of 31 March 1982 value to be brought into account in the re-basing calculation is that which the cost previously unallowed bears to the total cost, giving the same effect as if re-basing had applied to the part disposal. [*TCGA 1992, Sch 3 para 4(1)*].

(*c*) The Revenue will also accept an alternative basis of calculation on the part disposal of land. Under this method, the part disposed of is treated as a separate asset and any fair and reasonable method of apportioning part of the total cost to it will be accepted e.g. a reasonable valuation of that part at the acquisition date. (Revenue Statement of Practice SP D1.)

(*d*) The time apportionment calculation is applied to the gain *after* indexation (*Smith v Schofield HL 1993, 65 TC 669, [1993] STC 268*).

(*e*) Other than for the purposes of corporation tax on chargeable gains, indexation allowance is frozen at its April 1998 level. See 210 INDEXATION.

204.1 Assets held on 31 March 1982

204 Assets held on 31 March 1982

204.1 GENERAL COMPUTATION OF GAINS/LOSSES [*TCGA 1992, s 35, Sch 3*]

(A)
Rodney purchased a painting on 1 October 1979 for £50,000 (including costs of acquisition) and sold it at auction for £160,000 (net of selling expenses) on 15 August 2002 (his only disposal in 2002/03). Its value at 31 March 1982 was £70,000 and the indexation factor for the period March 1982 to April 1998 is 1.047 (see note (*f*)).

	£	£
Net sale proceeds	160,000	160,000
Cost	50,000	
Market value 31.3.82		70,000
Unindexed gain	110,000	90,000
Indexation allowance £70,000 × 1.047	73,290	73,290
Gain after indexation	£36,710	£16,710

	£
Chargeable gain (subject to taper relief)	16,710
Deduct Taper Relief	
(£16,710 @ 15% — non-business asset held 4 + 1 years)	2,507
Chargeable gain	£14,203

Notes

(*a*) The asset is deemed to have been sold and immediately re-acquired at its market value at 31 March 1982. [*TCGA 1992, s 35(1)(2)*].

(*b*) Re-basing does not apply if it would produce a larger gain or larger loss than would otherwise be the case, nor if it would turn a gain into a loss or vice versa, nor if the disposal would otherwise be a no gain/no loss disposal. [*TCGA 1992, s 35(3)(4)*].

(*c*) An *irrevocable* election may be made to treat, broadly speaking, *all* assets held on 31 March 1982 as having been sold and re-acquired at their market value on that date, in which case the restrictions in (*b*) above will not apply. [*TCGA 1992, s 35(5)*]. If the election had been made in this example, the gain would still be £16,710, but there would have been no need to compute the gain by reference to cost and make a comparison with that using re-basing.

There are some minor exclusions from the rule that the election must extend to all assets. [*TCGA 1992, Sch 3 para 7*]. There are also special rules for groups of companies. [*TCGA 1992, Sch 3 paras 8, 9*].

(*d*) Indexation is automatically based on 31 March 1982 value, without the need to claim such treatment, unless a greater allowance would be produced by reference to cost. [*TCGA 1992, s 55(1)(2)*]. See also 210.1(C) INDEXATION.

(*e*) See also 203 ASSETS HELD ON 6 APRIL 1965 for the general application of the re-basing provisions to such assets. See 210.2(A)(C) INDEXATION for the position as regards an asset acquired by means of a no gain/no loss transfer from a person who held it at 31 March 1982.

(*f*) Other than for the purposes of corporation tax on chargeable gains, indexation allowance is frozen at its April 1998 level. Therefore, the indexation factor for April 1998 is used in respect of disposals in a later month. See 210 INDEXATION.

Assets held on 31 March 1982 204.1

(B)
The facts are as in (A) above, except that net sale proceeds amount to £60,000.

	£	£
Net sale proceeds	60,000	60,000
Cost	50,000	
Market value 31.3.82		70,000
Unindexed gain/(loss)	10,000	(10,000)
Indexation allowance (as in (A)) but restricted to	10,000	—
Gain/(loss)	Nil	£(10,000)
Chargeable gain/(allowable loss)		Nil

Notes
(a) Re-basing does not apply as it cannot disturb a no gain/no loss position. [*TCGA 1992, s 35(3)(c)*].

(b) An election under *TCGA 1992, s 35(5)* would produce an allowable loss of £10,000 (but must extend to all assets).

(C)
The facts are as in (A) above, except that net sale proceeds amount to £135,000.

	£	£
Net sale proceeds	135,000	135,000
Cost	50,000	
Market value 31.3.82		70,000
Unindexed gain	85,000	65,000
Indexation allowance (as in (A))	73,290	
Indexation allowance (as in (A)) but restricted to		65,000
Gain	£11,710	Nil
Chargeable gain/(allowable loss)		Nil

Note
(a) Re-basing applies as it produces a no gain/no loss position compared to a gain otherwise.

204.1 Assets held on 31 March 1982

(D)
Albert acquired a holding of D plc quoted shares for £11,000 net in January 1980. At 31 March 1982, their value had fallen to £8,000. On 29 April 2002, Albert sold the entire holding for £25,000 net (his only disposal in 2002/03). The indexation factor for the period March 1982 to April 1998 (note (*d*)) is 1.047.

	£	£
Proceeds	25,000	25,000
Cost	11,000	
Market value 31.3.82		8,000
Unindexed gain	14,000	17,000
Indexation allowance £11,000 × 1.047	11,517	11,517
Gain after indexation	£2,483	£5,483

	£
Chargeable gain (subject to taper relief)	2,483
Deduct Taper Relief	
(£2,483 @ 15% — non-business asset held 4 + 1 years)	372
Chargeable gain	£2,111

Notes
(*a*) Re-basing does not apply as its effect would be to increase a gain.

(*b*) Indexation is based on cost as that is greater than 31 March 1982 value.

(*c*) If a universal re-basing election had been made (under *TCGA 1992, s 35(5)*), the chargeable gain (before taper relief) would have been £5,483.

(*d*) Other than for the purposes of corporation tax on chargeable gains, indexation allowance is frozen at its April 1998 level. See 210 INDEXATION.

(E)
Cassandra acquired a holding of E Ltd shares for £14,000 net in January 1980. At 31 March 1982, their value stood at £17,000. Cassandra sold the shares in April 2002 for £10,000 net.

	£	£
Proceeds	10,000	10,000
Cost	14,000	
Market value 31.3.82		17,000
Unindexed loss (no indexation due)	£4,000	£7,000
Allowable loss	£4,000	

Notes
(*a*) Re-basing does not apply as its effect would be to increase a loss.

(*b*) Indexation is not available in either calculation as it cannot increase a loss.

(*c*) If a universal re-basing election had been made (under *TCGA 1992, s 35(5)*), the allowable loss would have been £7,000, but the election must extend to all assets.

Assets held on 31 March 1982   204.2

204.2 **DEFERRED CHARGES ON GAINS BEFORE 31 MARCH 1982** [*TCGA 1992, s 36, Sch 4*]

Kirk purchased 3,000 unquoted ordinary shares in W Limited for £18,000 on 1 January 1980 and later gave them to his son, Michael, claiming gifts hold-over relief under legislation then in force. Michael sells the shares for £50,000 (net) on 10 June 2002. The shares had a value of £22,000 at 31 March 1982.

Assuming the gift to have taken place on

    (i)   1 February 1982 (market value of shares £21,000),
    (ii)   30 April 1994 (market value £42,000), and
    (iii)   1 June 1985 (market value £30,000),

the capital gains position is as set out below. The relevant indexation factors are

March 1982 to June 1985	0.202
March 1982 to April 1994	0.815
March 1982 to April 1998 (note (*e*))	1.047
June 1985 to April 1998 (note (*e*))	0.704
April 1994 to April 1998 (note (*e*))	0.128

(i) Gift on 1 February 1982

Kirk's chargeable gain (deferred) (£21,000 − £18,000)		£3,000
Michael's acquisition cost (£21,000 − £3,000)		£18,000

Michael's chargeable gain is

	£	£
Proceeds 10.6.02	50,000	50,000
Cost (as above)	18,000	
Market value 31.3.82		22,000
Unindexed gain	32,000	28,000
Indexation allowance £22,000 × 1.047	23,034	23,034
Gain after indexation	£8,966	£4,966
Chargeable gain 2002/03 (note (*f*))		£4,966

The deferred gain of £3,000 effectively falls out of charge as Michael held the shares at 31.3.82 and thus receives the benefit of re-basing to 1982.

(ii) Gift on 30 April 1994

Kirk's chargeable gain is

	£	£
Disposal value	42,000	42,000
Cost	18,000	
Market value 31.3.82		22,000
Unindexed gain	24,000	20,000
Indexation allowance £22,000 × 0.815	17,930	17,930
Gain after indexation	£6,070	£2,070
Chargeable gain (deferred)		£2,070

204.2 Assets held on 31 March 1982

Michael's chargeable gain is

	£	£
Proceeds 10.6.02		50,000
Cost	42,000	
Deduct deferred gain	2,070	
	39,930	
Indexation allowance £39,930 × 0.128	5,111	45,041
Chargeable gain 2002/03 (note (*f*))		£4,959

Michael cannot re-base to 1982 as he did not hold the shares at 31.3.82. However, as the deferred gain was itself computed by reference to the 31.3.82 value, he has effectively received full relief for the uplift in value between 1.1.80 and 31.3.82. The small difference between his gain of £4,959 and that of £4,966 in (i) above is due to the rounding of indexation factors to three decimal places.

(iii) Gift on 1 June 1985

Kirk's chargeable gain is

	£	£
Disposal value		30,000
Cost	18,000	
Indexation allowance £22,000 × 0.202	4,444	22,444
Chargeable gain (deferred)		£7,556

It is assumed that a claim would have been made to base indexation on the 31.3.82 value, this being greater than cost.

Michael's chargeable gain is

	£	£
Proceeds 10.6.02		50,000
Cost	30,000	
Deduct one-half of deferred gain £7,556 × ½	3,778	
	26,222	
Indexation allowance £26,222 × 0.704	18,460	44,682
Chargeable gain 2002/03 (note (*f*))		£5,318

Michael cannot benefit from re-basing to 1982 as he did not hold the shares at 31.3.82, nor is the deferred gain itself calculated by reference to the re-basing rules as the disposal (i.e. the gift) took place before 6.4.88. Under *TCGA 1992, s 36, Sch 4 para 1(a), para 2*, the deduction in respect of a deferred gain is halved where the deferral took place after 31.3.82 and before 6.4.88 and was, wholly or partly, in respect of a chargeable gain accruing on an asset held at 31.3.82, thus giving some relief, albeit on an arbitrary basis.

Notes
(*a*)   A claim for the deduction to be halved must be made by the first anniversary of 31 January following the year of assessment in which the ultimate disposal takes place. [*TCGA 1992, Sch 4 para 9; FA 1996, Sch 21 para 43*].

(*b*)   These provisions apply not only to gifts hold-over relief but to a number of situations in which gains are held over or rolled over, as listed in *TCGA 1992, Sch 4 para 2(5)*, of which the other most common example is rollover relief on

Assets held on 31 March 1982 204.2

      replacement of business assets under *TCGA 1992, s 152*. [*TCGA 1992, Sch 4 para 1(a), para 2*].

(*c*)   There are special rules where the disposal giving rise to the deferral is preceded by a no gain/no loss disposal (as defined by *TCGA 1992, s 35(3)(d)*) and where the ultimate disposal is preceded by a no gain/no loss disposal. [*TCGA 1992, Sch 4 paras 5–7*].

(*d*)   See 209 HOLD-OVER RELIEFS and 223 ROLLOVER RELIEF for the general application of these reliefs.

(*e*)   Other than for the purposes of corporation tax on chargeable gains, indexation allowance is frozen at its April 1998 level. Therefore, the indexation factor for April 1998 is used in respect of disposals in a later month (and expenditure incurred in April 1998 or later does not attract indexation allowance at all). See 210 INDEXATION.

(*f*)   In all cases, the 2002/03 chargeable gain is subject to TAPER RELIEF (227), which is given by reference to the *donee's* post-5 April 1998 period of ownership.

205.1 Companies

205 Companies

Cross-references. See also CT 104 CAPITAL GAINS.

205.1 CAPITAL LOSSES

P Ltd, which makes up accounts to 30 June annually, changes its accounting date to 31 December. It makes up 18-month accounts to 31 December 2002, and its chargeable gains and allowable losses are as follows

	Gains/(losses) £
31.7.01	4,600
19.10.01	11,500
1.12.01	3,500
28.3.02	(8,300)
21.7.02	8,500
1.9.02	(25,000)
20.12.02	7,000

The period of account is split into two accounting periods

1.7.01 – 30.6.02
Net chargeable gain £11,300
1.7.02 – 31.12.02
Net allowable loss £9,500

Notes

(*a*) The loss cannot be set off against the £11,300 net gain in the earlier accounting period (but *can* be carried forward against subsequent gains).

(*b*) For a further example, see CT 104.1 CAPITAL GAINS.

205.2 SHARES — ACQUISITIONS AND DISPOSALS WITHIN SHORT PERIOD [*TCGA 1992, s 106; FA 2000, Sch 29 para 18*]

S Ltd has the following transactions in shares in Q plc, a quoted company with share capital of £1m divided into 25p ordinary shares.

	Date	Number of shares	Price £
Purchase	1.6.99	100,000	62,000
Purchase	1.8.02	50,000	49,000
Sale	15.8.02	80,000	60,000
Purchase	31.8.02	50,000	35,000

The position is as follows

The shares sold on 15.8.02 are identified with the two purchases on 1.8.02 and 31.8.02 (in that order).

£

(i) Purchase on 1.8.02

	£
Proceeds $\frac{50,000}{80,000} \times £60,000$	37,500
Cost	49,000
Allowable loss	£11,500

(ii) Purchase on 31.8.02

	£
Proceeds $\frac{30,000}{80,000} \times £60,000$	22,500
Cost $\frac{30,000}{50,000} \times £35,000$	21,000
Chargeable gain	£1,500

	£
Net allowable loss on transaction	£10,000

Notes

(*a*) Where a company disposes of shares (including securities other than gilt-edged securities) and acquires similar shares within one month before or after the disposal through a stock exchange or within six months in other circumstances, the shares acquired and disposed of are matched. For these rules to apply, the number of shares held at some time in the one month (or six months) before the disposal must be not less than 2% of the number issued. Shares acquired within one month (or six months) before or after the disposal are called 'available shares'.

(*b*) Subject to *TCGA 1992, s 105* (matching of same day acquisitions and disposals), disposals are identified first from 'available shares', taking acquisitions before the disposal (latest first) before acquisitions after the disposal (earliest first). Once all 'available shares' have been matched with the disposal, the identification of any remaining shares disposed of follows the ordinary rules.

206.1 Disposal

206 Disposal

206.1 ALLOWABLE AND NON-ALLOWABLE EXPENDITURE

(A) Allowable expenditure [*TCGA 1992, s 38*]

In 2002/03 T sold a house which he had owned since 1991 and which was let throughout the period of ownership (other than as furnished holiday accommodation). The house cost £34,000, with legal costs of £900, in June 1991. T spent £2,000 on initial dilapidations in July 1991. In November 1998, he added an extension at a cost of £5,500 for which he received a local authority grant of £2,500 on completion. Legal costs of £500 were incurred on obtaining vacant possession at the end of the final tenancy in May 2002. The sale proceeds were £70,000 before deducting incidental costs (including valuation fees) of £1,200. There are no other disposals in 2002/03.

Indexation factors	June 1991 to April 1998 (note (*b*))			0.213	
	July 1991 to April 1998			0.215	

			£	£	£
Sale proceeds				70,000	
Deduct Costs of sale				1,200	68,800
Cost of house				34,000	
Add Incidental costs of purchase				900	
				34,900	
Improvement costs:					
Initial dilapidations	(note (*a*))		2,000		
Extension, less grant			3,000	5,000	
Cost of obtaining vacant possession (enhancement cost)				500	40,400
Unindexed gain					28,400
Indexation allowance:					
£34,900 × 0.213				7,434	
£2,000 × 0.215				430	
					7,864
Pre-tapered gain					20,536
Deduct Taper relief £20,536 × 15%					
(non-business asset rate)					3,081
Chargeable gain 2002/03					£17,455

Notes

(*a*) It is assumed that the cost of the initial dilapidations were disallowed for Schedule A purposes under the rule in *Law Shipping Co Ltd v CIR, CS 1923, 12 TC 621* (but see Revenue Booklet IR 150, paras 154–156). If any of the expenditure had been so allowed, a deduction would to that extent be precluded as an allowable deduction for CGT purposes by *TCGA 1992, s 39*.

(*b*) Other than for the purposes of corporation tax on chargeable gains, indexation allowance is frozen at its April 1998 level and is not given at all on post-March 1998 expenditure. See 210 INDEXATION.

(B) Non-allowable expenditure — capital allowances [*TCGA 1992, s 41; FA 2000, Sch 29 para 12; CAA 2001, Sch 2 para 78*]

S Ltd acquired land in March 1997 for £90,000 on which it constructed a factory for use in its manufacturing trade. The cost of construction was £45,000 incurred in June 1997. In June 2002, the company sold the freehold factory for £140,000, of which £100,000 related to the land and £40,000 to the building. Industrial buildings allowances of £9,000 had been given and there was a balancing charge of £4,000. The indexation factor for the period March 1997 to June 2002 is 0.134.

	Land £	Building £	£
Disposal consideration	100,000		40,000
Allowable cost	90,000	45,000	
Deduct net allowances given		5,000	40,000
Unindexed gain	10,000		Nil
Indexation allowance £90,000 × 0.134 = £12,060, but restricted to	10,000		
Chargeable gain/(allowable loss)	Nil		Nil

206.2 PART DISPOSALS [*TCGA 1992, s 42*]

Note. See also 213.1 LAND for small part disposals of land.

(A)

T purchased a 300-acre estate in March 1988 for £1m plus legal and other costs of £50,000. In January 1991 he spent £47,000 on improvements to the main house on the estate (not his main residence), which he sells in September 2002 for £660,000. The costs of sale are £40,000. The value of the remaining land is £2.34m. The indexation factor from March 1988 to April 1998 is 0.562, and that for January 1991 to April 1998 is 0.249 (see note (*b*)).

	£	£
Sale proceeds		660,000
Deduct incidental costs		40,000
		620,000
Cost £1,050,000 × $\dfrac{660,000}{660,000 + 2,340,000}$	231,000	
Improvement costs	47,000	278,000
Unindexed gain		342,000
Indexation allowance:		
£231,000 × 0.562	129,822	
£47,000 × 0.249	11,703	141,525
Chargeable gain (subject to TAPER RELIEF (227))		£200,475

Notes

(*a*) The improvements expenditure is not apportioned as it relates entirely to the part of the estate being sold. [*TCGA 1992, s 42(4)*].

206.2 Disposal

(*b*) Other than for the purposes of corporation tax on chargeable gains, indexation allowance is frozen at its April 1998 level. Therefore, the indexation factor for April 1998 is used in respect of disposals in a later month (and expenditure incurred in April 1998 or later does not attract indexation allowance at all). See 210 INDEXATION.

(B)
U inherited some land at a probate value of £500,000 in November 1981. Its market value at 31 March 1982 was £540,000. In November 1987, he sold part of the land for £240,000, the remaining land then being worth £480,000. He sells the remaining land in April 2002 for £600,000 and elects under *TCGA 1992, s 35(5)* for all his assets held at 31 March 1982 to be treated as sold and re-acquired by him at their market value on that date.

The gain, subject to indexation, on the part disposal in November 1987 is

	£
Proceeds	240,000
Cost £500,000 × $\dfrac{240,000}{240,000 + 480,000}$	166,667
Gain subject to indexation	£73,333

The gain, subject to indexation and taper relief, on the disposal in April 2002 is

	£
Proceeds	600,000
Market value 31.3.82	
£540,000 × $\dfrac{480,000}{240,000 + 480,000}$	360,000
Gain subject to indexation to April 1998 and taper relief	£240,000

Note
(*a*) Where re-basing applies and there has been a part disposal after 31 March 1982 and before 6 April 1988, the proportion of 31 March 1982 value to be brought into account on the ultimate disposal is the same as the proportion of cost unallowed on the part disposal, as if the re-basing provisions had applied to the part disposal. [*TCGA 1992, Sch 3 para 4(1)*].

(C)
V bought the film rights of a novel for £50,000 in May 1997. A one-third share of the rights was sold to W Ltd in March 1998 for £20,000, when the rights retained had a value of £45,000. In December 2002, V's rights were sold to a film company for £100,000 plus a right to royalties, such right being estimated to be worth £150,000. The indexation factor for the periods May 1997 to March 1998 and May 1997 to April 1998 (see note (*b*)) are 0.025 and 0.036 respectively.

March 1998	£
Sale proceeds	20,000
Cost £50,000 × $\dfrac{20,000}{20,000 + 45,000}$	15,385
Unindexed gain	4,615
Indexation allowance £15,385 × 0.025	385
Chargeable gain 1997/98	£4,230

December 2002	£
Sale proceeds (£100,000 + £150,000)	250,000
Cost (£50,000 − £15,385)	34,615
Unindexed gain	215,385
Indexation allowance £34,615 × 0.036	1,246
Chargeable gain (subject to TAPER RELIEF (227))	£214,139

Notes

(*a*) The right to royalties is itself an asset and could be the subject of a future disposal by V. See 206.3(B) below and, where applicable, 228 WASTING ASSETS.

(*b*) Other than for the purposes of corporation tax on chargeable gains, indexation allowance is frozen at its April 1998 level. Therefore, the indexation factor for April 1998 is used in respect of disposals in a later month (and expenditure incurred in April 1998 or later does not attract indexation allowance at all). See 210 INDEXATION.

206.2 Disposal

(D)
C inherited land valued at £72,000 in May 1989. He granted rights of way over the land to a neighbouring landowner in March 1994, in consideration for a parcel of land adjacent to his, valued at £21,000. The value of the original land, subject to the right of way, was then £147,000. In March 2003, C sold the whole of the land for £170,000.

Indexation factors	May 1989 to March 1994	0.239
	May 1989 to April 1998 (note (*c*))	0.414
	March 1994 to April 1998 (note (*c*))	0.141

Part disposal in March 1994 £
Disposal consideration 21,000
Allowable expenditure

$$\frac{21{,}000}{21{,}000 + 147{,}000} \times £72{,}000 \qquad 9{,}000$$

Unindexed gain	12,000
Indexation allowance £9,000 × 0.239	2,151
Chargeable gain 1993/94	£9,849

Disposal in March 2003   £
Disposal consideration		170,000
Deduct Original land £(72,000 − 9,000)	63,000	
Addition	21,000	84,000
Unindexed gain		86,000
Indexation allowance		
(*a*) Original land £63,000 × 0.414	26,082	
(*b*) Addition £21,000 × 0.141	2,961	
		29,043
Chargeable gain (subject to TAPER RELIEF (227))		£56,957

Notes

(*a*) It is assumed that the additional land is merged with the existing land to give a single asset.

(*b*) A claim under *TCGA 1992, s 242* (small part disposals of land — see 213.1 LAND) could not be made in respect of the March 1994 part disposal as the consideration exceeded £20,000.

(*c*) Other than for the purposes of corporation tax on chargeable gains, indexation allowance is frozen at its April 1998 level. Therefore, the indexation factor for April 1998 is used in respect of disposals in a later month (and expenditure incurred in April 1998 or later does not attract indexation allowance at all). See 210 INDEXATION.

Disposal 206.3

206.3 CAPITAL SUMS DERIVED FROM ASSETS [*TCGA 1992, s 22(1)*]

(A) General

A Ltd holds the remainder of a 99-year lease of land, under which it has mineral rights. The lease, which commenced in 1986, was acquired in April 1995 by assignment for £80,000. Following a proposal to extract minerals, the freeholder pays A Ltd £100,000 in June 2002 in consideration of relinquishing the mineral rights, in order to prevent such development. The value of the lease after the alteration is £150,000.

	£
Disposal proceeds	100,000
Allowable cost $\dfrac{100,000}{100,000 + 150,000} \times £80,000$	32,000
Gain subject to indexation from April 1995 to June 2002	£68,000

(B) Deferred consideration

Z owns 2,000 £1 ordinary shares in B Ltd, for which he subscribed at par in August 1992. On 31 March 1997, he and the other shareholders in B Ltd sold their shares to another company for £10 per share plus a further unquantified cash amount calculated by means of a formula relating to the future profits of B Ltd. The value in March 1997 of the deferred consideration was estimated at £2 per share. On 30 April 2002, Z receives a further £4.20 per share under the sale agreement. The indexation factor for the period August 1992 to March 1997 is 0.119, and for the period March 1997 to April 1998 (note (*c*)) is 0.046.

1996/97

	£	£
Disposal proceeds 2,000 at £10	20,000	
Value of rights 2,000 at £2	4,000	24,000
Cost of acquisition		2,000
Unindexed gain		22,000
Indexation allowance £2,000 × 0.119		238
Chargeable gain		£21,762

2002/03

	£
Disposal of rights to deferred consideration	
Proceeds 2,000 × £4.20	8,400
Deemed cost of acquiring rights	4,000
Unindexed gain	4,400
Indexation allowance	
£4,000 × 0.046	184
Chargeable gain (subject to TAPER RELIEF (227))	£4,216

Notes

(*a*) A right to unquantified and contingent future consideration on the disposal of an asset is itself an asset, and the future consideration when received is a capital sum derived from that asset (*Marren v Ingles HL 1980, 54 TC 76* and *Marson v Marriage Ch D 1979, 54 TC 59*).

206.3 Disposal

(b) See 225.4(C) SHARES AND SECURITIES for position where deferred consideration is to be satisfied in shares and/or debentures in the acquiring company.

(c) Other than for the purposes of corporation tax on chargeable gains, indexation allowance is frozen at its April 1998 level. See 210 INDEXATION.

(C)
Suppose that in the previous example, the deferred consideration was valued at £4.20 per share in March 1997, but only £2 per share was received on 30 April 2002.

1996/97

	£	£
Disposal proceeds	20,000	
Value of rights	8,400	28,400
Cost of acquisition		2,000
Unindexed gain		26,400
Indexation allowance £2,000 × 0.119		238
Chargeable gain		£26,162

2002/03

	£
Disposal of rights 2,000 × £2	4,000
Deemed acquisition cost	8,400
Allowable loss	£4,400

Note

(a) There is no provision for reopening the 1996/97 assessment or setting off the 2002/03 loss against the 1996/97 gain.

Disposal 206.4

206.4 RECEIPT OF COMPENSATION [*TCGA 1992, ss 22, 23*]

(A)
C owns a freehold warehouse which is badly damaged by fire as a result of inflammable goods having been inadequately packaged. The value of the warehouse after the fire is £90,000, and it cost £120,000 in 1992. The owner of the goods is held liable for the damage and pays C £60,000 compensation in October 2002.

	£
Disposal proceeds	60,000
Allowable cost $\dfrac{60,000}{60,000 + 90,000} \times £120,000$	48,000
Chargeable gain 2002/03 subject to indexation to April 1998 and taper relief	£12,000

(B) Restoration using insurance moneys
A diamond necklace owned by D cost £100,000 in 1994. D is involved in a motor accident in which the necklace is damaged. Its value is reduced to £80,000. D receives £40,000 under an insurance policy in May 2002 and spends £45,000 on having the necklace restored.

(i) No claim under *TCGA 1992, s 23*

	£
Disposal proceeds	40,000
Allowable cost $\dfrac{40,000}{40,000 + 80,000} \times £100,000$	33,333
Chargeable gain 2002/03 subject to indexation to April 1998 and taper relief	£6,667
Allowable cost in relation to subsequent disposal £100,000 − £33,333 + £45,000	£111,667

(ii) Claim under *TCGA 1992, s 23*
No chargeable gain arises in 2002/03

Allowable cost originally	100,000
Deduct Amount received on claim	40,000
	60,000
Add Expenditure on restoration	45,000
Allowable cost in relation to subsequent disposal	£105,000

206.4 Disposal

(C) Part application of capital sum received
E Ltd is the owner of a large estate consisting mainly of parkland which he acquired for £150,000 in August 1990. It grants a one-year licence in August 2002 to an exploration company to prospect for minerals, in consideration for a capital sum of £50,000. The exploration proves unsuccessful and on expiry of the licence E Ltd spends £20,000 on restoration of the drilling sites to their former state. The market value of the estate after granting the licence is £350,000, and it is £400,000 after restoration.

(i) No claim under *TCGA 1992, s 23(3)*

	£
Disposal proceeds	50,000
Deduct Allowable cost $\dfrac{50,000}{50,000 + 350,000} \times £150,000$	18,750
Gain subject to indexation from August 1990 to August 2002	£31,250
Allowable expenditure remaining £150,000 − £18,750 + £20,000	£151,250

(ii) Claim made under *TCGA 1992, s 23(3)*

	£
Deemed disposal proceeds (£50,000 − £20,000)	30,000
Deduct Allowable cost $\dfrac{30,000}{30,000 + 400,000} \times £(150,000 + 20,000)$	11,860
Gain subject to indexation to August 2002	£18,140
Allowable expenditure remaining £150,000 − £20,000 − £11,860 + £20,000	£138,140

(D) Capital sum exceeding allowable expenditure
F inherited a painting in 1980 when it was valued at £2,000. Its value at 31 March 1982 was £3,000. In March 1987, by which time its value had increased considerably, the painting suffered damage whilst on loan to an art gallery and F received £10,000 compensation. The value of the painting was then £30,000. It then cost F £9,800 to have the painting restored. In June 2002, he sells the painting for £50,000.

(i) No election under *TCGA 1992, s 23(2)*

	£
Disposal proceeds March 1987	10,000
Allowable cost $\dfrac{10,000}{10,000 + 30,000} \times £2,000$	500
Gain subject to indexation 1986/87	£9,500
Allowable cost in relation to subsequent disposal £2,000 − £500 + £9,800	£11,300

	£	£
	------	------
Disposal proceeds June 2002	50,000	50,000
Allowable cost without re-basing	11,300	
Allowable cost with re-basing		
$£3,000 \times \dfrac{30,000}{10,000 + 30,000} = £2,250 + £9,800$		12,050
Gain subject to indexation 2002/03	£38,700	£37,950

It is clear that re-basing will apply and the pre-tapered gain will be £37,950 less indexation allowance to April 1998, based on £12,050.

(ii) Election under *TCGA 1992, s 23(2)*

	£
Disposal proceeds March 1987	10,000
Less allowable expenditure	2,000
Gain subject to indexation 1986/87	£8,000
Allowable cost in relation to subsequent disposal £2,000 − £2,000 + £9,800	£9,800

	£	£
Disposal proceeds June 2002	50,000	50,000
Allowable cost without re-basing	9,800	
Allowable cost with re-basing (note (*b*))		
£3,000 − £2,000 + £9,800		10,800
Gain subject to indexation 2002/03	£40,200	£39,200

Again, re-basing will clearly apply and the pre-tapered gain will be £39,200 less indexation allowance to April 1998, based on £10,800.

Notes

(*a*) Although not illustrated in this example, indexation allowance must be deducted before comparing the positions with and without re-basing in order to ascertain whether or not re-basing applies.

(*b*) Where there is a disposal after 5 April 1989 to which re-basing applies and, if re-basing had not applied, the allowable expenditure would have fallen to be reduced under *TCGA 1992, s 23(2)* by reference to a capital sum received after 31 March 1982 but before 6 April 1988, the 31 March 1982 value is reduced by the amount previously allowed against the capital sum. [*TCGA 1992, Sch 3 para 4(2)*].

(E) Indexation allowance and taper relief [*TCGA 1992, s 2A, s 53(1)(1A)(3), s 57; FA 1998, s 121, s 122(1)(6)(7); FA 2002, s 46*]

A owns a freehold factory which cost £100,000 in June 1987. Because of mining operations nearby, part of the factory is severely damaged by subsidence and has to be demolished and rebuilt. The value of the factory after the damage is £150,000. The risk is not covered under A's insurance policy but the mining company agrees to pay compensation of £50,000 in full settlement, received in February 1998. The cost of demolition and rebuilding is £60,000, incurred in May 1998. The factory is sold in March 2003 for £300,000. The factory is a business asset throughout for taper relief purposes.

206.4 Disposal

Indexation factors	June 1987 to February 1998	0.573
	June 1987 to April 1998 (note (c))	0.596
	February 1998 to April 1998 (note (c))	0.014

(i) No claim under *TCGA 1992, s 23(1)*

(a) Part disposal February 1998   £

Disposal proceeds	50,000
Deduct Allowable cost $\dfrac{50,000}{50,000 + 150,000} \times £100,000$	25,000
Unindexed gain	25,000
Indexation allowance £25,000 × 0.573	14,325
Chargeable gain 1997/98	£10,675

(b) Disposal March 2003

Disposal proceeds		300,000
Deduct Allowable cost		
£(100,000 − 25,000) + £60,000		135,000
Unindexed gain		165,000
Indexation allowance:		
original cost £(100,000 − 25,000) × 0.596	44,700	
rebuilding cost (note (c))	—	44,700
Pre-tapered gain		120,300
Deduct Taper relief £120,300 × 75% (note (a))		90,225
Chargeable gain 2002/03		£30,075

(ii) Claim under *TCGA 1992, s 23(1)*

(a) No chargeable gain in February 1998   £

Allowable cost	100,000
Rebuilding cost	60,000
	160,000
Deduct Receipt rolled over	50,000
Revised allowable cost	£110,000

(b) Disposal March 2003

Disposal proceeds		300,000
Deduct Allowable cost		110,000
Unindexed gain		190,000
Indexation allowance:		
original cost £100,000 × 0.596	59,600	
rebuilding cost (note (c))	—	
	59,600	
Deduct		
Receipt rolled over £50,000 × 0.014	(700)	58,900
Pre-tapered gain		131,100
Deduct Taper relief £131,100 × 75% (note (a))		98,325
Chargeable gain 2002/03		£32,775

Disposal 206.4

Notes

(*a*) Business asset taper relief (for disposals in 2002/03 onwards) is 75% — by reference to a qualifying holding period of two whole years or more after 5 April 1998. In practice, any losses on other 2002/03 disposals must be taken into account before taper relief is applied to the gain (see 227.1(B) TAPER RELIEF).

(*b*) Note that, as well as deferring what would have been the gain on the part disposal, the effect of the claim under *TCGA 1992, s 23(1)* in this case is to increase the quantum of taper relief available on the ultimate disposal.

(*c*) Other than for the purposes of corporation tax on chargeable gains, indexation allowance is frozen at its April 1998 level. Therefore, the indexation factor for April 1998 is used in respect of disposals in a later month, and expenditure incurred in April 1998 or later does not attract indexation allowance at all. See 210 INDEXATION.

206.5 Disposal

206.5 OPTIONS [*TCGA 1992, ss 44, 46, 144, 145; FA 1998, s 122(5)–(7)*]

Cross-reference. See also 228.2 WASTING ASSETS.

On 1 February 1998 F granted an option to G for £10,000 to acquire freehold land bought by F for £50,000 in September 1994. The option is for a period of 5 years, and the option price is £100,000 plus 1% thereof for each month since the option was granted. On 1 February 2000, G sold the option to H for £20,000. On 30 June 2002, H exercises the option and pays F £141,000 for the land. Neither G nor H intended to use the land for the purposes of a trade.

Indexation factors September 1994 to April 1998 (note (*c*)) 0.121
February 1998 to April 1998 0.014

1998 Grant of option by F

	£
Disposal proceeds	10,000
Allowable cost	—
Chargeable gain 1997/98	£10,000

2000 Disposal of option by G

	£	
Disposal proceeds		20,000
Allowable cost	10,000	
Less: Wasted — £10,000 × $\frac{2}{5}$	4,000	6,000
Unindexed gain		14,000
Indexation allowance £6,000 × 0.014		84
Chargeable gain 1999/2000		£13,916

2002 Exercise of option

	£
(i) Earlier assessment on F vacated	
(ii) Aggregate disposal proceeds (£10,000 + £141,000)	151,000
Allowable cost of land	50,000
Unindexed gain	101,000
Indexation allowance £50,000 × 0.121	6,050
Chargeable gain (on F) 2002/03 (subject to TAPER RELIEF (227))	£94,950

H's allowable expenditure is

	£
Cost of option (acquired February 2000, so no indexation due)	20,000
Cost of land (acquired June 2002, so no indexation due)	141,000
	£161,000

Notes

(*a*) The wasting asset rules (see 228 WASTING ASSETS) apply on the disposal of the option by G (though certain options are exempted from these rules — see *TCGA 1992, s 144*). As these rules can only apply on a disposal, they cannot apply on the

Disposal 206.5

exercise of the option by H (as the exercise of an option is not treated as a disposal), so his acquisition cost remains intact.

(b) For the purposes of computing taper relief on a future disposal, H's acquisition of the land is deemed to have occurred on 30 June 2002, i.e. the date he exercised the option and not the date he acquired it. [*TCGA 1992, Sch A1 para 13(3); FA 1998, s 121, Sch 20*].

(c) Other than for the purposes of corporation tax on chargeable gains, indexation allowance is frozen at its April 1998 level. Therefore, the indexation factor for April 1998 is used in respect of disposals in a later month, and expenditure incurred in April 1998 or later does not attract indexation allowance at all. See 210 INDEXATION.

207.1 Enterprise Investment Scheme

207 Enterprise Investment Scheme

Cross-reference. See also IT 6.2 ENTERPRISE INVESTMENT SCHEME.

207.1 DISPOSAL OF EIS SHARES MORE THAN THREE YEARS AFTER ISSUE [*TCGA 1992, s 150A(2)(3); ICTA 1988, s 312(1A)(a); FA 1994, Sch 15 paras 28, 30; FA 1995, Sch 13 para 2(1)(3); FA 1998, Sch 13 para 24(1); FA 2000, Sch 17 para 6(4), para 8*]

On 8 November 2002 P subscribes £450,000 for 300,000 shares in the EIS company, S Ltd, and obtains an EIS income tax deduction of £30,000 (£150,000 × 20%) for 2002/03. On 3 April 2007 he sells the entire holding for £810,000. The shares are business assets throughout for the purposes of taper relief.

The chargeable gain arising is calculated as follows

	£
Disposal proceeds	810,000
Cost	450,000
Gain	360,000
Less TCGA 1992, s 150A(2)(3) exemption	
£360,000 × $\frac{30,000}{90,000}$ note (*b*)	120,000
Chargeable gain	240,000
Less taper relief @ 75% (note (*d*))	180,000
Taxable gain 2006/07	£60,000

Notes

(*a*) Gains arising on the sale more than three years after issue of shares qualifying for EIS income tax relief (five years for shares issued before 6 April 2000) are not chargeable gains unless the EIS relief is fully withdrawn before disposal. The exemption begins three years after the date of commencement of the qualifying trade if this is later than three years after issue.

(*b*) Where the income tax relief is not given on the full EIS subscription (otherwise than because of insufficient income), capital gains tax relief is given on a proportion of the gain on the disposal or part disposal.

The gain is reduced by the multiple A/B where

A = the actual income tax reduction and
B = the tax at the lower rate for the year of relief on the amount subscribed for the issue.

A = £150,000 × 20% = £30,000
B = £450,000 × 20% = £90,000

(*c*) Expenditure incurred after 31 March 1998 other than by companies does not attract indexation allowance. [*TCGA 1992, ss 53(1A), 54(1)(1A); FA 1998, s 121(1)–(3)*].

(*d*) Business asset taper relief is the maximum 75% — by reference to a qualifying holding period of at least two years (for disposals after 5 April 2002). In practice, any losses on other 2006/07 disposals must be taken into account before taper relief is applied to the gain (see 227.1(B) TAPER RELIEF).

Enterprise Investment Scheme 207.2

207.2 LOSS ON DISPOSAL OF EIS SHARES [*TCGA 1992, s 150A(1)(2A); FA 1994, Sch 15 paras 28, 30; FA 1995, Sch 13 para 2(1)(2); FA 1998, Sch 13 para 24(1)*]

(A) Disposal more than three years after issue

Assuming the facts otherwise remain the same as in 207.1 above but that the shares are sold for £300,000 on 3 April 2007.

The allowable loss arising is calculated as follows

	£	£
Disposal proceeds		300,000
Less Cost	450,000	
Less Income tax relief given (and not withdrawn)	30,000	420,000
Allowable loss 2006/07		£120,000

Note

(a) Any loss arising is reduced by deducting the amount of the EIS relief (given and not withdrawn) from the acquisition cost. On the question of income tax withdrawal, see note (b) to (B) below.

(B) Disposal within three years of issue

The facts are otherwise as in (A) above except that the shares are sold in an arm's length bargain on 3 April 2004, i.e. within three years after their issue.

Income tax relief given for 2002/03 is withdrawn as follows

Relief attributable (£150,000 @ 20%) £30,000 (1)

$$\text{Consideration } £300,000 \times \frac{30,000 \ (£150,000 \ @ \ 20\%)}{90,000 \ (£450,000 \ @ \ 20\%)} \ @ \ 20\% \quad £20,000 \ (2)$$

The amount at (1) is greater than that at (2), so income tax relief of £20,000 is withdrawn. [*ICTA 1988, s 299(1)–(4); FA 1994, Sch 15 para 12; FA 1998, s 74, Sch 13 para 12(1)–(3)(8)*].

The relief not withdrawn is therefore £(30,000 − 20,000) =   £10,000

The allowable loss arising is calculated as follows

	£	£
Disposal proceeds		300,000
Less Cost	450,000	
Less Income tax relief not withdrawn	10,000	440,000
Allowable loss 2003/04		£140,000

Notes

(a) For the purposes of computing an allowable loss, the consideration is reduced by the relief attributable to the shares. [*TCGA 1992, s 150A(1)*]. The relief attributable is that remaining following any withdrawal of relief.

(b) A withdrawal of income tax relief arises on a disposal of EIS shares within the relevant period under *ICTA 1988, s 312(1A)(a)*, i.e. within three years after their issue or, if later, within the period ending immediately before the third anniversary of the date of commencement of the qualifying trade (within five years after issue in the case of shares issued before 6 April 2000). [*ICTA 1988, s 299(1)*].

207.3 Enterprise Investment Scheme

207.3 **EIS DEFERRAL RELIEF** [*TCGA 1992, Schs 5B, 5BA; FA 1995, Sch 13 para 4(3)(4); FA 1998, s 74, Sch 13 paras 26–36; FA 1999, ss 72, 73, Schs 7, 8; FA 2000, Sch 17 para 7(2)(3), para 8; FA 2001, Sch 15 paras 25–37, 40*]

(A)

On 1 June 2002, X realises a gain of £300,000 (before taper relief) on the disposal of an asset. He had owned the asset since September 2000 and it had been a business asset throughout for taper relief purposes. X makes no other disposals in 2002/03 and does not qualify for retirement relief. On 1 February 2004, X acquires by subscription 65% of the issued ordinary share capital of ABC Ltd at a total subscription price of £248,000. This is a qualifying investment for the purposes of EIS deferral relief, and the ABC shares are also a business asset throughout for taper relief purposes. X makes a claim to defer the maximum £248,000 of the June 2002 gain against the qualifying investment.

On 1 July 2008, X sells 40% of his holding in ABC Ltd for £199,200. He makes no other disposals in 2008/09.

X's CGT position for 2002/03 is as follows

	£
Indexed gain	300,000
Less EIS deferral relief	248,000
	52,000
Less taper relief £52,000 @ 50%	26,000
	26,000
Less annual exemption	7,700
Taxable gain 2002/03	£18,300

X's CGT position for 2008/09 is as follows

	£
Gain on ABC Ltd shares	
Disposal proceeds	199,200
Less cost (£248,000 @ 40%)	99,200
	100,000
Less taper relief £100,000 @ 75%	75,000
Chargeable gain	£25,000
Deferred gain brought into charge	
Total gain deferred	£248,000
	£
Clawback restricted to expenditure to which disposal relates	99,200
Less taper relief £99,200 @ 50%	49,600
Gain	£49,600
Taxable gains 2008/09 (subject to annual exemption) (£25,000 + £49,600)	£74,600
Gain remaining deferred until any future chargeable event (£248,000 − £99,200)	£148,800

Enterprise Investment Scheme 207.3

Notes

(a) No part of X's subscription for ABC Ltd shares can qualify for EIS income tax relief. X is connected with the company by virtue of his shareholding being greater than 30%. (In practice, the holdings of his associates, e.g. wife and children, must also be taken into account in applying the 30% limit.) [*ICTA 1988, s 291(1), ss 291B, 312(1); FA 1998, s 74, Sch 13 para 6(1); FA 2001, Sch 15 paras 10, 40*].

(b) As the ABC Ltd shares do not qualify for income tax relief, there is no CGT exemption for the gain arising on disposal even though the shares were held for the requisite three-year period.

(c) Business asset taper relief is given by reference to the number of complete years an asset has been held after 5 April 1998. See 227 TAPER RELIEF. Taper relief on the deferred gain becoming chargeable is given by reference to the time and circumstances of the original disposal, not the disposal of the EIS shares giving rise to the chargeable event (but see (B) below re cases of serial reinvestment). [*TCGA 1992, Sch A1 para 16; FA 1998, s 121, Sch 20*].

(B) Serial reinvestment

On 1 June 2002, Anna realises a gain of £300,000 (after indexation but before taper relief) on the disposal of a complete holding of shares in ABC Ltd (an EIS company) for which she had subscribed on 1 June 2001 and in respect of which she had deferred a gain of £10,000 which would otherwise have accrued in 1999/2000 on a disposal of quoted shares. The ABC Ltd shares were a business asset throughout for taper relief purposes. Anna makes no other disposals in 2002/03. On 1 December 2003, she subscribes £260,000 for new ordinary shares in a new company, EIS Ltd. The investment is a qualifying investment for the purposes of EIS deferral relief (but not income tax relief) and a business asset throughout for the purposes of taper relief. Anna makes a claim to defer the maximum £260,000 of the June 2002 gain against her investment in EIS Ltd.

On 1 June 2007, Anna sells her holding of EIS Ltd shares for £540,000. She makes no other disposals in 2007/08.

Anna's CGT position for 2002/03 is as follows

	£
Gain on ABC Ltd shares	300,000
Less deferred under EIS provisions	260,000
	40,000
Less taper relief £40,000 @ 50% (Qualifying holding period 1.6.01–1.6.02 = 1 year)	20,000
	20,000
Previously deferred gain now chargeable (note (*c*))	10,000
	30,000
Less annual exemption	7,700
Taxable gain 2002/03	£22,300

207.3 Enterprise Investment Scheme

Anna's CGT position for 2007/08 is as follows

	£
Gain on EIS Ltd shares	
Disposal proceeds	540,000
Less cost	260,000
	280,000
Less taper relief £280,000 @ 75% (Qualifying holding period 1.12.03 – 1.6.07 = 3 years)	210,000
Gain	£70,000

	£
Deferred gain brought into charge	
Gain deferred	260,000
Less taper relief @ 75%*	195,000
Gain	£65,000

*Qualifying holding period
1.6.01–1.6.02 — 1 year
1.12.03–1.6.07 — 3.5 years
Total — 4.5 years (i.e. 4 whole years)

Taxable gains 2007/08 (subject to annual exemption) (£70,000 + £65,000)	£135,000

Notes

(*a*) A special taper relief rule applies in cases of serial EIS investment. It applies in consequence of the disposal after 5 April 1999 of a holding of EIS shares (the initial investment) (which were issued after 5 April 1998 and to which either CGT deferral relief or income tax relief (or both) is attributable) where the whole or part of the gain otherwise accruing is deferred by reinvestment in further EIS shares (the second investment). Upon a disposal of the second investment, with the result that the deferred gain on the initial investment is revived, taper relief is calculated in respect of the revived gain as if the holding periods of the two investments were combined. [*TCGA 1992, s 150D, Sch 5BA; FA 1999, s 72, Sch 7*]. See generally 227 TAPER RELIEF.

(*b*) Where the revived gain is itself deferred by means of a third EIS investment (not illustrated in this example), the holding periods of all three investments are combined for taper relief purposes, and so on as regards fourth and subsequent investments.

(*c*) The taper relief period for the first asset (a non-EIS investment) ends on the date of disposal of that asset (see (A) above) and does not fall to be extended under the serial reinvestment provisions. No taper relief is due in this case as the asset is a non-business asset held for less than three years after 5 April 1998.

208 Exemptions and Reliefs

Cross-references. See also 220 PRIVATE RESIDENCES, 221 QUALIFYING CORPORATE BONDS and 228 WASTING ASSETS.

208.1 CHATTELS

(A) Marginal relief [*TCGA 1992, s 262(2)*]

On 1 April 1988, Y acquired by inheritance a painting valued for probate at £900. He sold it for £7,200 on 30 October 2002, incurring costs of £150. The indexation factor for the period April 1988 to April 1998 (note (*a*)) is 0.537.

	£	£
Disposal proceeds	7,200	
Incidental costs	150	7,050
Acquisition cost		900
Unindexed gain		6,150
Indexation allowance £900 × 0.537		483
Chargeable gain		£5,667
Marginal relief		
Chargeable gain limited to $\frac{5}{3}$ × (£7,200 − £6,000)		£2,000

Notes

(*a*) Other than for the purposes of corporation tax on chargeable gains, indexation allowance is frozen at its April 1998 level. Therefore, the indexation factor for April 1998 is used in respect of disposals in a later month (and expenditure incurred in April 1998 or later does not attract indexation allowance at all). See 210 INDEXATION.

(*b*) The chargeable gain of £2,000 is subject to taper relief at the non-business asset rate of 15% (asset held four years after 5 April 1998 plus one bonus year), reducing it to £1,700. (Any losses available must be set against gains before applying taper relief — see 227.1(B) TAPER RELIEF.).

(B) Loss relief [*TCGA 1992, s 262(3)*]

Z bought a piece of antique jewellery for £7,000 in February 1991. In January 2003, he is forced to sell it, but at auction it realises only £1,500 and Z incurs costs of £100.

	£	£
Deemed disposal consideration		6,000
Cost of disposal	100	
Cost of acquisition	7,000	7,100
Allowable loss		£1,100

Note

(*a*) Where the disposal consideration for tangible movable property is less than £6,000 and there would otherwise be a loss, the consideration is deemed to be £6,000.

208.1 Exemptions and Reliefs

(C) Partial disposal of assets forming sets [*TCGA 1992, s 262(4)*]

AB purchased a set of six 18th century dining chairs in 1979 for £1,200. After incurring restoration costs of £300 in 1981, he sold two of them in May 1998 to an unconnected person for £2,900. In October 2002, he sold the other four to the same buyer for £4,900. The value of the complete set at 31 March 1982 was £1,800.

Indexation factor   March 1982 to April 1998 (note (c))   1.047

The two disposals are treated as one for the purposes of the chattel exemption and marginal relief, the consideration for which is £7,800. Marginal relief on this basis would give a total chargeable gain of £3,000 ([£7,800 − £6,000] × $\frac{5}{3}$) which is to be compared with the following:

May 1998	£	£	£
Disposal proceeds		2,900	2,900
Acquisition cost	1,200		
Enhancement cost	300		
	1,500		
Cost of two chairs sold £1,500 × $\frac{2}{6}$		500	
Market value 31.3.82 £1,800 × $\frac{2}{6}$			600
Unindexed gain		2,400	2,300
Indexation allowance £600 × 1.047		628	628
Gain after indexation		£1,772	£1,672
Chargeable gain			£1,672

October 2002	£	£
Disposal proceeds	4,900	4,900
Allowable cost £1,500 × $\frac{4}{6}$	1,000	
Market value 31.3.82 £1,800 × $\frac{4}{6}$		1,200
Unindexed gain	3,900	3,700
Indexation allowance £1,200 × 1.047	1,256	1,256
Gain after indexation	£2,644	£2,444
Chargeable gain		£2,444

Total chargeable gains (£1,672 + £2,444)	£4,116

The total gain of £4,116 compares with a gain of £3,000 using marginal relief. Marginal relief is therefore effective and the total chargeable gain is £3,000.

The gain is apportioned to tax years as follows (note (*b*))

1998/99 £3,000 × $\frac{2,900}{7,800}$ =   £1,115

2002/03 £3,000 × $\frac{4,900}{7,800}$ =   £1,885 (note (*d*))

Exemptions and Reliefs 208.1

Notes

(*a*) Prior to the second disposal, the first disposal would have been exempt, the proceeds being within the £6,000 chattel exemption.

(*b*) The gain as reduced by marginal relief is apportioned between tax years in the same ratio as the proportion of total sale proceeds applicable to each year (Revenue Capital Gains Manual, CG 76637).

(*c*) Other than for the purposes of corporation tax on chargeable gains, indexation allowance is frozen at its April 1998 level. Therefore, the indexation factor for April 1998 is used in respect of disposals in a later month (and expenditure incurred in April 1998 or later does not attract indexation allowance at all). See 210 INDEXATION.

(*d*) The 2002/03 gain of £1,885 is subject to TAPER RELIEF (227).

(*e*) See also 202.4 ANTI-AVOIDANCE.

209 Hold-Over Reliefs

209.1 RELIEF FOR GIFTS [*TCGA 1992, s 260*]

(A) Chargeable lifetime transfers

B owns a house which he has not occupied as a private residence. He purchased the house for £15,200 inclusive of costs in 1979 and in January 2003 he gives it to a discretionary trust of which he is the settlor. The market value of the house is agreed to be £60,000 at the date of transfer, and B incurs transfer costs of £1,000. The indexation factor for the period March 1982 to April 1998 (note (*c*)) is 1.047. The house had a value of £21,000 at 31 March 1982.

	£	£
Disposal consideration	60,000	60,000
Deduct Costs of disposal	1,000	1,000
	59,000	59,000
Cost	15,200	
Market value 31.3.82		21,000
Unindexed gain	43,800	38,000
Indexation allowance £21,000 × 1.047	21,987	21,987
Gain after indexation	£21,813	£16,013
Chargeable gain (subject to TAPER RELIEF (227))		£16,013

If B elects under *TCGA 1992, s 260*, his chargeable gain is reduced to nil, and the trustees' acquisition cost of the house is treated as £43,987 (£60,000 − £16,013). No taper relief is then due (note (*d*)).

Notes

(*a*) Relief under *TCGA 1992, s 260* is restricted, generally, to transfers which are, or would but for annual exemptions be, chargeable lifetime transfers for inheritance tax purposes.

(*b*) There are special rules where deferral took place after 31 March 1982 but before 6 April 1988, for which see 204.2 ASSETS HELD ON 31 MARCH 1982.

(*c*) Other than for the purposes of corporation tax on chargeable gains, indexation allowance is frozen at its April 1998 level. Therefore, the indexation factor for April 1998 is used in respect of disposals in a later month (and expenditure incurred in April 1998 or later does not attract indexation allowance at all). See 210 INDEXATION.

(*d*) A held-over gain cannot attract taper relief. On a future disposal by the donee, any gain will be tapered by reference only to the donee's period of ownership.

(*e*) Separate rules apply to transfers of assets between MARRIED PERSONS (215).

Hold-Over Reliefs 209.1

(B) Disposal consideration [*TCGA 1992, s 260(5)*]
The facts are as in (A) above except that B sells the house to the trustees for £30,000.

	£	£
Chargeable gain (as above) (note (*a*))		16,013
Deduct		
Actual consideration passing	30,000	
B's allowable costs (note (*b*))	(22,000)	
		8,000
Held-over gain		£8,013
(i) B's chargeable gain is reduced to £16,013 − £8,013		£8,000
(ii) The trustees' allowable cost is reduced to £60,000 − £8,013		£51,987

Notes
(*a*) The disposal consideration is taken as the open market value of the house at the date of disposal because B and the trustees are connected persons. Thus, the computation of the gain is as in (A) above.

(*b*) B's allowable costs are those allowable under *TCGA 1992, s 38* (costs of acquisition and disposal), which do not include indexation allowance.

(C) Relief for IHT [*TCGA 1992, s 260(7)*]
The facts are as in (A) above. Before transferring the house, B had made substantial chargeable transfers. Inheritance tax of £12,000 is payable on the transfer. The trustees sell the house in December 2003 for £55,000.

	£	£
Disposal proceeds		55,000
Acquisition cost	60,000	
Deduct held-over gain	16,013	
		43,987
Gain		11,013
IHT attributable to earlier transfer (restricted)		11,013
Chargeable gain		Nil

Notes
(*a*) The IHT deduction is limited to the amount of the gain and cannot create or increase a loss. [*TCGA 1992, s 260(7)*].

(*b*) A similar inheritance tax relief operates where the original gain was held over under *TCGA 1992, s 165* or *FA 1980, s 79*. [*TCGA 1992, ss 67, 165(10)*].

(*c*) Expenditure incurred (or deemed to be incurred) in April 1998 or later (other than by companies) does not attract indexation allowance. [*TCGA 1992, s 53(1A), s 54(1A); FA 1998, s 122(1)–(3)*].

209.2 Hold-Over Reliefs

209.2 **RELIEF FOR GIFTS OF BUSINESS ASSETS** [*TCGA 1992, s 165, Sch 7; FA 1993, Sch 7 para 1; FA 1996, s 176*]

(A) Partial consideration

Zoë owns a freehold property which she lets to the family trading company, Sphere Ltd, in which she and her father each own half the shares and voting rights. Zoë inherited the property in April 1990 at a probate value of £50,000, and since then the whole of the property has been used for the purposes of the company's trade. In November 2002, Zoë transfers the property to her boyfriend. Its market value at that time is £115,000. The intention is that he should give sufficient consideration to leave Zoë with a chargeable gain exactly equal to the annual exempt amount (there being no other disposals in 2002/03). The indexation factor for the period April 1990 to April 1998 is 0.300.

Actual consideration should be £80,800 as shown by the following computation

	£	£
Deemed consideration		115,000
Deduct: Cost	50,000	
Indexation allowance £50,000 × 0.300	15,000	65,000
Unrelieved gain		50,000
Held-over gain (see below)		19,200
Pre-tapered gain		30,800
Taper relief £30,800 × 75%		
(business asset held at least 2 years)		23,100
Chargeable gain covered by annual exemption		£7,700

Computation of held-over gain

	£	£
Unrelieved gain		50,000
Actual consideration	80,800	
Less allowable expenditure (excluding indexation)	50,000	30,800
Held-over gain		£19,200

Notes

(a) On a subsequent disposal of the property, the allowable expenditure would be £95,800 (deemed proceeds of £115,000 less held-over gain of £19,200). The actual consideration given does not enter into this calculation. No indexation allowance will be due as the expenditure was incurred after March 1998 (see 210 INDEXATION).

(b) If no part of the unrelieved gain were held over, business asset taper relief of 75% would have been available on the full amount. As a result of the hold-over claim, taper relief is forgone on the amount held over, and the transferee does not inherit the transferor's period of ownership. The availability and quantum of taper relief need to be taken into account in the decision-making. See 227 TAPER RELIEF. One consideration is whether the transferee's period of ownership and use of the asset are expected to be such as to obtain the maximum potential taper relief.

Hold-Over Reliefs 209.2

(B) Transfer of assets to a company — interaction with retirement relief
S has carried on his antique dealing business for 10 years. The assets of the business are valued as follows

	£
Freehold shop and office	140,000
Goodwill	40,000
Stocks	50,000
Debtors	9,500
Cash	4,500

Before the business began, S let the shop premises for one year. In October 2002, S transfers the business as a going concern to a company which he has formed with share capital of £1,000, held wholly by him. The transfer consideration is £1. At the time of the transfer S is 51. The gain arising in respect of the freehold is £55,000 and on goodwill it is £15,000 (both after deducting indexation allowance to April 1998).

	£	£
Gains eligible for retirement relief		
(£55,000 + £15,000)		70,000
Relief £50,000 × 100%	50,000	
£20,000 × 50%	10,000	60,000
Chargeable gain		£10,000

If S and the company jointly claim relief under *TCGA 1992, s 165*, part of the chargeable gain may be rolled over, as follows

	Freehold	Goodwill	
	£	£	£
Total gain	55,000	15,000	
Reduction for non-trade use [*TCGA 1992,*			
Sch 7 para 5] ($\frac{1}{11}$)	5,000		
	£50,000	£15,000	
Held-over gain before adjustment			65,000
Chargeable gain after retirement relief [*TCGA*			
1992, Sch 7 para 8]			10,000
Excess			£55,000
Held-over gain (£65,000 − £55,000)			£10,000
Chargeable gain			Nil

209.2 Hold-Over Reliefs

Notes

(a) There is no statutory formula for apportioning the held-over gain after retirement relief between different assets. The following is one possible method of computing the revised base costs in the hands of the company.

Freehold

Gain held over $\dfrac{55,000}{70,000} \times £10,000$ £7,857

Revised base cost (£140,000 − £7,857) £132,143

Goodwill

Gain held over $\dfrac{15,000}{70,000} \times £10,000$ £2,143

Revised base cost (£40,000 − £2,143) £37,857

(b) If S had transferred the business to the company in consideration for the issue of shares, *TCGA 1992, s 162* (see 209.3 below) would have applied, but business assets relief under *TCGA 1992, s 165* would not. Retirement relief would still have applied in priority, so that the chargeable gain would have been £10,000. This gain would then have been rolled over against the base cost of the shares acquired by S. Alternatively, the *section 162* treatment could have been disapplied by election (see 209.3(B) below).

(c) If the chargeable gain, after retirement relief, of £10,000 were not held over, business asset taper relief at 75% would have reduced it to £2,500. As a result of the hold-over claim, taper relief is forgone. The availability and quantum of taper relief need to be taken into account in the decision-making. See 227 TAPER RELIEF.

(d) In the hands of the company, the goodwill will not qualify for the special treatment of intangible assets of companies introduced by *FA 2002, s 84, Sch 29*, because it was acquired from a related party and was created before 1 April 2002 (by virtue of the business having been carried on before that date). [*FA 2002, Sch 29 paras 95, 117, 118, 121*].

(e) See 204.2 ASSETS HELD ON 31 MARCH 1982 for the relief given under *TCGA 1992, Sch 4* where gains were held over after 31 March 1982 and before 6 April 1988 and a disposal occurs after 5 April 1988. This relief applies, inter alia, to gains held over under the business gifts relief rules illustrated above.

(C) Chargeable business asset restriction

K holds 10,000 shares in her personal trading company, LO Ltd, which she acquired by inheritance in April 1998 at a probate value of £205,000. On 30 April 2002, she gifts 4,000 shares to her daughter, her only CGT disposal in 2002/03. Their market value is £160,000 and the market value of K's remaining 6,000 shares is £240,000. K is 50 years of age at the time of the gift. K and her daughter jointly claim hold-over relief under *TCGA 1992, s 165*. At the date of disposal, the market values of the company's assets are as follows

	Assets	Chargeable assets	
		Business	Non-business
	£	£	£
Business premises	240,000	240,000	
Goodwill	30,000	30,000	
Trading stock	30,000		
Debtors	10,000		
Cash	10,000		
Investments	90,000		90,000
Fixtures (all valued at less than £6,000)	20,000		
		£270,000	£90,000

Despite the presence of investments, the company has always derived at least 80% of its income from trading activities and is accepted by the Revenue as having been a trading company for taper relief purposes throughout K's period of ownership of the shares. See *TCGA 1992, Sch A1 para 22A; FA 2002, Sch 10 para 9* and Revenue Tax Bulletin June 2001 pp 852–856.

The gain on the gift of shares is calculated as follows

	£
Deemed consideration	160,000
Cost £205,000 × $\dfrac{160,000}{160,000 + 240,000}$	82,000
Gain	£78,000

The gain eligible for retirement relief is as follows

$$\frac{\text{Chargeable business assets}}{\text{Chargeable assets}} = \frac{270,000}{360,000} \times £78,000 \qquad £58,500$$

The maximum amount qualifying for retirement relief at 100% is calculated by reference to a four-year qualifying period and is thus £50,000 × 40% = £20,000. The balance of £38,500 qualifies at 50%. Thus, retirement relief of £39,250 is available, leaving a chargeable gain of £38,750 (£78,000 – £39,250).

The gain available for hold-over relief (disregarding retirement relief) is calculated as follows

$$£78,000 \times \frac{270,000}{360,000} \quad [TCGA\ 1992,\ Sch\ 7\ para\ 7] \qquad £58,500$$

However, the held-over gain is not to exceed the 'relevant proportion' of the *chargeable* gain disregarding hold-over relief under *TCGA 1992, s 165*. [*TCGA 1992, Sch 7 para 8(3)*]. The maximum available for hold-over is thus

$$£38,750 \times \frac{270,000}{360,000} \qquad £29,063$$

209.2 Hold-Over Reliefs

The final position is thus as follows

	£	£
Total gain		78,000
Deduct: retirement relief	39,250	
hold-over relief	29,063	68,313
Pre tapered gain		9,687
Deduct Taper relief £9,687 @ 75% (period of ownership at least 2 years)		7,265
		£2,422

The base cost of the 4,000 shares in the hands of K's daughter is £130,937 (market value of £160,000 less held-over gain of £29,063).

Notes

(a) This example illustrates the provisions of *TCGA 1992, Sch 7 para 7* (restriction of held-over gain under *TCGA 1992, s 165* on disposal of shares where some of the company's chargeable assets are not chargeable business assets) and those of *TCGA 1992, Sch 7 para 8(3)* (interaction of hold-over relief and retirement relief).

(b) If the appropriate proportion (i.e. chargeable business assets over chargeable assets) of the gain had been fully covered by retirement relief, hold-over relief would have been precluded by *TCGA 1992, s 165(3)(b)*.

(c) See also 222.2 RETIREMENT RELIEF for the calculation of gains qualifying for relief.

(d) This example is based on a strict, but favourable, interpretation of *TCGA 1992, Sch 7 para 8(3)*. An alternative view is that the gain left in charge should not be less than £19,500 (£78,000 − £58,500), with hold-over relief being restricted accordingly.

209.3 TRANSFER OF BUSINESS TO A COMPANY

(A) Incorporation relief [TCGA 1992, s 162]

W carries on an antiquarian bookselling business. He decides to form an unquoted company, P Ltd, to carry on the business. He transfers, in August 2002, the whole of the business undertaking, assets and liabilities to P Ltd, in consideration for the issue of shares, plus an amount left outstanding on interest-free loan. The business assets and liabilities transferred are valued as follows

	£	Value £	Chargeable gain (after indexation to April 1998) £
Freehold shop premises (acquired in 1990)		80,000	52,000
Goodwill		36,000	26,000
Fixtures and fittings		4,000	—
Trading stock		52,000	—
Debtors		28,000	—
		200,000	
Mortgage on shop	50,000		
Trade creditors	20,000	70,000	—
		£130,000	£78,000

The company issues 100,000 £1 ordinary shares, valued at par, to W in August 2002, and the amount left outstanding is £30,000. In March 2003, W sells 20,000 of his shares for £45,000 to X. W's remaining shareholding is then worth, say, £155,000.

(i) Amount of chargeable gain rolled over on transfer of the business

$$\frac{100,000}{130,000} \times £78,000 \qquad £60,000$$

Of the chargeable gain, £18,000 (£78,000 – £60,000) remains taxable, but is subject to taper relief at 75%, reducing it to £4,500 (see note (*b*)).

The allowable cost of W's shares is £40,000 (£100,000 – £60,000).

(ii) On the sale of shares to X, W realises a chargeable gain

	£
Disposal consideration	45,000
Allowable cost £40,000 × $\frac{45,000}{45,000 + 155,000}$	9,000
Chargeable gain (no taper relief as shares held less than 12 months)	£36,000

Notes

(*a*) Relief under *TCGA 1992, s 162* is given automatically and without the need for a claim (but see (B) below).

(*b*) Where part of the aggregate chargeable gain on the old assets remains in charge, after giving relief under *TCGA 1992, s 162*, the Revenue will accept a computation of taper relief on this amount by reference to the holding period(s) of *any* of the *chargeable* assets transferred (Revenue Capital Gains Manual CG 65821, 65826).

209.3 Hold-Over Reliefs

The shop premises have been held by W for at least two years after 5 April 1998, and thus the whole gain qualifies at 75%.

(c) In the hands of the company, the goodwill will not qualify for the special treatment of intangible assets of companies introduced by *FA 2002, s 84, Sch 29*, because it was acquired from a related party and was created before 1 April 2002 (by virtue of the business having been carried on before that date). [*FA 2002, Sch 29 paras 95, 117, 118, 121*].

(d) See 204.2 ASSETS HELD ON 31 MARCH 1982 for the relief given under *TCGA 1992, Sch 4* where gains were held over after 31 March 1982 and before 6 April 1988 and a disposal occurs after 5 April 1988. This relief applies, inter alia, to gains held over under the rules illustrated above.

(e) Expenditure incurred (or deemed to be incurred) in April 1998 or later (other than by companies) does not attract indexation allowance. [*TCGA 1992, s 53(1A), s 54(1A); FA 1998, s 122(1)–(3)*].

(B) Election to disapply incorporation relief [*TCGA 1992, s 162A; FA 2002, s 49*]
The facts are as in (A) above, except that W considers an election under *TCGA 1992, s 162A* to disapply *TCGA 1992, s 162*. With an election, the computations in (A) are revised as follows.

(i) Chargeable gain on transfer of the business

	£
Gain after indexation but before taper relief	78,000
Less Taper relief £78,000 @ 75% (asset held at least 2 years)	58,500
Chargeable gain	£19,500

(ii) Chargeable gain on sale of shares

	£
Disposal consideration	45,000
Allowable cost £100,000 × $\dfrac{45,000}{45,000 + 155,000}$	22,500
Chargeable gain (no taper relief as shares held less than 12 months)	£22,500

On the face of it, the election is not beneficial, producing aggregate gains of £42,000 (£19,500 + £22,500) as against £40,500 (£4,500 + £36,000) in (A) above.

If, however, W then sells his remaining 80,000 shares for £155,000 in, say, May 2003, he will have, as illustrated below, a chargeable gain for 2003/04 of £124,000 without the election or £77,500 with the election. There is now an overall saving of £45,000 if the election is made; this is the benefit of the increased taper relief on the disposal to the company (i.e. £60,000 @ 75% = £45,000). If W had retained the shares for at least one year, such that 50% taper relief would have been available on sale, the overall saving with an election would have been reduced accordingly. See also note (*b*).

Chargeable gain on sale of 80,000 shares in May 2003

Without the election

	£
Disposal consideration	155,000
Allowable cost (£40,000 – £9,000)	31,000
Chargeable gain (no taper relief as shares held less than 12 months)	£124,000

With the election

	£
Disposal consideration	155,000
Allowable cost (£100,000 – £22,500)	77,500
Chargeable gain (no taper relief as shares held less than 12 months)	£77,500

Notes

(a) On a transfer (of a business) that is otherwise within the scope of *TCGA 1992, s 162* at (A) above and takes place after 5 April 2002, the transferor may make an election under *TCGA 1992, s 162A* to forgo incorporation relief.

(b) If instead of making the early sales illustrated in this example, W had retained all 100,000 shares for two years, such that the gain on eventual disposal would have qualified for the maximum 75% business asset taper relief, the election would have been neutral. This is because the taper relief forgone on incorporation (i.e. without an election) would have been fully recovered. (This does assume that the shares retain their status as business assets for taper relief purposes throughout W's ownership.)

210.1 Indexation

210 Indexation

Cross-references. See 225.9 SHARES AND SECURITIES for indexation on a building society share account where cash bonus received on takeover or conversion, 226 SHARES AND SECURITIES — IDENTIFICATION RULES.

210.1 **INDEXATION ALLOWANCE — GENERAL RULES** [*TCGA 1992, ss 53–56; FA 1994, s 93(1)–(5)(11); FA 1998, s 122(1)–(3)(6)(7)*]

(A) Calculation of indexation factor — companies

M Ltd bought a freehold factory in December 1984 for £500,000. Further buildings are erected at a cost of £200,000 in May 1992. In May 2002 the factory is sold for £2m. The retail price index (RPI) was re-based in January 1987 from 394.5 to 100 and the relevant values are as follows

December	1984	358.5
May	1992	139.3
May	2002	176.2

	£	£
Disposal consideration		2,000,000
Deduct Cost of factory and site	500,000	
Cost of additions	200,000	700,000
Unindexed gain		1,300,000
Indexation allowance		

(i) Factory and site
   Indexation factor

$$\left(\frac{394.5 \times 176.2}{358.5} \right) - 100 = 93.9\%$$

   Indexed rise
   £500,000 × 0.939 — 469,500

(ii) Additions
   Indexation factor

$$\frac{176.2 - 139.3}{139.3} = 0.265$$

   Indexed rise
   £200,000 × 0.265 — 53,000 — 522,500

   Gain chargeable to corporation tax — £777,500

Note

(*a*) Alternatively the indexation factor on the pre-January 1987 expenditure can be calculated using the revised RPI figures so that, for example,

   December 1984 = 90.87
   May 2002 = 176.2

   Indexation from December 1984 to May 2002 = $\dfrac{176.2 - 90.87}{90.87} = 0.939$

Indexation 210.1

(B) Calculation of indexation factor — individuals etc.

All the facts are as in (A) above except that M is an individual rather than a company. Additional information: the value of the RPI for April 1998 (see note (*a*)) was 162.6, and the factory is a business asset throughout for taper relief purposes.

		£	£
Disposal consideration (May 2002)			2,000,000
Deduct Expenditure (December 1984)		500,000	
Expenditure (May 1992)		200,000	700,000
Unindexed gain			1,300,000

Indexation allowance

(i) Expenditure (December 1984)
   Indexation factor

$$\frac{162.6 - 90.87}{90.87} = 0.789$$

   Indexed rise
   £500,000 × 0.789 394,500

(ii) Expenditure (May 1991)
   Indexation factor

$$\frac{162.6 - 139.3}{139.3} = 0.167$$

   Indexed rise
   £200,000 × 0.167 .... 33,400 ... 427,900

Gain			872,100
Deduct Taper relief (£872,100 × 75%)			654,075
Chargeable gain 2002/03			£218,025

Notes

(*a*) For individuals, trustees and personal representatives (but not for companies), indexation allowance is frozen at its April 1998 level. Therefore, the indexation factor for April 1998 is used in respect of disposals in a later month (and expenditure incurred in April 1998 or later does not attract indexation allowance at all). [*TCGA 1992, s 53(1A), s 54(1A); FA 1998, s 122(1)–(3)*].

(*b*) Business asset taper relief is given by reference to the number of complete years an asset has been held after 5 April 1998. See 227 TAPER RELIEF. Taper relief is applied to the otherwise chargeable gain (*after* indexation to April 1998).

(*c*) In practice, any losses on other 2002/03 disposals must be taken into account before taper relief is applied to the net gain (see 227.1(B) TAPER RELIEF).

210.1 Indexation

(C) Disposal of asset held on 31 March 1982
X acquired an antique for £6,000 in August 1979. He sold it for £17,000 in December 2002. The agreed market value of the clock at 31 March 1982 is £7,500. The indexation factor for March 1982 to April 1998 (see note (*a*) to (B) above) is 1.047.

	£	£
Disposal consideration	17,000	17,000
Deduct Cost	6,000	
Market value 31.3.82		7,500
Unindexed gain	11,000	9,500
Indexation allowance £7,500 × 1.047	7,853	7,853
Gain after indexation	£3,147	£1,647
Chargeable gain (subject to TAPER RELIEF (227))		£1,647

Notes
(*a*) In both the calculation using cost and that using 31 March 1982 value, indexation is automatically based on 31 March 1982 value. If, however, a greater allowance would have been produced by basing indexation on cost, that would automatically have applied instead. If, however, an irrevocable election were to be made under *TCGA 1992, s 35(5)* for all assets to be treated as sold and re-acquired at 31 March 1982, indexation must then be based on 31 March 1982 value whether it is beneficial or not. [*TCGA 1992, s 55(1)(2)*].

(*b*) See also 204.1 ASSETS HELD ON 31 MARCH 1982.

(D) Losses — indexation allowance restriction [*TCGA 1992, s 53(1)(b)(2A); FA 1994, s 93(1)–(3)(11)*]
In June 1990, M had purchased two paintings, each for £25,000. In September 2002, he sells the paintings for £30,000 (A) and £23,000 (B) respectively. Incidental costs of purchase and sale are ignored for the purposes of this example. The indexation factor for the period June 1990 to April 1998 (see note (*a*) to (B) above) is 0.283.

The gains/losses on the sales are as follows

	(A) £	(B) £
Proceeds	30,000	23,000
Cost	25,000	25,000
Unindexed gain/(loss)	5,000	(2,000)
Indexation allowance £25,000 × 0.283 = £7,075 but restricted to	(5,000)	Nil
Chargeable gain/(allowable loss)	Nil	£(2,000)

Note
(*a*) Indexation allowance can reduce an unindexed gain to nil but cannot create or increase a loss.

210.2 NO GAIN/NO LOSS TRANSFERS

(A) Inter-spouse transfers — asset acquired by first spouse before 1 April 1982 — no indexation allowance restriction on ultimate disposal [*TCGA 1992, s 55(5)(6), s 56(2), s 58; FA 1994, s 93(5)(11)*]

Mr N inherited a country cottage in 1977 at a probate value of £12,000. Its market value at 31 March 1982 was £30,000. In July 1988, Mr N incurred enhancement expenditure of £5,000 on the cottage. In May 1990, he gave the cottage to his wife. In November 2002, Mrs N sells it for £85,000. At no time was the cottage the main residence of either spouse. The relevant indexation factors are as follows

March 1982 to May 1990	0.589
July 1988 to May 1990	0.183
March 1982 to April 1998 (note (*d*))	1.047
July 1988 to April 1998 (note (*d*))	0.524

(i) Disposal in May 1990
Consideration deemed to be such that neither gain nor loss arises.

	£	£
Cost of cottage to Mr N		12,000
Enhancement expenditure		5,000
		17,000
Indexation allowance:		
£30,000 × 0.589	17,670	
£5,000 × 0.183	915	18,585
Cost of cottage to Mrs N		£35,585

(ii) Disposal in November 2002

	£	£	£
Sale proceeds		85,000	85,000
Cost	35,585		
Deduct Indexation allowance previously given	18,585		
	17,000		
Deduct Enhancement expenditure	5,000	(12,000)	
Market value 31.3.82			(30,000)
Enhancement expenditure (July 1988)		(5,000)	(5,000)
Unindexed gain		68,000	50,000
Indexation allowance:			
£30,000 × 1.047		(31,410)	(31,410)
£5,000 × 0.524		(2,620)	(2,620)
Gain after indexation		£33,970	£15,970
Chargeable gain 2002/03 (subject to TAPER RELIEF (227))			£15,970

Notes

(*a*) Having acquired the asset by means of a no gain/no loss disposal, under *CGTA 1979, s 44* (now *TCGA 1992, s 58*), from her husband, who held it at 31 March 1982, Mrs N is deemed to have held the asset at 31 March 1982 for the purpose of the re-basing provisions, and also the provisions under which indexation allowance is computed using value at 31 March 1982. [*TCGA 1992, s 55(5)(6), Sch 3 para 1*].

210.2 Indexation

(b) Where for re-basing/indexation purposes a person is deemed to have held an asset at 31 March 1982, that person can also be treated as having incurred enhancement expenditure which was in fact incurred after that date by a previous holder of the asset. (Revenue Tax Bulletin August 1992 p 32).

(c) Re-basing does not apply to the no gain/no loss disposal. [*TCGA 1992, s 35(3)(d)(i)*].

(d) Other than for the purposes of corporation tax on chargeable gains, indexation allowance is frozen at its April 1998 level. Therefore, the indexation factor for April 1998 is used in respect of disposals in a later month (and expenditure incurred in April 1998 or later does not attract indexation allowance at all). See 210.1(B) above.

(e) See also (B)–(D) below and 215 MARRIED PERSONS.

(B) Inter-spouse transfers — asset acquired by first spouse after 31 March 1982 — gain on ultimate disposal [*TCGA 1992, s 56(2)*]
The facts are as in (A) above except that Mr N inherited the cottage in April 1982 at a probate value of £30,000. The relevant indexation factors are

April 1982 to May 1990	0.557
July 1988 to May 1990	0.183
May 1990 to April 1998	0.288

(i) Disposal in May 1990
Consideration deemed to be such that neither gain nor loss arises.

	£	£
Cost of cottage to Mr N		30,000
Enhancement expenditure		5,000
		35,000
Indexation allowance:		
£30,000 × 0.557	16,710	
£5,000 × 0.183	915	17,625
Cost of cottage to Mrs N		£52,625

(ii) Disposal in November 2002

	£
Sale proceeds	85,000
Cost (as above)	52,625
Unindexed gain	32,375
Indexation allowance £52,625 × 0.288	15,156
Chargeable gain 2002/03 (subject to TAPER RELIEF (227))	£17,219

Note
(a) For further examples on inter-spouse transfers, see (A) above and 215 MARRIED PERSONS. The principles in (C) and (D) below also apply to inter-spouse transfers (except that, for inter-spouse transfers, indexation allowance cannot be computed beyond April 1998 — see note (d) to (A) above).

Indexation 210.2

(C) Intra-group transfers — asset acquired by group before 1 April 1982 — indexation allowance restricted on ultimate disposal [*TCGA 1992, s 55(5)–(9), s 56(2), 171; FA 1994, s 93(4)*]

J Ltd and K Ltd are 75% subsidiaries of H Ltd. J Ltd acquired a property in 1980 for £20,000. Its market value at 31 March 1982 was £25,000. In May 1990, J Ltd transferred the property to K Ltd. In May 2002, K Ltd sells the property outside the group. The sale proceeds are (1) £18,000 or (2) £29,000. The relevant indexation factors are as follows

March 1982 to May 1990	0.589
March 1982 to May 2002	1.218

(i) Disposal in May 1990
Consideration deemed to be such that neither gain nor loss arises.

	£
Cost of asset to J Ltd	20,000
Indexation allowance £25,000 × 0.589	14,725
Cost of asset to K Ltd	£34,725

(ii) Disposal in May 2002

(1) Proceeds £18,000

	£	£	£
Proceeds		18,000	18,000
Cost	34,725		
Deduct Indexation allowance previously given	14,725	(20,000)	
Market value 31.3.82			(25,000)
		(2,000)	(7,000)
Add Rolled-up indexation		(14,725)	(14,725)
Loss after rolled-up indexation		£(16,725)	£(21,725)
Allowable loss		£16,725	

210.2 Indexation

(2) Proceeds £29,000

	£	£	£
Proceeds		29,000	29,000
Cost	34,725		
Deduct Indexation allowance previously given	14,725		
		(20,000)	
Market value 31.3.82			(25,000)
Unindexed gain		9,000	4,000
Indexation allowance:			
£25,000 × 1.218 = £30,450 but restricted to		(9,000)	(4,000)
		Nil	Nil
Excess of rolled-up indexation (£14,725) over indexation allowance given above		(5,725)	(10,725)
Loss after rolled-up indexation		£(5,725)	£(10,725)
Allowable loss		£5,725	

Notes

(*a*) The calculation first follows that in (A) above. [*TCGA 1992, s 55(5)(6)*]. As the ultimate disposal is after 29 November 1993 and indexation allowance is either unavailable as in (1) above or restricted as in (2) above, special provisions enable the person making the disposal to obtain the benefit of any indexation allowance already accrued on no gain/no loss transfers made *before* 30 November 1993 (called 'rolled-up indexation'). [*TCGA 1992, s 55(7)–(9); FA 1994, s 93(4)*].

(*b*) The principles illustrated in this example apply equally to inter-spouse transfers (except that, for inter-spouse transfers, indexation allowance cannot be computed beyond April 1998 — see note (*d*) to (A) above).

Indexation 210.2

(D) Intra-group transfers — asset acquired by group after 31 March 1982 — loss on ultimate disposal [*TCGA 1992, s 56(2)–(4), s 171; FA 1994, s 93(5)*]

L Ltd, M Ltd and N Ltd are members of a 75% group of companies. L Ltd acquired a property in June 1990 for £50,000 and transferred it to M Ltd in June 1993. M Ltd transferred the property to N Ltd in June 1996, and N Ltd sold it outside the group in June 2002 for £55,000. The relevant indexation factors are as follows

June 1990 to June 1993	0.113
June 1993 to June 1996	0.085

(i) Disposal in June 1993
Consideration deemed to be such that neither gain nor loss arises.

	£
Cost of asset to L Ltd	50,000
Indexation allowance £50,000 × 0.113	5,650
Cost of asset to M Ltd	£55,650

(ii) Disposal in June 1996

Cost of asset to M Ltd	55,650
Indexation allowance £55,650 × 0.085	4,730
Cost of asset to N Ltd	£60,380

(iii) Disposal in June 2002

Proceeds	55,000
Cost (as above)	60,380
Loss before adjustment under *TCGA 1992, s 56(3)*	5,380
Deduct Indexation on June 1996 disposal	4,730
Allowable loss	£650

Notes

(*a*) Where a loss accrues on the ultimate disposal, it is reduced by any indexation allowance included in the cost of the asset by virtue of a no gain/no loss disposal made *after* 29 November 1993. If this adjustment would otherwise convert a loss into a gain, the disposal is treated as giving rise to neither a gain nor a loss. [*TCGA 1992, s 56(3); FA 1994, s 93(5)*].

(*b*) The principles illustrated in this example apply equally to inter-spouse transfers (except that, for inter-spouse transfers, indexation allowance cannot be computed beyond April 1998 — see note (*d*) to (A) above).

211.1 Interest on Overpaid Tax

211 Interest on Overpaid Tax

211.1 **SELF-ASSESSMENT** [*TCGA 1992, s 283; FA 1994, Sch 19 para 46, Sch 26 Pt V(23); FA 1997, s 92(5)(6)*]

M's tax return for 2000/2001 included a chargeable gain of £53,200 on the sale of some unquoted shares. His self-assessment showed capital gains tax payable of £18,400, i.e. £53,200 − £7,200 (annual exemption) = £46,000 @ 40% (M's marginal rate of income tax). M submitted the return and paid the tax on 27 January 2002. However, the computation included an estimated valuation of the shares as at 31 March 1982 and, following negotiations, the value was finally agreed at a figure in excess of M's estimate, resulting in a reduction of £8,000 in the chargeable gain. Thus, tax of £3,200 (£8,000 @ 40%) became repayable to M, and repayment was duly made on 9 August 2002.

The rate of interest on overpaid capital gains tax remained at 2.5% p.a. from 6 November 2001 to 9 August 2002 and beyond. *Purely for illustration purposes*, it is assumed that it was increased to 2.75% from 6 May 2002.

Repayment supplement is as follows

27.1.02 − 5.5.02	£3,200 × 2.5% × $\frac{99}{365}$	21.70
6.5.02 − 9.8.02	£3,200 × 2.75% × $\frac{95}{365}$	22.90
		£44.60

Note

(a) Supplement runs from the date the tax was paid (even if before the due date — 31 January 2002 in this case) to the date the repayment order is issued, though it should be noted that the Revenue do not pay supplement on any amount deliberately overpaid (Revenue Press Release 12 November 1996).

212 Interest and Surcharges on Unpaid Tax

212.1 SELF-ASSESSMENT [*TMA 1970, ss 59C, 86; FA 1994, ss 194, 196, 199, Sch 19 para 20; FA 1995, ss 109, 110*]

Mr Watson's 2000/2001 capital gains tax liability as shown in his self-assessment amounts to £5,000. On 1 June 2002 Mr Watson pays £2,000 and on 3 August 2002 he pays the £3,000 balance.

The rate of interest on overdue capital gains tax remained at 6.5% p.a. from 6 November 2001 to 3 August 2002 and beyond. *Purely for illustration purposes*, it is assumed that it was increased to 7% from 6 May 2002.

Mr Watson will be charged as follows

Interest and Surcharge due

	£	£
Interest		
£2,000 × 6.5% × $\frac{95}{365}$ (31.1.02 – 5.5.02)	33.83	
£2,000 × 7.0% × $\frac{26}{365}$ (6.5.02 – 1.6.02)	9.97	43.80
£3,000 × 6.5% × $\frac{95}{365}$ (31.1.02 – 5.5.02)	50.75	
£3,000 × 7.0% × $\frac{89}{365}$ (6.5.02 – 3.8.02)	51.21	101.96
		£145.76
Surcharge		
Initial surcharge — £5,000 × 5%		250.00
Additional surcharge — £3,000 × 5%		150.00
		£400.00

Notes

(a) Under self-assessment, capital gains tax is normally due on 31 January following the year of assessment. [*TMA 1970, s 59B(4); FA 1994, ss 193, 199*].

(b) If any tax is paid more than 28 days late, a 5% surcharge is levied in addition to interest. An additional surcharge is also levied on tax outstanding for more than 6 months. On appeal, surcharges may be set aside if the Commissioners accept that the taxpayer had a 'reasonable excuse' for late payment. Interest is chargeable on a surcharge and accrues from a date which is 30 days after the surcharge is imposed. [*TMA 1970, s 59C; FA 1994, s 194; FA 1995, s 109*].

213.1 Land

213 Land

213.1 SMALL PART DISPOSALS [*TCGA 1992, s 242; FA 1996, Sch 21 para 37*]
C owns farmland which cost £134,000 in May 1988 and which is a business asset throughout for the purposes of TAPER RELIEF (227). In February 1996, a small plot of land is exchanged with an adjoining landowner for another piece of land. The value placed on the transaction is £18,000. The value of the remaining estate excluding the new piece of land is estimated at £250,000. In March 2003, C sells the whole estate for £300,000. He makes no other disposals in 2002/03.

Indexation factors		
May 1988 to February 1996		0.421
February 1996 to April 1998 (note (*e*))		0.078
May 1988 to April 1998 (note (*e*))		0.531

(i) No claim made under *TCGA 1992, s 242(2)*

		£	£
(*a*)	Disposal in February 1996		
	Disposal proceeds		18,000
	Allowable cost $\dfrac{18,000}{18,000 + 250,000} \times £134,000$		9,000
	Unindexed gain		9,000
	Indexation allowance £9,000 × 0.421		3,789
	Chargeable gain 1995/96		£5,211
(*b*)	Disposal in March 2003		
	Disposal proceeds		300,000
	Allowable cost		
	Original land £(134,000 − 9,000)	125,000	
	Exchanged land	18,000	143,000
	Unindexed gain		157,000
	Indexation allowance		
	Original land £125,000 × 0.531	66,375	
	Exchanged land £18,000 × 0.078	1,404	67,779
	Pre-tapered gain		89,221
	Business asset taper relief @ 75%		66,916
	Chargeable gain 2002/03		£22,305

(ii) Claim made under *TCGA 1992, s 242(2)*

(*a*)	No disposal in February 1996	
	Allowable cost of original land	134,000
	Deduct Disposal proceeds	18,000
	Adjusted allowable cost	£116,000
	Allowable cost of additional land	£18,000

Land 213.1

		£	£
(b)	*Disposal in March 2003*		
	Disposal proceeds		300,000
	Allowable cost		
	Original land	116,000	
	Additional land	18,000	134,000
	Unindexed gain		166,000
	Indexation allowance		
	Original land £134,000 × 0.531	71,154	
	Additional land £18,000 × 0.078	1,404	
		72,558	
	Receipt set-off £18,000 × 0.078	1,404	71,154
	Pre-tapered gain		94,846
	Business asset taper relief @ 75%		71,135
	Chargeable gain 2002/03		£23,711

Notes

(a) A claim under *TCGA 1992, s 242* may be made where the consideration for the part disposal does not exceed one-fifth of the value of the whole, up to a maximum of £20,000.

(b) If the second disposal had also been made in 1995/96 no claim under *section 242(2)* could have been made on the part disposal as proceeds of all disposals of land in the year would have exceeded £20,000.

(c) Although (ii) above gives the lower overall gain, (i) above would be preferable if there are little or no other gains for 1995/96, such that the 1995/96 gain in (i) above is fully covered by the annual exemption for that year.

(d) If the original land had been held at 31 March 1982 and the part disposal took place after that date, the disposal proceeds, on a claim under *section 242(2)*, would be deducted from the 31 March 1982 value for the purpose of the re-basing provisions.

(e) Other than for the purposes of corporation tax on chargeable gains, indexation allowance is frozen at its April 1998 level. Therefore, the indexation factor for April 1998 is used in respect of disposals in a later month (and expenditure incurred in April 1998 or later does not attract indexation allowance at all). See 210 INDEXATION.

213.2 Land

213.2 **COMPULSORY PURCHASE** [*TCGA 1992, ss 243–248; FA 1996, s 141(4)(6), Sch 21 para 38*]

(A) Rollover where new land acquired

(i) Rollover not claimed

D owns freehold land purchased for £77,000 in 1978. Part of the land is made the subject of a compulsory purchase order. The compensation of £70,000 is agreed on 10 August 2002. The market value of the remaining land is £175,000. The value of the total freehold land at 31 March 1982 was £98,000. The indexation factor for the period March 1982 to April 1998 (see note (*a*)) is 1.047.

	£	£
Disposal consideration	70,000	70,000
Cost £77,000 × $\dfrac{70,000}{70,000 + 175,000}$	22,000	
Market value 31.3.82		
£98,000 × $\dfrac{70,000}{70,000 + 175,000}$		28,000
Unindexed gain	48,000	42,000
Indexation allowance £28,000 × 1.047	29,316	29,316
Gain after indexation	£18,684	£12,684
Chargeable gain 2002/03 (subject to TAPER RELIEF (227))		£12,684

(ii) Rollover claimed under *TCGA 1992*, s 247

If, in (i), D acquires new land costing, say, £80,000 in, say, December 2002, relief may be claimed as follows.

	£
Allowable cost of land compulsorily purchased	28,000
Indexation allowance	29,316
Deemed consideration for disposal	57,316
Actual consideration	70,000
Chargeable gain rolled over	£12,684
Allowable cost of new land (£80,000 − £12,684)	£67,316

Note

(*a*) Other than for the purposes of corporation tax on chargeable gains, indexation allowance is frozen at its April 1998 level. Therefore, the indexation factor for April 1998 is used in respect of disposals in a later month (and expenditure incurred in April 1998 or later does not attract indexation allowance at all). See 210 INDEXATION.

(B) Small disposals

(i) No rollover relief claimed

T inherited land in June 1988 at a probate value of £290,000. Under a compulsory purchase order, a part of the land is acquired for highway improvements. Compensation of £32,000 and a further £10,000 for severance, neither sum including any amount in respect of loss of profits, is agreed on 15 May 2002. The value of the remaining land is £900,000. Prior to the compulsory purchase, the value of all the land had been £950,000. The indexation factor for the period June 1988 to April 1998 (note (*c*)) is 0.525.

	£
Total consideration for disposal (£32,000 + £10,000)	42,000
Deduct Allowable cost $\dfrac{42,000}{42,000 + 900,000} \times £290,000$	12,930
Unindexed gain	29,070
Indexation allowance £12,930 × 0.525	6,788
Chargeable gain 2002/03 (subject to TAPER RELIEF (227))	£22,282

(ii) Rollover relief claimed under *TCGA 1992, s 243*

Total consideration for disposal is £42,000, less than 5% of the value of the estate before the disposal (£950,000). T may therefore claim that the consideration be deducted from the allowable cost of the estate.

Revised allowable cost (£290,000 − £42,000)   £248,000

No chargeable gain then arises in 2002/03.

Notes

(*a*) An indexation adjustment in respect of the amount deducted will be required on a subsequent disposal of the estate. [*TCGA 1992, s 53(3), s 57*]. For an example of the computation, see 206.4(E) DISPOSAL.

(*b*) The Revenue additionally regard consideration of £3,000 or less as 'small', whether or not it would pass the 5% test illustrated here. (Revenue Tax Bulletin February 1997, p 397).

(*c*) Other than for the purposes of corporation tax on chargeable gains, indexation allowance is frozen at its April 1998 level. Therefore, the indexation factor for April 1998 is used in respect of disposals in a later month (and expenditure incurred in April 1998 or later does not attract indexation allowance at all). See 210 INDEXATION.

213.3 Land

213.3 **LEASES**

(A) Short leases which are not initially wasting assets [*TCGA 1992, Sch 8 para 1*]
On 31 August 1997, N purchased the remaining term of a lease of commercial premises for £55,000. The lease was subject to a 25-year sub-lease granted on 1 July 1975 at a fixed rental of £1,000 a year. The market rental was estimated at £15,000 a year. The term of the lease held by N is 60 years from 1 April 1973. The value of the lease in 2000, when the sub-lease expired, was estimated at 31 August 1997 as being £70,000. Immediately upon expiry of the sub-lease, N has refurbishment work done at a cost of £50,000, of which £40,000 qualifies as enhancement expenditure. On 31 March 2003, N sells the lease for £130,000.

Indexation factor	August 1997 to April 1998 (note (*b*))	0.026
Term of lease at date of expiry of sub-lease		32 years 9 months
Relevant percentage $89.354 + \frac{9}{12} \times (90.280 - 89.354)$		90.049%
Term of lease at date of assignment		30 years
Relevant percentage		87.330%

	£	£
Disposal consideration		130,000
Deduct Allowable cost	55,000	
Enhancement costs	40,000	
	95,000	
Less Wasted		
$\dfrac{90.049 - 87.330}{90.049} \times 95,000$	2,868	
		92,132
Unindexed gain		37,868
Indexation allowance:		
Cost of lease		
$0.026 \times \dfrac{55,000}{95,000} \times £92,132$	1,387	
Enhancement costs (note (*b*))	—	
		1,387
Chargeable gain 2001/02 (subject to TAPER RELIEF (227))		£36,481

Notes
(*a*) The head-lease becomes a wasting asset on the expiry of the sub-lease. [*TCGA 1992, Sch 8 para 1(2)*].

(*b*) Other than for the purposes of corporation tax on chargeable gains, indexation allowance is frozen at its April 1998 level. Therefore, the indexation factor for April 1998 is used in respect of disposals in a later month (and expenditure incurred in April 1998 or later does not attract indexation allowance at all). See 210 INDEXATION.

Land   213.3

(B) Grant of long lease [*TCGA 1992, s 42, Sch 8 para 2*]
In 1980, K acquired a long lease by assignment for £24,000. At the time he acquired it, the lease had an unexpired term of 82 years. On 10 April 2002, he granted a 55-year sub-lease for a premium of £110,000 and a peppercorn rent. The value of the reversion plus the capitalised value of the rents is £10,000. The value of the lease at 31 March 1982 was estimated at £54,000. The indexation factor for the period March 1982 to April 1998 (see note (*b*) to (A) above) is 1.047.

	£	£
Disposal consideration	110,000	110,000
Cost £24,000 × $\dfrac{110{,}000}{110{,}000 + 10{,}000}$	22,000	
Market value 31.3.82		
£54,000 × $\dfrac{110{,}000}{110{,}000 + 10{,}000}$		49,500
Unindexed gain	88,000	60,500
Indexation allowance £49,500 × 1.047	51,827	51,827
Gain after indexation	£36,173	£8,673
Chargeable gain 2002/03 (subject to TAPER RELIEF (227))		£8,673

213.3 Land

(C) Grant of short lease [*ICTA 1988, s 34; TCGA 1992, Sch 8 paras 2, 5; FA 1998, s 40, Sch 5 paras 15, 63*]

L is the owner of a freehold factory which he leases for a term of 25 years commencing in December 2002. The cost of the factory was £100,000 in April 1995. The lease is granted for a premium of £30,000 and an annual rent. The reversion to the lease plus the capitalised value of the rents amount to £120,000. The indexation factor for April 1995 to April 1998 (see note (*c*)) is 0.091.

	£	£
Amount chargeable to income tax		
Amount of premium		30,000
Deduct Excluded $\dfrac{25-1}{50} \times £30,000$		14,400
Amount chargeable to income tax		£15,600
Chargeable gain		
Premium received	30,000	
Deduct Charged to income tax	15,600	
		14,400
Allowable cost $\dfrac{14,400}{30,000 + 120,000} \times £100,000$		9,600
Unindexed gain		4,800
Indexation allowance £9,600 × 0.091		874
Chargeable gain 2002/03 (subject to TAPER RELIEF (227))		£3,926

Notes

(*a*) A short lease is one the duration of which, at the time of grant, does not exceed 50 years.

(*b*) The amount chargeable to income tax is not deducted from the amount of premium appearing in the denominator of the CGT apportionment fraction.

(*c*) Other than for the purposes of corporation tax on chargeable gains, indexation allowance is frozen at its April 1998 level. Therefore, the indexation factor for April 1998 is used in respect of disposals in a later month (and expenditure incurred in April 1998 or later does not attract indexation allowance at all). See 210 INDEXATION.

(D) Disposal by assignment of short lease: without enhancement expenditure [*TCGA 1992, Sch 8 para 1*]

X buys a lease for £200,000 on 1 October 1998. The lease commenced on 1 June 1989 for a term of 60 years. X assigns the lease for £300,000 at the end of March 2003.

Term of lease unexpired at date of acquisition	50 years 8 months
Relevant percentage	100%
Term of lease unexpired at date of assignment	46 years 2 months
Relevant percentage $98.490 + \frac{2}{12} \times (98.902 - 98.490)$	98.559%

	£	£
Disposal consideration		300,000
Allowable cost	200,000	
Deduct Wasted $\dfrac{100 - 98.559}{100} \times £200,000$	2,882	
		197,118
Chargeable gain 2002/03 (subject to TAPER RELIEF (227))		£102,882

Note
(a) Expenditure incurred in April 1998 or later does not attract indexation allowance. See 210 INDEXATION.

(E) Disposal by assignment of short lease held at 31 March 1982 [*TCGA 1992, s 35, Sch 8 para 1*]

A buys a lease for £100,000 on 1 March 1981. The lease commenced on 31 March 1971 for a term of 60 years. Its value at 31 March 1982 was estimated at £104,000. On 31 March 2003, A assigns the lease for £240,000. The indexation factor for the period March 1982 to April 1998 (note (*d*)) is 1.047.

(i) The computation without re-basing to 1982 is as follows

Term of lease unexpired at date of acquisition (1.3.81)	50 years 1 month
Relevant percentage	100%
Term of lease unexpired at date of assignment	28 years 0 months
Relevant percentage	85.053%

213.3 Land

	£	£
Disposal consideration		240,000
Cost	100,000	
Deduct Wasted $\dfrac{100 - 85.053}{100} \times £100{,}000$	14,947	85,053
Unindexed gain		154,947
Indexation allowance (see (ii) below)		92,932
Gain after indexation		£62,015

(ii) The computation with re-basing to 1982 is as follows

Term of lease unexpired at deemed date of acquisition (31.3.82)	49 years
Relevant percentage	99.657%
Term of lease unexpired at date of assignment	28 years
Relevant percentage	85.053%

	£	£
Disposal consideration		240,000
Market value 31.3.82	104,000	
Deduct Wasted $\dfrac{99.657 - 85.053}{99.657} \times £104{,}000$	15,240	88,760
Unindexed gain		151,240
Indexation allowance £88,760 × 1.047		92,932
Gain after indexation		£58,308
Chargeable gain 2002/03 (subject to TAPER RELIEF (227))		£58,308

Notes

(*a*) A is deemed, under *TCGA 1992, s 35*, to have disposed of and immediately re-acquired the lease on 31 March 1982 at its market value at that date.

(*b*) Both calculations produce a gain with the re-basing calculation producing the smaller gain. Therefore, re-basing applies. [*TCGA 1992, s 35(2)(3)(a)*].

(*c*) Indexation is based, in both calculations, on the assumption that the asset was sold and re-acquired at market value on 31 March 1982 since this gives a greater allowance than if based on original cost as reduced by the wasting asset provisions. [*TCGA 1992, s 55(1)(2)*].

(*d*) Other than for the purposes of corporation tax on chargeable gains, indexation allowance is frozen at its April 1998 level. Therefore, the indexation factor for April 1998 is used in respect of disposals in a later month (and expenditure incurred in April 1998 or later does not attract indexation allowance at all). See 210 INDEXATION.

(F) Disposal by assignment of short lease: with enhancement expenditure [*TCGA 1992, Sch 8 para 1*]

D Ltd acquires the lease of office premises for £100,000 on 1 July 1994. On 1 January 1996, the company contracts for complete refurbishment of the premises at a total cost of £180,000, of which £120,000 can be regarded as capital enhancement expenditure. The work is done at the beginning of January 1996, and the money is payable in equal tranches in March 1996 and May 1996. The lease is for a term of 50 years commencing 1 April 1987. On 1 January 2003, the lease is assigned to a new lessee for £450,000.

Indexation factors (assumed)		
July 1994 to January 2003		0.250
March 1996 to January 2003		0.180
May 1996 to January 2003		0.170

Term of lease unexpired at date of acquisition — 42 years 9 months
Relevant percentage $96.593 + \frac{9}{12} \times (97.107 - 96.593)$ — 96.978%

Term of lease unexpired at date of expenditure incurred (January 1995 — see note (*a*)) — 41 years 3 months
Relevant percentage $96.041 + \frac{3}{12} \times (96.593 - 96.041)$ — 96.179%

Term of lease unexpired at date of assignment — 34 years 3 months
Relevant percentage $91.156 + \frac{3}{12} \times (91.981 - 91.156)$ — 91.362%

	£	£	£
Disposal consideration			450,000
Cost of acquisition	100,000		
Deduct Wasted			
$\dfrac{96.978 - 91.362}{96.978} \times 100{,}000$	5,791	94,209	
Enhancement expenditure	120,000		
Deduct Wasted			
$\dfrac{96.179 - 91.362}{96.179} \times 120{,}000$	6,010	113,990	208,199
Unindexed gain			241,801
Indexation allowance			
Cost of lease £94,209 × 0.250		23,552	
Enhancement costs			
March 1995 £56,995 × 0.180		10,259	
May 1995 £56,995 × 0.170		9,689	
			43,500
Chargeable gain			£198,301

Note

(*a*) The wasting provisions apply to enhancement expenditure by reference to the time when it is first reflected in the nature of the lease. The indexation provisions apply by reference to the date the expenditure became due and payable. [*TCGA 1992, s 54(4)(b), Sch 8 para 1(4)(b)*].

213.3 Land

(G) Disposal of short lease where premium partly relieved under *ICTA 1988, s 87*
Butcher acquired a 36-year lease of shop premises from Baker on 1 July 1995 at a premium of £33,000. Butcher prepares trading accounts to 30 June each year. On 1 July 2002, when the unexpired term of the lease is 29 years and property values have risen sharply in the locality, he assigns the lease for £65,000. He makes no other chargeable disposals in 2002/03 and is not entitled to retirement relief. The indexation factor for the period July 1995 to April 1998 (note (*c*)) is 0.091.

The annual trading deduction under *ICTA 1988, s 87* is computed as follows

	£
Premium on 36-year lease	33,000
Deduct (36 − 1) × 2% × £33,000	23,100
Premium chargeable under Schedule A on Baker	£9,900

In addition to actual rent payable under the lease, Butcher is treated for Schedule D, CaseI income tax purposes as paying rent, accruing on a day-to-day basis for up to 36 years, of

$$\frac{£9,900}{36} = £275 \text{ p.a.}$$

In his seven accounting years to 30 June 2002, Butcher has thus received a total deduction under *ICTA 1988, s 87* of (£275 × 7) = £1,925

The chargeable gain on disposal of the lease in July 2002 is computed as below.

Term of lease unexpired at date of acquisition	36 years	
Relevant percentage	92.761%	
Term of lease unexpired at date of disposal	29 years	
Relevant percentage	86.226%	
	£	£
Disposal consideration		65,000
Cost of acquisition	33,000	
Deduct Income tax relief given (see above)	1,925	(note (*a*))
	31,075	
Deduct Wasted $\dfrac{92.761 - 86.226}{92.761}$ × £31,075	2,189	28,886
Unindexed gain		36,114
Deduct Indexation allowance £28,886 × 0.091		2,629
Pre-tapered gain		33,485
Deduct Business asset taper relief for 3 years (£33,485 × 75%)		25,114
Chargeable gain		8,371
Deduct Annual exemption		7,700
Taxable gains 2002/03		£671

Notes

(*a*) The allowable expenditure for CGT is reduced, by virtue of *TCGA 1992, s 39* (exclusion of double relief), by the amount on which income tax relief has been given. This reduction is made *before* the wasting asset reduction required by *TCGA 1992, Sch 8 para 1(4)* (Revenue Capital Gains Manual CG 71201).

(*b*) For further examples on the *income tax* treatment of lease premiums, see (C) above, (H) and (J) below, and IT 20.4 SCHEDULE A.

(*c*) Other than for the purposes of corporation tax on chargeable gains, indexation allowance is frozen at its April 1998 level. See 210 INDEXATION.

213.3 Land

(H) Sub-lease granted out of short lease: premium not less than potential premium
[*TCGA 1992, Sch 8 paras 4, 5; FA 1998, Sch 5 para 63*]
On 1 November 2000, S purchased a lease of shop premises then having 50 years to run for a premium of £100,000 and an annual rental of £40,000. After occupying the premises for the purposes of his own business, S granted a sub-lease to N Ltd. The sub-lease was for a term of 21 years commencing on 1 August 2002, for a premium of £50,000 and an annual rental of £30,000. It is agreed that, had the rent under the sub-lease been £40,000, the premium obtainable would have been £20,000.

Term of lease at date granted	50 years
Relevant percentage	100%
Term of lease at date sub-lease granted	48 years 3 months
Relevant percentage $99.289 + \frac{3}{12} \times (99.657 - 99.289)$	99.381%
Term of lease at date sub-lease expires	27 years 3 months
Relevant percentage $83.816 + \frac{3}{12} \times (85.053 - 83.816)$	84.125%

Premium chargeable on S under Schedule A	£
Amount of premium	50,000
Deduct $\dfrac{21-1}{50} \times £50{,}000$	20,000
Amount chargeable under Schedule A	£30,000
Chargeable gain	
Disposal consideration	50,000
Allowable expenditure	
$£100{,}000 \times \dfrac{99.381 - 84.125}{100}$	15,256
Chargeable gain	34,744
Deduct Amount chargeable under Schedule A	30,000
Net chargeable gain 2002/03 (subject to TAPER RELIEF (227))	£4,744

Notes
(*a*) If the amount chargeable under Schedule A had exceeded the chargeable gain, the net gain would have been nil. The deduction cannot create or increase a loss. [*TCGA 1992, Sch 8 para 5(2)*].

(*b*) Other than for the purposes of corporation tax on chargeable gains, expenditure incurred in April 1998 or later does not attract indexation allowance (see 210 INDEXATION).

Land 213.3

(J) Sub-lease granted out of short lease: premium less than potential premium
[*TCGA 1992, Sch 8 paras 4, 5; FA 1998, Sch 5 para 63*]
C bought a lease of a house on 1 May 1998, when the unexpired term was 49 years. The cost of the lease was £20,000, and the ground rent payable is £500 p.a. C then let the house on a monthly tenancy until 30 November 2002 when he granted a 10-year lease for a premium of £5,000 and an annual rent of £8,000. Had the rent under the sub-lease been £500 a year, the premium obtainable would have been £40,000. C does not at any time occupy the house as a private residence.

Term of lease at date of acquisition	49 years
Relevant percentage	99.657%
Term of lease when sub-lease granted	44 years 5 months
Relevant percentage $97.595 + \frac{5}{12} \times (98.059 - 97.595)$	97.788%
Term of lease when sub-lease expires	34 years 5 months
Relevant percentage $91.156 + \frac{5}{12} \times (91.981 - 91.156)$	91.500%

Amount chargeable under Schedule A	£
Amount of premium	5,000
Deduct Exclusion $\frac{10-1}{50} \times £5,000$	900
Chargeable under Schedule A	£4,100

Chargeable gain	
Disposal consideration	5,000
Deduct Allowable expenditure	
$£20,000 \times \frac{97.788 - 91.500}{99.657} \times \frac{5,000}{40,000}$	158
Gain	4,842
Deduct Amount chargeable under Schedule A	4,100
Net chargeable gain 2002/03 (subject to TAPER RELIEF (227))	£742

Notes
(*a*) If the amount chargeable under Schedule A had exceeded the chargeable gain, the net gain would have been nil. The deduction cannot create or increase a loss. [*TCGA 1992, Sch 8 para 5(2)*].

(*b*) Expenditure incurred in April 1998 or later does not attract indexation allowance). See 210 INDEXATION.

214 Losses

Cross-references. See IT 10.2 LOSSES for the set-off of trading losses against chargeable gains made by individuals. See 201.2 ANNUAL RATES AND EXEMPTIONS for the interaction between losses and the annual exemption. See also 227.1(B) TAPER RELIEF.

214.1 GENERAL

On 30 April 2002 Q sells for £40,000 a part of the land which he owns. The market value of the remaining estate is £160,000. Q bought the land for £250,000 in March 1992.

	£
Disposal consideration	40,000
Allowable cost $\dfrac{40,000}{40,000 + 160,000} \times £250,000$	50,000
Allowable loss	£10,000

Note

(*a*) Indexation allowance cannot increase or create a loss for CGT purposes. [*TCGA 1992, s 53; FA 1994, s 93(1)–(3)*].

214.2 PERSONAL LOSSES SET AGAINST ATTRIBUTED SETTLEMENT GAINS

[*TCGA 1992, ss 2(4)–(8), 77; FA 1998, Sch 21 para 2; FA 2002, s 51, Sch 11 paras 2, 3, 7, 8*].

In 1997, R created a UK–resident settlement in which he retained the reversionary interest. It is accepted that *TCGA 1992, s 77* applies to the settlement such that any chargeable gains accruing to the trustees are chargeable on R as settlor (see also 224.2 SETTLEMENTS). In 2002/03, the trustees realised a pre-tapered gain of £14,118 on a disposal of quoted securities, a non-business asset for taper relief purposes which they had held since creation of the settlement. They made no other disposal in the year. R, meanwhile, made two disposals in 2002/03 on which he realised a chargeable gain of £4,000 (attracting potential 10% taper relief) and an allowable loss of £9,000. Neither the trustees nor R have any losses brought forward from earlier years. R has taxable income in excess of the basic rate limit.

Without an election under *FA 2002, Sch 11 para 8***, R's CGT position for 2002/03 is as follows** (see also 201.2(B)(C) ANNUAL RATES AND EXEMPTIONS).

Before being attributed to R, the trustees' gain of £14,118 attracts 15% TAPER RELIEF (227) (non-business asset held for 4 years after 5 April 1998 + 1 bonus year) and is thus reduced to £12,000 (£14,118 @ 85%).

Losses 214.2

	£
Personal gains	4,000
Attributed gains (up to the annual exempt amount)	7,700
	11,700
Deduct Personal losses (against personal gains only)	4,000
	7,700
Deduct Annual exempt amount	7,700
	Nil
Add Attributed gains not included above (£12,000 – 7,700)	4,300
Taxable gains (no further taper relief available)	£4,300
CGT payable by R at 40% (recoverable from trustees)	£1,720.00
Personal losses carried forward (£9,000 – £4,000)	£5,000

With an election, R's CGT position becomes as follows.

	£
Personal gains	4,000
Deduct Personal losses (part) (note (*b*))	4,000
	Nil
Attributed gains (note (*c*))	14,118
Deduct Personal losses (balance) (£9,000 – £4,000)	5,000
	9,118
Deduct Taper relief £9,118 @ 15% (note (*c*))	1,368
	7,750
Deduct Annual exempt amount	7,700
Taxable gains	£50
CGT payable by R at 40% (recoverable from trustees)	£20.00
Personal losses carried forward	Nil

Notes

(*a*) The election under *FA 2002, Sch 11 para 8* is available for any one or more of the years 2000/01, 2001/02 and 2002/03 and must be made no later than 31 January 2005. [*FA 2002, Sch 11 para 8*]. For 2003/04 onwards, personal losses are deductible without election from *TCGA 1992, s 77* gains. For 1998/99 and 1999/2000, they were not deductible from such gains at all.

(*b*) Personal losses must be set against personal gains for any particular tax year in priority to attributed gains treated as accruing to the person in that year.

(*c*) Where personal losses are set against an attributed gain, the gain is initially attributed without regard to taper relief. After offsetting the losses, the net attributed gain is then tapered by reference to the period the asset was held by the trustees and its status (business or non-business asset) in their hands.

(*d*) Similar rules apply in the case of gains attributed under *TCGA 1992, s 86* (offshore settlements with settlor interest).

214.3 Losses

214.3 LOSSES ON SHARES IN UNLISTED TRADING COMPANIES [*ICTA 1988, ss 574–576; FA 1994, s 210, Sch 20 para 8; FA 1996, Sch 38 para 6(1)(2)(9); FA 1998, s 80; FA 2000, s 63(2)(3), Sch 16 para 3(3)*]

P subscribed for 3,000 £1 ordinary shares at par in W Ltd, a qualifying trading company, in June 1988. In September 1995, P acquired a further 2,200 shares at £3 per share from another shareholder. In December 2002, P sold 3,900 shares at 40p per share.

Indexation factors	June 1988 to September 1995	0.413
	September 1995 to April 1998 (note (*c*))	0.080

Procedure

Firstly, establish the '*section 104* holding' pool.

	Shares	Qualifying expenditure £	Indexed pool £
June 1988 subscription	3,000	3,000	3,000
Indexation to September 1995 £3,000 × 0.413			1,239
September 1995 acquisition	2,200	6,600	6,600
	5,200	9,600	10,839
Indexed rise: September 1995 to April 1998 £10,839 × 0.080			867
	5,200	9,600	11,706
December 2002 disposal	(3,900)	(7,200)	(8,780)
Pool carried forward	1,300	£2,400	£2,926

Step 1. Calculate the CGT loss in the normal way, as follows

	£
Disposal consideration 3,900 × £0.40	1,560
Allowable cost $\dfrac{3,900}{5,200} \times £9,600$	7,200
Allowable loss	£5,640

Step 2. Applying a LIFO basis, identify the qualifying shares (1,700) and the non-qualifying shares (2,200) comprised in the disposal.

Step 3. Calculate the proportion of the loss attributable to the qualifying shares.

Loss referable to 1,700 qualifying shares $\dfrac{1,700}{3,900} \times £5,640$ £2,458

Step 4. Compare the loss in Step 3 with the actual cost of the qualifying shares, *viz.*

Cost of 1,700 qualifying shares $\dfrac{1,700}{3,000} \times £3,000$ £1,700

The loss available against income is restricted to £1,700 (being lower than £2,458).

The loss not relieved against income remains an allowable loss for CGT purposes.

£5,640 − £1,700 =   £3,940

Losses 214.3

Notes

(*a*) Steps 1 to 4 illustrated in this example are those identified by the Revenue Capital Gains Manual at CG 58377 and Venture Capital Schemes Manual at VCM 47150.

(*b*) For shares issued after 5 April 1998 (not illustrated above), a company is a qualifying trading company for the purposes of this relief only if it would be a qualifying company for the purposes of the Enterprise Investment Scheme (EIS), although it is not a condition that the company issued the shares under the EIS or that any EIS income tax relief has been, or could have been, claimed in respect of them. [*ICTA 1988, s 576(4)–(4B); FA 1998, s 80(3)(5); FA 2001, Sch 15 para 38*].

(*c*) Other than for the purposes of corporation tax on chargeable gains, indexation allowance is frozen at its April 1998 level. Therefore, the indexation factor for April 1998 is used in respect of disposals in a later month (and expenditure incurred in April 1998 or later does not attract indexation allowance at all). See 210 INDEXATION.

(*d*) For further examples on this topic, see IT 10.5 LOSSES and CT 118.4 LOSSES.

215.1 Married Persons

215 Married Persons

Cross-reference. See 227.3 TAPER RELIEF.

215.1 INTER-SPOUSE TRANSFERS AND RATES OF TAX [*TCGA 1992, ss 4, 58*]

(A) No inter-spouse transfer
Paul and Heidi are a married couple with total income of £31,800 and £36,800 respectively for 2002/03. On 4 April 2003, Heidi sells a painting which she had acquired in June 1994 at a cost of £5,000. Net sale proceeds amount to £19,200 and the indexation factor for the period June 1994 to April 1998 (note (*a*)) is 0.124. Neither spouse disposed of any other chargeable assets during 2002/03.

Chargeable gain — Heidi

	£
Net proceeds	19,200
Cost	5,000
Unindexed gain	14,200
Indexation allowance £5,000 × 0.124	620
Pre-tapered gain	13,580
Taper relief @ 15%	2,037
	11,543
Annual exemption	7,700
Taxable gain	£3,843

	£
Total income	36,800
Personal allowance	4,615
Taxable income	£32,185

Basic rate limit = £29,900, so gain of £3,843 is all taxed at 40%.

Tax payable £3,843 × 40%   £1,537.20

Note
(*a*) Other than for the purposes of corporation tax on chargeable gains, indexation allowance is frozen at its April 1998 level. Therefore, the indexation factor for April 1998 is used in respect of disposals in a later month (and expenditure incurred in April 1998 or later does not attract indexation allowance at all). See 210 INDEXATION.

(B) Inter-spouse transfer
The facts are as in (A) above except that in January 2003, Heidi gives the painting to Paul who then makes the sale on 4 April 2003.

Chargeable gain — Heidi

	£
Deemed consideration (January 2003)	5,620
Cost	5,000
Unindexed gain carried forward	620

Married Persons 215.1

	£
Unindexed gain brought forward	620
Indexation allowance (to April 1998) £5,000 × 0.124	620
Chargeable gain	Nil

Chargeable gain — Paul

	£
Net proceeds (4.4.03)	19,200
Cost (January 2003)	5,620
Pre-tapered gain	13,580
Taper relief @ 15% (note (*b*))	2,037
	11,543
Annual exemption	7,700
Taxable gain	£3,843
Total income	31,800
Personal allowance	(4,615)
Taxable income	£27,185

Taxable income falls short of the basic rate limit (£29,900) by £2,715, so gain of £3,843 is taxed as follows

£2,715 at 20%	543.00
£1,128 at 40%	451.20
Tax payable	£994.20
Tax saving compared with (A) above	£543.00

Notes

(*a*) The inter-spouse transfer is deemed to be for such consideration as to ensure that no gain or loss accrues. [*TCGA 1992, s 58*]. Effectively, the consideration is equal to cost plus indexation (to April 1998 see 210.1 INDEXATION). See 210.2(A)(B) INDEXATION for further examples. The principles in 210.2(C)(D) INDEXATION also apply.

(*b*) Taper relief is computed by reference to the combined period of ownership after 5 April 1998 (see 227.3 TAPER RELIEF). In this instance, relief is at the non-business asset rate of 15% by reference to a qualifying holding period of five complete years (including the bonus year for assets acquired before 17 March 1998).

(*c*) The fact that transfers of assets between husband and wife are no gain/no loss transfers enables savings to be made by ensuring that disposals are made by a spouse with an unused annual exemption and/or basic rate band.

(*d*) An inter-spouse transfer followed by a sale could be attacked by the Revenue as an anti-avoidance device. To minimise the risk, there should be a clear time interval between the two transactions and no arrangements made to effect the ultimate sale until after the transfer. The gift should be outright with no strings attached and with no 'arrangement' for eventual proceeds to be passed to the transferor.

215.2 Married Persons

215.2 JOINTLY OWNED ASSETS

Derek and Raquel are a married couple. Derek had for many years owned an investment property which he purchased for £70,000 in May 1988. On 5 January 1996, he transferred to Raquel a 10% share in the property which was thereafter held in their joint names as tenants in common. At the time of the transfer, a 10% share of the property is worth £10,000 on the open market and a 90% share is worth £90,000. No declaration is made for income tax purposes under *ICTA 1988, s 282B*, with the result that the rental income from the property is treated, by virtue of *ICTA 1988, s 282A* as arising in equal shares. On 29 June 2002, the property is sold for £140,000.

Indexation factors May 1988 to January 1996	0.414
May 1988 to April 1998 (note (*d*))	0.531
January 1996 to April 1998 (note (*d*))	0.083

(i) Inter-spouse transfer

	£
Deemed consideration (January 1996)	9,898
Cost £70,000 × $\frac{10,000}{10,000 + 90,000}$ (see note (*c*))	7,000
Unindexed gain	2,898
Indexation allowance £7,000 × 0.414	2,898
Chargeable gain 1995/96	Nil

(ii) 2002/03 disposal

	Derek £	Raquel £
Disposal proceeds	126,000	14,000
Cost: Derek (£70,000 − £7,000)	63,000	
Raquel (see (i) above)		9,898
Unindexed gain	63,000	4,102
Indexation allowance: £63,000 × 0.531	33,453	
£9,898 × 0.083		822
Chargeable gains 2002/03 (subject to TAPER RELIEF (227))	£29,547	£3,280

Notes

(*a*) Where a joint declaration of unequal beneficial interests is made under *ICTA 1988, s 282B*, it is presumed that the same split applies for capital gains tax purposes. In the absence of a declaration, and regardless of the income tax treatment of income derived from the asset, a gain on an asset held in the joint names of husband and wife is apportioned in accordance with their respective beneficial interests at the time of disposal. (Revenue Press Release 21 November 1990).

(*b*) See 215.1 above as to how the consideration for the inter-spouse transfer is arrived at.

(*c*) The allowable expenditure on the inter-spouse transfer is apportioned in accordance with the part disposal rules in *TCGA 1992, s 42* (see 206.2 DISPOSAL).

(*d*) Other than for the purposes of corporation tax on chargeable gains, indexation allowance is frozen at its April 1998 level. Therefore, the indexation factor for April 1998 is used in respect of disposals in a later month (and expenditure incurred in April 1998 or later does not attract indexation allowance at all). See 210 INDEXATION.

216 Mineral Royalties

Cross-reference. See also IT 12.1 MINERAL ROYALTIES.

216.1 GENERAL [*ICTA 1988, s 122; TCGA 1992, ss 201–203*]

L Ltd, an investment company preparing accounts to 31 December, is the holder of a lease of land acquired in 1989 for £66,000, when the lease had an unexpired term of 65 years. In January 1997, L Ltd grants a 10-year licence to a mining company to search for and exploit minerals beneath the land. The licence is granted for £60,000 plus a mineral royalty calculated on the basis of the value of any minerals won by the licensee. The market value of the retained land (exclusive of the mineral rights) is then £10,000. L Ltd receives mineral royalties as follows

		£
Year ended	31 December 1997	12,000
	31 December 1998	19,000
	31 December 1999	29,000
	31 December 2000	38,000
	31 December 2001	17,000
	31 December 2002	10,000

On 2 January 2003, L Ltd relinquishes its rights under the lease and receives no consideration from the lessor.

(i) Chargeable gains 1997

		£
(a)	Disposal proceeds	60,000
	Allowable cost $\dfrac{60,000}{60,000 + 10,000} \times £66,000$	56,571
	Chargeable gain subject to indexation	£3,429
(b)	$\tfrac{1}{2} \times £12,000$	£6,000

(ii) Chargeable gains 1998 to 2002

		£
1998	$\tfrac{1}{2} \times £19,000$	9,500
1999	$\tfrac{1}{2} \times £29,000$	14,500
2000	$\tfrac{1}{2} \times £38,000$	19,000
2001	$\tfrac{1}{2} \times £17,000$	8,500
2002	$\tfrac{1}{2} \times £10,000$	5,000

(iii) Loss 2003

	£
Proceeds of disposal of lease	Nil
Allowable cost £66,000 – £56,571	9,429
Allowable loss	£9,429

216.1 Mineral Royalties

(iv) The loss may be set off against the chargeable gains arising on the mineral royalties as follows

	£
2002 (whole)	5,000
2001 (part)	4,429
	£9,429

Note
(a) Under *ICTA 1988, s 122* and *TCGA 1992, s 201*, one half of mineral royalties is taxed as income and one half as a chargeable gain. The gain is deemed to accrue in the year of assessment or company accounting period for which the royalties are receivable and is not capable of being reduced by any expenditure or by indexation allowance.

217 Offshore Settlements

Cross-reference. See also 214.2 LOSSES.

217.1 CHARGE ON BENEFICIARY IN RECEIPT OF CAPITAL PAYMENTS

(A) Charge under *TCGA 1992, s 87*

M, resident and domiciled in the UK, is the sole beneficiary of a discretionary settlement administered in the Cayman Islands. The trustees are all individuals resident in the Cayman Islands. The settlement was created in 1987 by M's father, who is resident and domiciled in the UK throughout. For 1987/88 to 2001/02 the trustees have chargeable gains and allowable losses, and make capital payments to M, as follows

	Chargeable gains £	Allowable losses £	Capital payments £
1987/88	50,000	60,000	20,000
1988/89	80,000	30,000	50,000
1989/90	105,000	—	—
1990/91	—	—	35,000
1991/92	32,000	7,000	20,000
1992/93	—	—	27,000
1993/94–2001/02	101,000	—	—

See also (B) below.

	£	£
1987/88		
Trust gains (£50,000 – £60,000)		—
Capital payment		20,000
Balance of capital payment carried forward		£20,000
Trust losses carried forward		£10,000
1988/89		
Trust gains (£80,000 – £30,000 – £10,000)		£40,000
Capital payment	50,000	
Brought forward	20,000	£70,000
Chargeable gains assessable on M		£40,000
Capital payment carried forward (£70,000 – £40,000)		£30,000
1989/90		
Trust gains		£105,000
Capital payment brought forward		£30,000
Chargeable gains assessable on M		£30,000
Trust gains carried forward (£105,000 – £30,000)		£75,000

217.1 Offshore Settlements

1990/91	£
Trust gains	—
Trust gains brought forward	75,000
	£75,000
Capital payment	£35,000
Chargeable gains assessable on M	£35,000
Trust gains carried forward (£75,000 − £35,000)	£40,000

1991/92	£
Trust gains (£32,000 − £7,000)	25,000
Trust gains brought forward	40,000
	£65,000
Capital payment	£20,000
Chargeable gains assessable on M	£20,000
Trust gains carried forward (£65,000 − £20,000)	£45,000

1992/93	£
Trust gains	—
Trust gains brought forward	45,000
	£45,000
Capital payment	£27,000
Chargeable gains assessable on M	£27,000
Trust gains carried forward	£18,000

1993/94–2001/02	£
Cumulative trust gains	101,000
Trust gains brought forward	18,000
Trust gains carried forward	£119,000

Note

(a) As regards gains and losses accruing to the trustees after 16 March 1998 and capital payments received by beneficiaries after that date, these provisions apply regardless of the domicile and residence status of the settlor when the settlement was made or during the tax year in question. [*TCGA 1992, s 87; FA 1998, s 130*].

Offshore Settlements 217.1

(B) Surcharge on CGT under *TCGA 1992, s 87* [*TCGA 1992, ss 91–93, 97*]
The facts are as in (A) above. In 2002/03, the trustees make a capital payment of £100,000. For both 1992/93 and 2002/03, M is liable to CGT at the rate of 40% on all chargeable gains.

(i) Determination of qualifying amounts [*TCGA 1992, s 92(1)(2)*]

Qualifying amount for 1990/91 (equivalent to trust gains carried forward at 5.4.91)	£40,000
Qualifying amount for 1991/92 (i.e. trust gains for that year only)	£25,000

(ii) Matching capital payments made after 5.4.91 [*TCGA 1992, s 92(3)–(6)*]
£20,000 paid in 1991/92 is matched (on first in, first out basis) with qualifying amount for 1990/91, leaving an unmatched qualifying amount of £20,000 for 1990/91.

£27,000 paid in 1992/93. £20,000 is matched with balance of qualifying amount for 1990/91 and £7,000 is matched with qualifying amount for 1991/92, leaving an unmatched qualifying amount of £18,000 for 1991/92.

£100,000 paid in 2002/03. £18,000 is matched with balance of qualifying amount for 1991/92 (leaving £82,000 to be matched with post-1991/92 qualifying amounts and £19,000 of gains unmatched).

(iii) Surcharge payable by M [*TCGA 1992, ss 91–93*]

1991/92
No surcharge is payable in respect of capital payments made before 6.4.92.

1992/93
As only part of the capital payment is matched with a qualifying amount for a year of assessment falling before that immediately preceding the year in which the payment is made, only that part (i.e. £20,000 — see (ii) above) is liable to surcharge, and the balance is ignored. [*TCGA 1992, s 93(3)*].

	£
CGT payable by M (subject to surcharge)	
(£27,000 − £5,800 annual exemption) × 40%	8,480
Surcharge (£20,000 − £5,800) × 40% = £5,680 × 10% × 2 years	
(1.12.91–30.11.93) [*TCGA 1992, s 91(3)(4)(5)(a)*]	1,136
Total tax payable	£9,616

2002/03	£
CGT payable by M (subject to surcharge)	
(£100,000 − £7,700 annual exemption) × 40%	36,920
Surcharge on part of payment matched with 1991/92 qualifying amount:	
(£18,000 − £7,700) × 40% = £4,120 × 10% × 6 years	
(maximum) [*TCGA 1992, s 91(3)(4)(5)(b)*]	2,472
Surcharge on balance of payment (not illustrated)	X
Total tax payable	X

217.1 Offshore Settlements

Notes

(a) The surcharge is 10% per annum for a maximum of 6 years. [*TCGA 1992, s 91(3)–(5)*].

(b) In arriving, for surcharge purposes, at the CGT payable by M on the capital payment, that payment is deemed to form the lowest slice of his total gains (and may be reduced by the annual exemption) (Revenue Helpsheet IR 301).

(c) For 1998/99 onwards, personal capital losses cannot be set against gains attributed to an individual under *TCGA 1992, s 87*. [*TCGA 1992, s 2(4)(5); FA 1998, s 121(3)(4), Sch 21 para 2*]. See also 201.2(B) ANNUAL RATES AND EXEMPTIONS.

(C) Charge under *TCGA 1992, s 87* — further example

T and M are the only beneficiaries under a Jersey settlement set up by their grandfather. None of the trustees is resident in the UK.

T is resident in the UK but M is neither resident nor ordinarily resident in the UK. Both beneficiaries have a UK domicile. In 2001/02, the trustees sell shares realising a chargeable gain of £102,000. No disposals are made in 2002/03.

The trustees make capital payments of £60,000 to M in 2001/02. In 2002/03 they make capital payments of £60,000 to T and £10,000 to M.

2001/02	£
Trust gains	102,000
Capital payment	60,000
Trust gains carried forward	£42,000

M has chargeable gains of £60,000 but is not subject to CGT.

2002/03	£
Trust gains (brought forward)	42,000
Capital payments (£60,000 + £10,000)	70,000
Balance of capital payments carried forward	£28,000

The chargeable gains are apportioned as follows

		£
T	$\dfrac{60,000}{70,000} \times £42,000$	36,000
M	$\dfrac{10,000}{70,000} \times £42,000$ (not assessable)	6,000
		£42,000

The capital payments carried forward are apportioned as follows

		£
T	£60,000 – £36,000	24,000
M	£10,000 – £6,000	4,000
		£28,000

Offshore Settlements 217.1

(D) Distributions of income and gains [*ICTA 1988, s 740(6); TCGA 1992, ss 87, 97*]
A Liechtenstein foundation was created in 1966 by a UK resident domiciled in Scotland. None of the trustees is resident in the UK and the trust administration is carried on in Switzerland. The foundation has the following income and chargeable gains for 2000/01 to 2002/03.

	Income £	Chargeable gains £
2000/01	15,000	5,000
2001/02	24,000	12,000
2002/03	30,000	3,000

L, who is resident and domiciled in the UK and is the only current beneficiary, receives payments of £28,000 in 2000/01 and £50,000 in 2002/03.

	Total £	Income £	Chargeable gains £
2000/01			
Total income/gains	20,000	15,000	5,000
Payment	28,000	15,000	5,000
Balance	Nil	Nil	Nil
Balance of payment c/f	£8,000		
2001/02			
Total income/gains	36,000	24,000	12,000
Payment (balance b/f)	8,000	8,000	—
Balance c/f	£28,000	£16,000	£12,000
2002/03			
Total income/gains	33,000	30,000	3,000
Brought forward	28,000	16,000	12,000
	61,000	46,000	15,000
Payment	50,000	46,000	4,000
Balance c/f against future payments	£11,000	—	£11,000

Summary of taxable amounts

	Schedule D, Case VI £	Chargeable gains £
2000/01	15,000	5,000
2001/02	8,000	—
2002/03	46,000	4,000

218.1 Overseas Matters

218 Overseas Matters

218.1 COMPANY MIGRATION [*TCGA 1992, ss 185, 187*]

Z Ltd is a company incorporated in Ruritania, but regarded as resident in the UK by virtue of its being managed and controlled in the UK. It is the 75% subsidiary of Y plc, a UK resident company. On 1 October 2002, the management and control of Z Ltd is transferred to Ruritania and it thus ceases to be UK resident, although it continues to trade in the UK, on a much reduced basis, via a UK branch.

Details of the company's chargeable assets immediately before 1 October 2002 were as follows.

	Market value £	Capital gain after indexation (where applicable) if all assets sold £
Factory in UK	480,000	230,000
Warehouse in UK	300,000	180,000
Factory in Ruritania	350,000	200,000
Warehouse in Ruritania	190,000	100,000
UK quoted investments	110,000	80,000
Foreign trade investments	100,000	Loss (60,000)

The UK warehouse continues to be used in the UK trade. The UK factory does not, and is later sold. On 1 June 2003, the Ruritanian warehouse is sold for the equivalent of £210,000. On 1 October 2004, Y plc sells its shareholding in Z Ltd.

Prior to becoming non-UK resident, Z Ltd had unrelieved capital losses brought forward of £40,000.

The corporation tax consequences assuming no election under *TCGA 1992, s 187* are as follows

Chargeable gain accruing to Z Ltd on 1.10.02

	£
Factory (UK)	230,000
Factory (Ruritania)	200,000
Warehouse (Ruritania)	100,000
UK quoted investments	80,000
Foreign trade investments	(60,000)
	550,000
Losses brought forward	40,000
Net gain chargeable to corporation tax	£510,000

The later sale of the UK factory does not attract corporation tax as the company is non-resident and the factory has not, since the deemed reacquisition immediately before 1 October 2002, been used in a trade carried on in the UK through a branch or agency. Similarly, the sale of the overseas warehouse, and of any other overseas assets, is outside the scope of corporation tax on chargeable gains. Any subsequent disposal of the UK warehouse *will* be within the charge to corporation tax, having been omitted from the deemed disposal on 1 October 2002, due to its being used in a trade carried on in the UK through a branch. On disposal, the gain will be computed by reference to original cost, or

31.3.82 value if appropriate, rather than to market value immediately before 1 October 2002 — see also note (*d*).

Y plc will realise a capital gain (or loss) on the sale of its shareholding in Z Ltd on 1 October 2004.

The corporation tax consequences if an election is made under *TCGA 1992*, *s 187* are as follows

Chargeable gain accruing to Z Ltd on 1.10.02

	£
Factory (UK)	230,000
UK quoted investments	80,000
	310,000
Losses brought forward	40,000
Net gain liable to corporation tax	£270,000

Postponed gain on foreign assets

	£
Factory (Ruritania)	200,000
Warehouse (Ruritania)	100,000
	300,000
Foreign trade investments	(60,000)
	£240,000

On 1 June 2003, a proportion of the postponed gain becomes chargeable as a result of the sale, within six years of Z Ltd's becoming non-resident, of one of the assets in respect of which the postponed gain accrued. The gain chargeable to corporation tax as at 1 June 2003 on Y plc is

$$\frac{100{,}000 \text{ (postponed gain on warehouse)}}{300{,}000 \text{ (aggregate of postponed gains)}} \times £240{,}000 = £80{,}000$$

On 1 October 2004, in addition to any gain or loss arising on the sale of the shares, Y plc will be chargeable to corporation tax on the remainder of the postponed gain, i.e. on £160,000 (£240,000 – £80,000), by virtue of Z Ltd having ceased to be its 75% subsidiary as a result of the sale of shares.

The position as regards the UK warehouse is the same as if no election had been made.

Notes

(*a*) The provisions of *TCGA 1992*, *s 185* apply where a company ceases to be resident in the UK. All companies incorporated in the UK are regarded as UK resident. As such a company cannot therefore cease to be resident, *Section 185* can apply only to companies incorporated abroad which are UK resident. See also Revenue Statement of Practice SP 1/90 as regards company residence generally.

(*b*) If, with an election, Z Ltd's unrelieved capital losses had exceeded its chargeable gains arising on 1 October 2002, the excess could have been allowed against postponed gains at the time when they become chargeable on Y plc, subject to the two companies making a joint election to that effect under *TCGA 1992, s 187(5)*.

218.2 Overseas Matters

(c) *FA 1988, ss 130–132* contain management provisions designed to secure payment of all outstanding tax liabilities on a company becoming non-UK resident. See also Revenue Statement of Practice SP 2/90.

(d) If the UK warehouse ceases to be a chargeable asset by virtue of Z Ltd's ceasing to carry on a trade in the UK through a branch or agency, there will be a deemed disposal at market value at that time, under *TCGA 1992, s 25*. See 218.2 below.

218.2 **NON-RESIDENTS CARRYING ON TRADE, ETC. THROUGH UK BRANCH OR AGENCY** [*TCGA 1992, ss 10, 25*]

X, who is not resident and not ordinarily resident in the UK, practises abroad as a tax consultant and also practises in the UK through a London branch, preparing accounts to 5 April. The assets of the UK branch include premises bought in 1988 for £60,000 and a computer acquired in March 2000 for £20,000. On 31 January 2003, the computer ceases to be used in the UK branch and is immediately shipped abroad, and on 28 February 2003, X closes down the UK branch. He sells the premises in June 2003 for £118,000. Capital allowances claimed on the computer up to and including 2001/02 were £13,250 and short-life asset treatment had been claimed.

Relevant market values of the assets are as follows

	£
Computer, at 31 January 2003	11,000
Premises, at 14 March 1989	65,000
at 28 February 2003	110,000
Indexation factor March 1989 to April 1998 (note (*h*))	0.448

The UK capital gains tax consequences are as follows

		£	£
Computer			
Market value 31.1.03			11,000
Deduct Cost		20,000	
Less capital allowances claimed (note (*f*))		9,000	11,000
Chargeable gain			Nil

	£
Premises	
Market value 28.2.03	110,000
Deduct Market value 14.3.89	65,000
Unindexed gain	45,000
Indexation allowance £65,000 × 0.448	29,120
Chargeable gain	£15,880
Net chargeable gains 2002/03 (subject to TAPER RELIEF (227))	£15,880

Notes

(a) X is within the charge to UK capital gains tax for disposals after 13 March 1989 by virtue of his carrying on a profession in the UK through a branch or agency. Previously, the charge applied only to non-residents carrying on a *trade* in this manner. X is deemed to have disposed of (with no capital gains tax consequences) and reacquired immediately before 14 March 1989 all chargeable assets used in the UK branch at market value, so that any subsequent CGT charge will be by reference only to post-13 March 1989 gains. [*FA 1989, s 126(3)–(5); TCGA 1992, s 10(5)*].

(b) There is a deemed disposal, at market value, of the computer on 31 January 2003 as a result of its ceasing to be a chargeable asset by virtue of its becoming situated outside the UK. [*TCGA 1992, s 25(1)*].

(c) There is a deemed disposal, at market value, of the premises on 28 February 2003 as a result of the asset ceasing to be a chargeable asset by virtue of X's ceasing to carry on a trade, profession or vocation in the UK through a branch or agency. [*TCGA 1992, s 25(3)(8)*]. See also note (g) below.

(d) There are no UK CGT consequences on the actual disposal of the premises in June 2003.

(e) X is entitled to the £7,700 annual exemption against UK gains, regardless of his residence status.

(f) Where a chargeable asset has qualified for capital allowances and a loss accrues on its disposal, the allowable expenditure is restricted, under *TCGA 1992, s 41*, by the net allowances given, which in this example amount to £9,000 (first-year and writing-down allowances £13,250 less balancing charge £4,250 arising on the asset's ceasing to be used in the trade).

(g) *TCGA 1992, s 25(3)* (see note (c) above) does not apply, on a claim under *TCGA 1992, s 172*, in relation to an asset where a non-UK resident company transfers its trade (carried on through a UK branch or agency) to a UK resident company in the same group. The asset is deemed to be transferred at no gain/no loss. For disposals after 31 March 2000, this applies automatically under *TCGA 1992, s 171* without the need for any claim. [*TCGA 1992, s 172; FA 2000, Sch 29 para 3*].

(h) Other than for the purposes of corporation tax on chargeable gains, indexation allowance is frozen at its April 1998 level. Therefore, the indexation factor for April 1998 is used in respect of disposals in a later month (and expenditure incurred in April 1998 or later does not attract indexation allowance at all). See 210 INDEXATION.

218.3 TRANSFER OF ASSETS TO NON-RESIDENT COMPANY [*TCGA 1992, s 140*]

Q Ltd, a UK resident company, carries on business in a foreign country through a branch there. In September 1996, it is decreed that all enterprises in that country be carried on by locally resident companies. Q Ltd forms a wholly-owned non-UK resident subsidiary R and transfers all the assets of the branch to R wholly in consideration for the issue of shares. The assets transferred include the following

218.3 Overseas Matters

	Value £	Chargeable gains £
Goodwill	100,000	95,000
Freehold land	200,000	120,000
Plant (items worth more than £6,000)	50,000	20,000
Other assets	150,000	—
	£500,000	£235,000

In March 1998, there is a compulsory acquisition of 50% of the share capital of R for £300,000 (market value). The value of the whole shareholding immediately before disposal is £750,000. The value of Q Ltd's remaining 50% holding is £300,000.

In June 2002, R is forced to sell its freehold land to the government.

Q Ltd's capital gains position is as follows

1996
The gain of £235,000 is deferred. The allowable cost of the shares in R is £500,000.

1998

	£
Consideration on disposal	300,000
Add Proportion of deferred gain £235,000 × $\dfrac{300,000}{750,000}$	94,000
	394,000
Deduct Cost of shares sold £500,000 × $\dfrac{300,000}{300,000 + 300,000}$	250,000
Gain subject to indexation	£144,000

2002

Proportion of deferred gain chargeable	£
Gain arising $\dfrac{120,000}{235,000}$ × £235,000	£120,000
Balance of gain still held over (£235,000 − £94,000 − £120,000)	£21,000

Notes

(a) The 2002 gain arises under *section 140(5)*. If the sale of freehold land had taken place more than six years after the original transfer of assets, no part of the deferred gain would have become chargeable as a result.

(b) The 1998 gain arises under *section 140(4)*. In this case, there is no time limit as in (a) above.

(c) The 1998 gain is subject to indexation allowance on £250,000 from September 1996 to March 1998.

219 Partnerships

219.1 ASSETS [*TCGA 1992, s 59*]

G, H and I trade in partnership. They share capital in the ratio 5:4:3. Land occupied by the firm is sold on 15 April 2002 for £240,000, having been acquired for £60,000 in 1981. The agreed market value of the land at 31 March 1982 is £54,000. G has elected under *TCGA 1992, s 35(5)* for his personal assets held on 31 March 1982 to be treated as disposed of and re-acquired at their market value on that date. G has personal gains in 2002/03 of £2,500, H has losses of £1,000 and I made no disposals of personal assets. None of the partners has any capital losses brought forward from earlier years. The partnership land was a business asset throughout for taper relief purposes but the personal assets sold by G and H were non-business assets (held in G's case for less than three years). The indexation factor for the period March 1982 to April 1998 (note (*b*)) is 1.047.

The gains of G, H and I, without re-basing to 1982, are as follows

	G ($\frac{5}{12}$) £	H ($\frac{4}{12}$) £	I ($\frac{3}{12}$) £
Disposal consideration	100,000	80,000	60,000
Cost	25,000	20,000	15,000
Unindexed gain	75,000	60,000	45,000
Indexation allowance Cost × 1.047	26,176	20,940	15,706
Gain after indexation	£48,824	£39,060	£29,294

The gains of G, H and I, with re-basing to 1982, are as follows

	G ($\frac{5}{12}$) £	H ($\frac{4}{12}$) £	I ($\frac{3}{12}$) £
Disposal consideration	100,000	80,000	60,000
Market value 31.3.82	22,500	18,000	13,500
Unindexed gain	77,500	62,000	46,500
Indexation allowance (as above)	26,176	20,940	15,706
Gain after indexation	£51,324	£41,060	£30,794

Summary

	G £	H £	I £
Share of partnership gain	48,824	39,060	29,294
Personal gains/(losses)	2,500	(1,000)	—
Chargeable gain	51,324	38,060	29,294
Taper relief @ 75% on £48,824/£38,060/£29,294	36,618	28,545	21,971
	14,706	9,515	7,323
Annual exemption	7,700	7,700	7,323
Taxable gain	£7,006	£1,815	Nil

Notes

(*a*) An individual partner's election under *TCGA 1992, s 35(5)* in respect of his personal assets does not extend to his share of partnership assets and *vice versa*, this

219.2 Partnerships

being by virtue of *TCGA 1992, s 35(7)*. (See Revenue Statement of Practice SP 4/92, para 10(i).)

(b) Other than for the purposes of corporation tax on chargeable gains, indexation allowance is frozen at its April 1998 level. See 210 INDEXATION.

219.2 CHANGES IN SHARING RATIOS

J and K have traded in partnership for several years, sharing capital and income equally. The acquisition costs and 31 March 1982 values of the chargeable assets of the firm are as follows

	Cost £	31.3.82 value £
Premises	60,000	150,000
Goodwill	10,000	50,000

The assets have not been revalued in the firm's balance sheet. On 1 June 2002, J and K admit L to the partnership, and the sharing ratio is J 35%, K 45% and L 20%. The indexation factor for March 1982 to April 1998 (note (d)) is 1.047.

J and K are regarded as disposing of part of their interest in the firm's assets to L as follows

	£	£
J		
Premises		
Deemed consideration		
£60,000 × (50% − 35%)	9,000	
Add indexation allowance (see below)	23,558	
Total deemed consideration	32,558	
Allowable cost	9,000	
Unindexed gain	23,558	
Indexation allowance (50% − 35%) × £150,000 × 1.047	23,558	—
Goodwill		
Deemed consideration		
£10,000 × (50% − 35%)	1,500	
Add indexation allowance (see below)	7,853	
Total deemed consideration	9,353	
Allowable cost	1,500	
Unindexed gain	7,853	
Indexation allowance (50% − 35%) × £50,000 × 1.047	7,853	—
Chargeable gain/allowable loss		Nil

K
Premises

Deemed consideration		
£60,000 × (50% − 45%)		3,000
Add indexation allowance (see below)		7,853
Total deemed consideration		10,853
Allowable cost		3,000
Unindexed gain		7,853
Indexation allowance (50% − 45%) × £150,000 × 1.047		7,853	—

Goodwill

Deemed consideration		
£10,000 × (50% − 45%)		500
Add indexation allowance (see below)		2,618
Total deemed consideration		3,118
Allowable cost		500
Unindexed gain		2,618
Indexation allowance (50% − 45%) × £50,000 × 1.047		2,618	—
Chargeable gain/allowable loss			Nil

The allowable costs (inclusive, in L's case, of indexation allowance to April 1998) of the three partners are now

		Freehold land £	Goodwill £
J		21,000	3,500
K		27,000	4,500
L	(note (c))	43,411	12,471

Notes

(a) The treatment illustrated above is taken from Revenue Statement of Practice SP D12 (17.1.75), para 4 as extended by SP 1/89. Each partner's disposal consideration is equal to his share of current balance sheet value of the asset concerned plus, for disposals after 5 April 1988, indexation allowance to April 1998, and each disposal treated as producing no gain and no loss.

(b) As the deemed disposals are no gain/no loss disposals, re-basing to 1982 does not apply. The incoming partner, having acquired his share in the assets by means of a no gain/no loss disposal after 31 March 1982 is regarded as having held the asset at that date for the purposes of re-basing on a subsequent disposal. (Revenue Statement of Practice SP 1/89).

(c) L's allowable costs comprise 20% of original cost, plus indexation allowance to April 1998 based on 20% of 31 March 1982 value.

(d) Other than for the purposes of corporation tax on chargeable gains, indexation allowance is frozen at its April 1998 level. Therefore, the indexation factor for April 1998 is used in respect of disposals in a later month (and expenditure incurred in April 1998 or later does not attract indexation allowance at all). See 210 INDEXATION.

(e) See 210.2(A)(C) INDEXATION for an example of the indexation adjustments required on a subsequent disposal other than a no gain/no loss disposal.

219.3 Partnerships

219.3 ACCOUNTING ADJUSTMENTS

A, B and C trade in partnership. They share income and capital profits equally. The firm's only chargeable asset is its premises which cost £51,000 in 1989. C, who is 49, decides to retire. The remaining partners agree to share profits equally. Before C retires (in May 2002), the premises are written up to market value in the accounts, agreed at £81,000. C does not receive any payment directly from the other partners on his retirement.

The capital gains tax consequences are

On retiring, C is regarded as having disposed of his interest in the firm's premises for a consideration equal to his share of the then book value.

		£
Disposal consideration	$\frac{1}{3} \times £81,000$	27,000
Acquisition cost	$\frac{1}{3} \times £51,000$	17,000
Gain subject to indexation to April 1998 and taper relief		£10,000

A and B will each be treated as acquiring a $\frac{1}{6}$ ($\frac{1}{2} \times \frac{1}{3}$) share in the premises, at a cost equal to one half of C's disposal consideration. Their acquisition costs are then

		A	B
		£	£
Cost of original share	$\frac{1}{3} \times £51,000$	17,000	17,000
Cost of new share	$\frac{1}{2} \times £27,000$	13,500	13,500
Total		£30,500	£30,500

Note

(a) If C's retirement is for reasons of ill-health, he may be entitled to RETIREMENT RELIEF (222).

219.4 CONSIDERATION OUTSIDE ACCOUNTS

D, E and F are partners in a firm of accountants who share all profits in the ratio 7:7:6. G is admitted as a partner in May 2002 and pays the other partners £10,000 for goodwill. The new partnership shares are D $\frac{3}{10}$, E $\frac{3}{10}$, F $\frac{1}{4}$ and G $\frac{3}{20}$. The book value of goodwill is £18,000, its cost on acquisition of the practice from the predecessor in 1990.

The partners are treated as having disposed of shares in goodwill as follows

D

$\frac{7}{20} - \frac{3}{10} = \frac{1}{20}$

	£	£
Disposal consideration		
Notional $\frac{1}{20} \times £18,000$	900	
Actual $\frac{7}{20} \times £10,000$	3,500	
		4,400
Allowable cost $\frac{1}{20} \times £18,000$		900
Unindexed gain		£3,500

E

$\frac{7}{20} - \frac{3}{10} = \frac{1}{20}$

	£
Disposal consideration (as for D)	4,400
Allowable cost (as for D)	900
Unindexed gain	£3,500

F

$\frac{6}{20} - \frac{1}{4} = \frac{1}{20}$

	£	£
Disposal consideration		
Notional $\frac{1}{20} \times £18,000$	900	
Actual $\frac{6}{20} \times £10,000$	3,000	
		3,900
Allowable cost		900
Unindexed gain		£3,000

G's allowable cost of his share of goodwill is therefore

	£
Actual consideration paid	10,000
Notional consideration paid $\frac{3}{20} \times £18,000$	2,700
	£12,700

Note

(a) In practice, the above calculations must be adjusted for indexation allowance to April 1998 which is added to the notional consideration and deducted from the unindexed gain — see 219.2 above and Revenue Statement of Practice SP 1/89. Any chargeable gains remaining after indexation are reduced by TAPER RELIEF (227).

219.5 Partnerships

219.5 SHARES ACQUIRED IN STAGES

Q is a partner in a medical practice. The partnership's only chargeable asset is a freehold house used as a surgery. The cost of the house to the partnership was £3,600 in 1962 and it was revalued in the partnership accounts to £50,000 in 1990. Q was admitted to the partnership in June 1964 with a share of $\frac{1}{6}$ of all profits. As a result of partnership changes, Q's profit share altered as follows

1970	$\frac{1}{5}$
1981	$\frac{1}{4}$
2002	$\frac{3}{10}$

For capital gains tax, Q's allowable cost of his share of the freehold house is calculated as follows

		£	
1964	$\frac{1}{6} \times £3,600$		£600
1970	$(\frac{1}{5} - \frac{1}{6}) \times £3,600$	120	
1981	$(\frac{1}{4} - \frac{1}{5}) \times £3,600$	180	
2002	$(\frac{3}{10} - \frac{1}{4}) \times £50,000$	2,500	£2,800

Notes

(*a*) The pre- and post-6.4.65 costs are not pooled.

(*b*) On Q's acquisition of an increased share of the property in 2002 (subsequent to the revaluation in 1990), any partner with a reduced share will be treated as having made a disposal and thus a gain or loss. The re-basing rules of *TCGA 1992, s 35* will apply to the disposal (subject to the usual comparison with the gain or loss without re-basing).

219.6 PARTNERSHIP ASSETS DISTRIBUTED IN KIND

R, S and T are partners sharing all profits in the ratio 4:3:3. Farmland owned by the firm is transferred in November 2002 to T for future use by him as a market gardening enterprise separate from the partnership business. No payment is made by T to the other partners but a reduction is made in T's future share of income profits. The book value of the farmland is £5,000, its cost in 1991, but the present market value is £15,000.

		£
R		
Deemed disposal consideration	$\frac{4}{10} \times £15{,}000$	6,000
Allowable cost	$\frac{4}{10} \times £5{,}000$	2,000
Gain (subject to indexation allowance to April 1998 and TAPER RELIEF (227))		£4,000
S		
Deemed disposal consideration	$\frac{3}{10} \times £15{,}000$	4,500
Allowable cost	$\frac{3}{10} \times £5{,}000$	1,500
Gain (subject to indexation allowance to April 1998 and TAPER RELIEF (227))		£3,000
T		
Partnership share	$\frac{3}{10} \times £5{,}000$	1,500
Market value of R's share		6,000
Market value of S's share		4,500
Allowable cost of land for future disposal		£12,000

220 Private Residences

220.1 PERIODS OF OWNERSHIP QUALIFYING FOR EXEMPTION AND LET PROPERTY EXEMPTION [*TCGA 1992, ss 222, 223*]

(A)

P sold a house on 1 July 2002 realising an otherwise chargeable gain (before taper relief) of £54,000. The house was purchased on 1 February 1980 and was occupied as a residence until 30 June 1987 when P moved to another residence, letting the house as residential accommodation. He did not re-occupy the house prior to its sale.

	£
Gain on sale	54,000
Deduct Exempt amount under main residence rules	
$\dfrac{5y\ 3m + 3y}{20y\ 3m} \times £54,000$	22,000
	32,000
Deduct Let property exemption	22,000
Net chargeable gain (subject to TAPER RELIEF (227))	£10,000

Notes

(*a*) The final three years of ownership are always included in the exempt period of ownership. [*TCGA 1992, s 223(1)*].

(*b*) The period of ownership for the exemption calculation does not include any period before 31 March 1982. This applies regardless of whether the gain has been calculated by reference to cost or to 31 March 1982 value under the re-basing rules. [*TCGA 1992, s 223(7)*].

(*c*) The gain attributable to the letting (£32,000) is exempt to the extent that it does not exceed the lesser of £40,000 and the gain otherwise exempt (£22,000 in this example). [*TCGA 1992, s 223(4)*].

(B)

Q bought a house on 1 August 1981 for £40,000 and used it as his main residence. On 10 February 1982, he was sent by his employer to manage the Melbourne branch of the firm and continued to work in Australia until 4 August 1987, the whole of his duties being performed outside the UK. The house was let as residential accommodation during that period. Q took up residence in the house once again following his return to the UK, but on 30 September 1994 moved to Switzerland for health reasons. On this occasion, the property was not let. He returned to the UK in August 1997, but did not reside in the house at any time prior to its being sold on 31 December 2002 for £252,350. The house had a market value of £50,000 at 31 March 1982 and the indexation factor for the period March 1982 to April 1998 (note (*f*)) is 1.047.

Private Residences 220.1

Computation of gain before applying exemptions

	£	£
Disposal consideration	252,350	252,350
Cost	40,000	
Market value 31.3.82		50,000
Unindexed gain	212,350	202,350
Indexation allowance £50,000 × 1.047	52,350	52,350
Gain after indexation	£160,000	£150,000
Gain before applying exemptions		£150,000

The gain is reduced by the main residence exemptions as follows

Period of ownership (excluding period before 31.3.82)		20y 9m
Exempt periods since 31.3.82:		
31.3.82 – 30.9.94	12y 6m	
1.1.2000 – 31.12.02 (last three years)	3y 0m	15y 6m

		£
Gain as above		150,000
Deduct Exempt amount under main residence rules		
$\dfrac{15\text{y 6m}}{20\text{y 9m}} \times £150{,}000$		112,048
		37,952
Deduct Let property exemption:		
Period of letting 31.3.82 – 4.8.87	5y 4m	
Gain attributable to letting $\dfrac{5\text{y 4m}}{20\text{y 9m}} \times £150{,}000 =$	£38,530	
Exemption (note (*e*))		37,952
Net chargeable gain		Nil

Notes

(*a*) Periods of ownership before 31 March 1982 are excluded in applying the main residence exemptions. This is the case even if re-basing to 1982 does not apply. [*TCGA 1992, s 223(7)*].

(*b*) The period spent in Australia (regardless of its length but excluding that part of it before 31 March 1982) counts as a period of residence, as Q worked in an employment all the duties of which were performed outside the UK and used the house as his main residence at some time before and after this period of absence. [*TCGA 1992, s 223(3)(b)*].

(*c*) The period spent in Switzerland would have been exempt, having not exceeded three years, but the exemption is lost as Q did not occupy the property as a main residence at any time after this period. [*TCGA 1992, s 223(3)(a)*].

(*d*) The last three years of ownership are always exempt providing the property has been used as the owner's only or main residence at some time during the period of

220.2 Private Residences

ownership, and for this purpose, 'period of ownership' is not restricted to the period after 30 March 1982. [*TCGA 1992, ss 222, 223(1)*].

(e) The let property exemption is the lesser of the gain attributable to the period of letting (£38,530), the gain otherwise exempt (£112,048 in this example) and £40,000. It is further restricted in this example to the amount of the gain otherwise unrelieved, as it cannot create a loss. It is available only if the property is let as residential accommodation. [*TCGA 1992, s 223(4)*].

(f) Other than for the purposes of corporation tax on chargeable gains, indexation allowance is frozen at its April 1998 level. Therefore, the indexation factor for April 1998 is used in respect of disposals in a later month (and expenditure incurred in April 1998 or later does not attract indexation allowance at all). See 210 INDEXATION.

220.2 ELECTION FOR MAIN RESIDENCE [*TCGA 1992, s 222(5); FA 1996, Sch 20 para 59, Sch 41 Pt V(10)*]

S purchased the long lease of a London flat on 1 June 1994. He occupied the flat as his sole residence until 31 July 1996 when he acquired a property in Shropshire. Both properties were thereafter occupied as residences by S until the lease of the London flat was sold on 28 February 2003, realising an otherwise chargeable gain of £75,000.

The possibilities open to S are

(i) Election for London flat to be treated as main residence throughout

Exempt gain £75,000

(ii) Election for Shropshire property to be treated as main residence from 31.7.96 onwards

Exempt gain £75,000 × $\dfrac{2y\ 2m + 3y}{8y\ 9m}$ £44,286

(iii) Election for London flat to be treated as main residence up to 28 February 2000, with election for the Shropshire property to be so treated thereafter

Exempt gain £75,000 × $\dfrac{5y\ 9m + 3y}{8y\ 9m}$ £75,000

Note

(a) The elections in (iii) are the most favourable, provided they could have been made by 31 July 1998 in respect of the London flat, and by 28 February 2002 in respect of the Shropshire property. Note that the last three years' ownership of the London flat is an exempt period in any case. The advantage of (iii) over (i) is that the period of ownership 1 March 2000 to 28 February 2003 of the Shropshire property will be treated as a period of residence as regards any future disposal of that property. Revenue practice is that the *initial* election (which can be varied) must be made within two years of acquisition of the second property, and this was upheld in *Griffin v Craig-Harvey Ch D 1993, 66 TC 396, [1994] STC 54.*

220.3 PART BUSINESS USE [TCGA 1992, s 224(1) (2); FA 1996, Sch 20 para 60]

T purchased a freehold property for £50,000 on 30 April 1986. It consists of living room, two bedrooms, kitchen, bathroom and spare room. T and his family occupy the house as their main residence. T runs a small accountancy practice for which he rented office accommodation until October 1988 when a rent review made it less economical. From 1 November 1988, he uses the spare room at home exclusively for business, also making use of the living room occasionally to receive clients. On 1 February 2003, T, who is then aged 46, sells the property for £190,000. T makes no other disposals in 2002/03. The indexation factor for the period April 1986 to April 1998 (note *d*)) is 0.665.

T's chargeable gain on disposal of the property may be computed as follows

	£	£
Net proceeds		190,000
Cost		50,000
Unindexed gain		140,000
Indexation allowance £50,000 × 0.665		33,250
Gain after indexation		106,750
Deduct Private residence exemption		
£106,750 × $\dfrac{2y\ 6m\ +\ 3y}{16y\ 9m}$ × 100% (note (*b*))	35,052	
£106,750 × $\dfrac{11y\ 3m}{16y\ 9m}$ × $\dfrac{5\ \text{rooms}}{6\ \text{rooms}}$ (notes (*a*)(*b*))	59,748	94,800
Gain attributable to business use		11,950
Deduct Business asset taper relief for 4 years		
£11,950 × 75% (note (*c*))		8,963
Chargeable gain		2,987
Deduct Annual exemption (maximum £7,700)		2,987
Taxable gain 2002/03		Nil

Notes

(*a*) Only the gain on the part of the house used *exclusively* for business is excluded from qualifying for the private residence exemption. [TCGA 1992, s 224(1)]. In this example, it is considered reasonable to compute that gain by apportioning the whole gain by reference to the use to which rooms are put. In a case where the value of the business part of mixed property is disproportionately higher than that of the private part, it would be more appropriate to apportion the proceeds by reference to respective values and compute two separate gains, only one of which will attract the exemption (see Revenue Capital Gains Manual CG 64670–64674).

(*b*) Where there has been change of use of part of a house, private residence relief is adjusted as is 'just and reasonable'. [TCGA 1992, s 224(2); FA 1996, Sch 20 para 60]. Simple time apportionment of the gain over the period of ownership is considered to give the most sensible result in this example. Note that because the business part of the house has *at some time* in the period of ownership been used as part of the main residence, the last three years of ownership are included in the 100% exempt period of ownership (see Revenue Capital Gains Manual CG 64765, 64988, 64989).

220.3 Private Residences

(c) The pre-tapered gain is entirely attributable to the business part of the property. This part has satisfied the conditions of *TCGA 1992, Sch A1 para 5(2)* throughout the relevant period of ownership (which runs from 6 April 1998 to date of disposal) and the gain should therefore fully qualify for taper relief at the business asset rate.

(d) Other than for the purposes of corporation tax on chargeable gains, indexation allowance is frozen at its April 1998 level. See 210 INDEXATION.

(e) If T were to purchase a replacement property which again has a part used exclusively for the business he could choose to roll over the pre-tapered gain against the cost of that part of the new property under the rules illustrated in 223 ROLLOVER RELIEF — REPLACEMENT OF BUSINESS ASSETS. In practice, he would clearly not do so as no tax is payable in any case.

221 Qualifying Corporate Bonds

[TCGA 1992, ss 115–117]

221.1 DEFINITION [*TCGA 1992, s 117; FA 1993, s 84(1)(3); FA 1995, s 50; FA 1996, ss 104, 105, Sch 14 para 61, Sch 41 Pt V(3)*]
B has the following transactions in 5% unsecured loan stock issued in 1983 by F Ltd.

		£
11.11.83	Purchase £2,000	1,800
10.7.89	Gift from wife £1,000 (original cost £800)	—
30.9.97	Purchase £2,000	2,100
5.6.02	Sale £4,000	(3,300)

Apart from the gift on 10.7.89, all acquisitions were arm's length purchases. B's wife acquired her £1,000 holding on 11.11.83. Indexation allowance of £266 arose on the transfer from wife to husband.

For the purposes of the accrued income scheme, the sale is without accrued interest and the rebate amount is £20. The stock is a corporate bond as defined by *TCGA 1992, s 117(1)* and a 'relevant security' as defined by *TCGA 1992, s 108(1)*.

Under the rules for matching relevant securities in *TCGA 1992, s 106A*, the stock disposed of is identified with acquisitions as follows.

(i) Identify £2,000 with purchase on 30.9.97 (LIFO)

	£
Disposal consideration £3,300 × $\frac{2,000}{4,000}$	1,650
Add rebate amount £20 × $\frac{2,000}{4,000}$	10
	1,660
Allowable cost	2,100
Loss	£440

The loss is *not* allowable as the £2,000 stock purchased on 30.9.97 is a qualifying corporate bond (note (*a*)). [*TCGA 1992, s 115*].

(ii) Identify £1,000 with acquisition on 10.7.89

	£
Disposal consideration £3,300 × $\frac{1,000}{4,000}$	825
Add rebate amount £20 × $\frac{1,000}{4,000}$	5
	830
Allowable cost (including indexation to 10.7.89)	1,066
Allowable loss	£236

The loss is allowable as the stock acquired on 10.7.89 is not a qualifying corporate bond (note (*b*)).

(iii) Identify £1,000 with purchase on 11.11.83

	£
Disposal consideration £3,300 × $\frac{1,000}{4,000}$	825
Add rebate amount £20 × $\frac{1,000}{4,000}$	5
	830
Allowable cost £1,800 × $\frac{1,000}{2,000}$	900
Allowable loss	£70

221.2 Qualifying Corporate Bonds

The loss is allowable as the stock acquired on 11.11.83 is not a qualifying corporate bond (note (c)).

Notes

(a) The acquisition on 30.9.97 is a qualifying corporate bond as it was acquired after 13 March 1984 otherwise than as a result of an excluded disposal. [*TCGA 1992, s 117(7)(b)*].

(b) The acquisition on 10.7.89 was the result of an excluded disposal, being a no gain/no loss transfer between spouses where the first spouse had acquired the stock before 14 March 1984. It is therefore not a qualifying corporate bond. [*TCGA 1992, s 117(7)(b)(8)*].

(c) Securities acquired before 14 March 1984 cannot be qualifying corporate bonds in the hands of the person who so acquired them.

(d) See IT 23.1 SCHEDULE D, CASE VI for the income tax effects of the accrued income scheme.

221.2 REORGANISATION OF SHARE CAPITAL [*TCGA 1992, s 116*]

D holds 5,000 £1 ordinary shares in H Ltd. He acquired the shares in April 1992 by subscription at par. On 1 August 1995, he accepted an offer for the shares from J plc. The terms of the offer were one 25p ordinary share of J plc and £10 J plc 10% unsecured loan stock (a qualifying corporate bond) for each H Ltd ordinary share. Both the shares and the loan stock are listed on the Stock Exchange. In December 2002, D sells £20,000 loan stock at its quoted price of £105 per cent.

The value of J plc ordinary shares at 1 August 1995 was £3.52 per share and the loan stock was £99.20 per cent. The indexation factor for April 1992 to August 1995 is 0.080.

The cost of the H Ltd shares must be apportioned between the J plc ordinary shares and loan stock.

	£
Value of J plc shares	
5,000 × £3.52	17,600
Value of J plc loan stock	
£50,000 × 99.2%	49,600
	£67,200

Allowable cost of J plc shares

$$\frac{17,600}{67,200} \times £5,000 \qquad £1,310$$

Allowable cost of J plc loan stock

$$\frac{49,600}{67,200} \times £5,000 \qquad £3,690$$

Chargeable gain on H Ltd shares attributable to J plc loan stock to date of exchange

	£
Deemed disposal consideration	49,600
Allowable cost	3,690
Unindexed gain	45,910
Indexation allowance £3,690 × 0.080	295
Deferred chargeable gain	£45,615

Deferred chargeable gain accruing on disposal of loan stock in December 2001

Loan stock sold (nominal)	£20,000
Total holding of loan stock before disposal (nominal)	£50,000

Deferred chargeable gain accruing in 2002/03

$$\frac{20{,}000}{50{,}000} \times £45{,}615 \qquad £18{,}246$$

Notes

(a) The gain on the sale of J plc loan stock is exempt (as the stock is a qualifying corporate bond) except for that part which relates to the gain on the previous holding of H Ltd shares. [*TCGA 1992, s 115, s 116(10)*]. There will also be income tax consequences under the accrued income scheme (see IT 23.1 SCHEDULE D, CASE VI).

(b) For taper relief purposes, the deferred gain is deemed to arise in August 1995 (and not in December 2002). [*TCGA 1992, Sch A1 para 16; FA 1998, s 121(2)(4), Sch 20*]. Thus, there can be no taper relief due in this example.

(c) The qualifying corporate bond is treated as acquired at the date of the reorganisation, so even if the original shares had been held at 31 March 1982, re-basing could *not* apply on the subsequent disposal of the loan stock. However, where the original shares were acquired before 31 March 1982, the reorganisation took place before 6 April 1988, and the qualifying corporate bonds are disposed of after 5 April 1988, the deferred chargeable gain is halved. [*TCGA 1992, Sch 4 para 4*].

(d) The exchange of J plc ordinary shares for H Ltd shares is dealt with under *TCGA 1992, ss 127–130*, and no gain or loss will arise until the J plc shares are disposed of. See 225.4 SHARES AND SECURITIES.

222.1 Retirement Relief

222 Retirement Relief

[*TCGA 1992, ss 163, 164, Sch 6; FA 1993, s 87, Sch 7 Pt I, Sch 23 Pt III(7); FA 1994, s 92; FA 1996, s 176; FA 1998, s 140, Sch 27 Pt III(31)*]

222.1 EXTENT OF RELIEF

(A) General provisions

N had been the proprietor of a retail business for more than ten years. In December 2002, when N was 51, he sold the whole of the business to a national group for £190,000. The consideration under the agreement is apportioned as follows

	£
Freehold shop	105,000
Flat over shop (occupied throughout by N as main residence)	30,000
Goodwill	40,000
Trading stock	6,000
Fixtures and fittings (one item over £6,000)	9,000
	£190,000

Chargeable gains after indexation to April 1998 are

	£
Freehold shop	88,500
Goodwill	26,000
Fixture	500
Aggregate	£115,000

Retirement relief is calculated as follows

Gain subject to relief	115,000
Maximum available for 100% relief	
Qualifying period — 10 years	
$\frac{10}{10} \times £50,000$	(50,000)
Maximum available for 50% relief (statutory maximum £150,000) £115,000 − £50,000 = £65,000	
£65,000 × $\frac{1}{2}$	(32,500)
Chargeable gain 2002/03 subject to TAPER RELIEF (227)	£32,500

Notes

(*a*) For disposals after 5 April 2002 and before 6 April 2003, the exemption is extended to one half of gains between £50,000 and £200,000, these limits being reduced by reference to qualifying periods of less than ten years. Retirement relief is abolished for disposals after 5 April 2003.

(*b*) The age from which a person may qualify for retirement relief, other than on ill-health grounds, is 50.

Retirement Relief 222.1

(c) The flat over the shop is exempt from capital gains tax as it has been N's main residence throughout the period of ownership.

(B) Retirement from business on ill-health grounds and relief restricted by reference to qualifying period [*TCGA 1992, s 163(1)–(3), Sch 6 paras 3, 13; FA 1994, s 92; FA 1996, Sch 20 para 66*]

After giving up salaried employment in June 1996 at the age of 41, R purchased a small philately business. In June 2002, R finds he is unable to continue running the business because of ill-health and sells for the following amounts.

	Proceeds	Chargeable gain (after indexation to April 1998)
	£	£
Premises	115,000	93,000
Goodwill	15,000	11,400
Fixtures and fittings	4,000	—
Stock	12,500	—
		£104,400

Retirement relief is given as follows

	£
Gains eligible for relief	104,400

Maximum available for 100% relief
Qualifying period — 6 years

$$\frac{6}{10} \times £50,000 \qquad (30,000)$$

Ceiling for 50% relief

$$\frac{6}{10} \times £200,000 = £120,000$$

£104,400 (being less than £120,000) − £30,000 = £74,400
£74,400 × ½   (37,200)

Chargeable gain 2002/03 subject to TAPER RELIEF (227)   £37,200

Note

(a) Relief is given where an individual has retired below the age of 50 on ill-health grounds provided he has ceased work and is likely to remain permanently incapable of that kind of work. Claims for relief on the grounds of ill-health must be made to the Board by the first anniversary of 31 January following the tax year in which the disposal occurred. [*TCGA 1992, Sch 6 paras 3, 5(2)(4); FA 1996, Sch 20 para 66, Sch 21 para 44(3)*].

222.1 Retirement Relief

(C) Operative date — ceasing to be a full-time working officer or employee [*TCGA 1992, s 163(5)(7), Sch 6 para 1; FA 1993, s 87, Sch 7 Pt I*]

Q gave up full-time work at the age of 51 in June 2002 when she had been a director of Q Ltd, her personal company, for five years. She continued as a director, working three four-hour mornings per week until January 2003 when she sold her 40% shareholding in Q Ltd realising a chargeable gain of £245,000.

Retirement relief is given as follows

	£
Gain eligible for relief	245,000

Maximum available for 100% relief
Qualifying period — 5 years

$\frac{5}{10} \times £50,000$ (25,000)

Ceiling for 50% relief

$\frac{5}{10} \times £200,000 = £100,000$

£100,000 − £25,000 = £75,000

£75,000 × $\frac{1}{2}$ (37,500)

Chargeable gain 2002/03 (subject to TAPER RELIEF (227)) £182,500

Note

(*a*) If an individual ceases to be a full-time working officer or employee of a company but remains an officer or employee and works an average of ten hours per week in a technical or managerial capacity until the date of disposal, the operative date is deemed to be the date of ceasing to be a full-time working officer or employee. This enables retirement relief to be given, but by reference to the qualifying period ended on that earlier date rather than on the date of disposal.

Retirement Relief 222.1

(D) Share for share exchange — relief available [*TCGA 1992, Sch 6 para 2; FA 1996, Sch 21 para 44(1)(2)*]

In November 2002, D, aged 67, accepts an offer to exchange his 60% holding of 1,200 shares in C Ltd for shares in M plc on the basis of 10 for 1. He has been a full-time working officer of C Ltd for 15 years. He receives 12,000 shares in M plc valued at £90,000. The holding in C Ltd cost £25,000 in August 1986. D elects *not* to treat the new shares and the holding disposed of as the same asset under *TCGA 1992, s 127*.

The indexation factor from August 1986 to April 1998 (note (*b*)) is 0.662.

C Ltd had no non-business assets.

The chargeable gain is calculated as follows

	£
Disposal consideration	90,000
Cost	25,000
Unindexed gain	65,000
Indexation allowance £25,000 × 0.662	16,550
Gain after indexation	£48,450
Gain subject to retirement relief	48,450
Retirement relief available (maximum £50,000 at 100% and £150,000 at 50%)	48,450
Chargeable gain	Nil

Notes

(*a*) The base cost for D's holding of M plc shares is £90,000.

(*b*) Other than for the purposes of corporation tax on chargeable gains, indexation allowance is frozen at its April 1998 level. Therefore, the indexation factor for April 1998 is used in respect of disposals in a later month (and expenditure incurred in April 1998 or later does not attract indexation allowance at all). See 210 INDEXATION.

222.2 Retirement Relief

222.2 GAINS QUALIFYING FOR RELIEF

(A) Non-business chargeable assets [*TCGA 1992, Sch 6 paras 6, 7, 12; FA 1993, s 87, Sch 7 Pt 1*]

P Ltd carries on a trade of printing and bookbinding. Its full-time working directors include C who owns 10% of the issued share capital and of the voting rights. In December 2002, on reaching the age of 63, C gives his shares to his sister. At the date of transfer, the company's assets are valued as follows

	£	£	Market value £	Cost £
Leasehold printing works			190,000	50,000
Goodwill			60,000	—
Stocks of materials			80,000	75,000
Plant				
Printing presses No 1	8,000			3,000
No 2	8,500			3,500
No 3	6,500	23,000		2,000
Typesetter		10,500		15,000
Binding machine		16,500		12,000
Small tools, type etc.		7,000		10,000
Motor cars		20,000		30,000
Office fixtures and fittings (items under £6,000)		9,000	86,000	15,000
Shares in associated publishing company			60,000	40,000
Cash at bank and in hand			7,500	—
Debtors			11,500	—

The pre-tapered chargeable gain (after indexation to April 1998) arising on the shares given to C's sister is £75,000.

The value of the company's chargeable assets is as follows

	Business £	Non-business £
Leasehold	190,000	—
Goodwill	60,000	—
Plant (£23,000 + £10,500 + £16,500)	50,000	—
Shares	—	60,000
	£300,000	£60,000

Gain eligible for retirement relief is therefore

$$£75,000 \times \frac{300,000}{300,000 + 60,000} \qquad £62,500$$

Notes

(a) Chargeable assets are all assets other than those on which any gain accruing on a disposal immediately before the end of the qualifying period would not be a chargeable gain.

(b) The balance of the gain after retirement relief will qualify for TAPER RELIEF (227).

Retirement Relief 222.2

(B) Shares in holding company — group holding non-business assets. [*TCGA 1992, Sch 6 paras 6, 8, 12; FA 1993, s 87, Sch 7 Pt I*]

D, a full-time working director aged 60, gives 20% of his shares in his personal company, N Ltd, to his son. The business of manufacturing and distributing double glazing units is carried on through two subsidiaries, X Ltd and Y Ltd. At the date of disposal in November 2002, the market value of the assets of the group are as follows

	Assets	Chargeable assets	
		Business	Non-business
	£	£	£
N Ltd			
Leasehold of factory	150,000	150,000	
Investment in subsidiaries			
X (100%)	60,000		
Y (60%)	40,000		
Quoted shares	10,000		10,000
X Ltd (100% owned)			
Plant	32,000	32,000	
Stock, debtors and cash	18,000		
		£182,000	£10,000
Y Ltd (60% owned)			
Freehold shop (half let)	50,000	25,000	25,000
Plant and machinery	15,000	15,000	
Stock, debtors and cash	9,000		
		£40,000	£25,000
60% thereof		£24,000	£15,000
Total		£206,000	£25,000

The chargeable gain (after indexation to April 1998) on the gift of shares is £57,750.

The gain eligible for retirement relief is therefore

$$£57,750 \times \frac{206,000}{206,000 + 25,000} = \underline{£51,500}$$

Notes

(a) A shareholding in another member of the trading group is not counted as a chargeable asset.

(b) Chargeable business and non-business assets of a part-owned subsidiary are reduced in proportion to the share capital owned.

(c) It is assumed that none of the items of plant and machinery are covered by the £6,000 chattel exemption.

(d) The balance of the gain after retirement relief will qualify for TAPER RELIEF (227).

222.2 Retirement Relief

(C) Associated disposal by trustees [*TCGA 1992, s 164(3)–(5), Sch 6 para 13; FA 1993, s 87, Sch 7 Pt I*]

B has carried on a business for more than ten years in premises held by a family trust in which he has a life interest of 40%.

In May 2001 B, who is then 54, sells the business, realising a chargeable gain of £47,000. The trustees sell the property on 30 April 2002, at a chargeable gain of £44,000.

Disposal by B

	£
Chargeable gain	47,000
Retirement relief (100%) (maximum £100,000)	(47,000)
Chargeable gain	Nil

Disposal by trustees

	£
Chargeable gain	44,000
Gain subject to retirement relief: 40% × £44,000 = £17,600	
Relief available at 100% £(50,000 – 47,000)	(3,000)
Relief available at 50% × £14,600 (17,600 – 3,000)	(7,300)
Chargeable gain (subect to TAPER RELIEF (227) and see note (c))	£33,700

Notes

(a) For the purposes of calculating the maximum available retirement relief, a trustees' disposal is regarded as a qualifying disposal by the beneficiary. If disposals by trustees and a beneficiary are made on the same day, relief is given first to the gain by the beneficiary.

(b) The qualifying period of full-time working must end not more than one year before the trustees' disposal. If the trustees' sale were deferred to, say, June 2002, no relief would be available except at the Board's discretion.

(c) For the period May 2001 to April 2002, the property is not a business asset for taper relief purposes by reference to the trustees' disposal. B remains an eligible beneficiary but no longer carries on a trade in which the asset is used. The gain must be apportioned using the method at 227.2 TAPER RELIEF.

(d) See also 222.3(B) below as regards two or more disposals qualifying for retirement relief.

Retirement Relief 222.2

(D) Associated disposal — restriction for non-business use, qualifying period and rent [*TCGA 1992, Sch 6 para 10; FA 1996, Sch 20 para 66(4)*]

In May 2002, X, who had been a full-time working officer for 10 years and was aged 53, sold his qualifying holding of shares in W Ltd, an unlisted company, realising a gain of £30,000. The company had, since 1992, used a warehouse acquired by X personally in 1987. It was agreed that whilst the company would continue to carry on the trade, it would vacate the warehouse (for which it paid a rent of 75% market rate) after six months. X then sold the warehouse in November 2002 realising a chargeable gain of £23,625.

Disposal of shares

	£
Chargeable gain	30,000
Retirement relief (100%)	(30,000)
	Nil

Disposal of warehouse

	£
Chargeable gain	23,625

Gain subject to retirement relief
(i) Proportion of business use

$$\frac{10 \text{ years}}{15 \text{ years}} \times £23,625 = £\underline{15,750}$$

(ii) Qualifying period of ownership

$$\frac{10}{10\frac{1}{2}} \times £15,750 = £\underline{15,000} \quad \text{(note } (b)\text{)}$$

(iii) Proportion rent-free
25% × £15,000 = £<u>3,750</u>

Balance of relief available (at 100%) £(50,000 − 30,000) = £20,000

Retirement relief (restricted to £3,750 × 100%)	3,750
Chargeable gain 2002/03 (subject to TAPER RELIEF (227))	£19,875

Notes

(a) Restricted retirement relief is available where the asset has not been used for business purposes throughout the period of ownership or where the individual was not concerned in carrying on the trade during part of the period of use in the business or where rent has been paid for the use of the asset. The part qualifying for relief is that which is 'just and reasonable'.

(b) For the final six months of use of the warehouse in the business, W Ltd was not X's personal company. (Note that for taper relief purposes after 5 April 2000, this will not restrict the period for which the warehouse is a business asset by reference to X's disposal — the fact that the company is unlisted is sufficient for the warehouse to retain its business asset status for those six months.)

(c) Note that where the material disposal occurs before 6 April 2003 and an associated disposal occurs on or after that date, the associated disposal will fall into 2003/04 and will not attract retirement relief (due to its abolition), though relief remains available for the material disposal. If, however, the associated disposal takes place before 6 April 2003 and the material disposal on or after that date, no relief can be due on *either* disposal.

222.2 Retirement Relief

(E) Partnerships [*TCGA 1992, s 163(8), Sch 6 para 10; FA 1996, Sch 20 para 66(4)*]
U, V and W trade in partnership. They have shared income and capital in the ratio 5:3:2 since 1979. On 30 April 2002, V retires aged 63 after 30 years as a partner and receives a lump sum of £50,000 from the other partners. Of the £50,000, £35,000 is expressed to relate to V's interest in the freehold depot, £10,000 to goodwill and £5,000 to non-chargeable assets. V also transfers to the firm, for £120,000, office premises which the firm has occupied for business purposes, paying an annual rent to V of £3,000. The open market rent for the property is £5,000 per annum. V's chargeable gain on the property is £82,000. The book values of the firm's chargeable assets are as follows

Freehold depot	£40,000 (cost on 1.5.88)
Goodwill	£10,000 (valuation on 31.3.82)

Indexation factors May 1988 to April 1998	0.531
March 1982 to April 1998	1.047

Gains eligible for retirement relief are

	£	£	£
Freehold depot: Consideration	35,000		
Allowable cost $\frac{3}{10}$ × £40,000	12,000		
Unindexed gain		23,000	
Indexation allowance £12,000 × 0.531		6,372	
			16,628
Goodwill: Consideration	10,000		
Allowable cost $\frac{3}{10}$ × £10,000	3,000		
Unindexed gain		7,000	
Indexation allowance £3,000 × 1.047		3,141	
			3,859
Office premises			
Gain	£82,000		
Fraction eligible			
$\frac{3}{10} + \left(\frac{7}{10} \times \frac{5,000 - 3,000}{5,000}\right) = \frac{29}{50} \times £82,000$			47,560
			£68,047

V's chargeable gains for 2002/03 are as follows

	£	£
Gains as above £(16,628 + 3,859 + 82,000)		102,487
Retirement relief at 100% (maximum £50,000)	50,000	
Retirement relief at 50% (on a maximum £150,000, but restricted to £18,047)	9,024	59,024
Gains subject to TAPER RELIEF (227)		£43,463

Notes
(*a*) Where rent, but at less than market rent, is paid by the partnership, *TCGA 1992, Sch 6 para 10* gives relief for a 'just and reasonable' amount of the gain. The formula shown above is used by the Revenue (Revenue Capital Gains Manual, CG 63836, CG 63838).

(*b*) See (D) above for restriction of retirement relief where an asset has not been used for business purposes throughout the period of ownership.

222.2 Retirement Relief

(F) Capital distribution [*TCGA 1992, s 163(1)(2)(4), Sch 6 paras 11, 12(5)(6); FA 1993, s 87, Sch 7 Pt I; FA 1996, Sch 21 para 44(4)*].

At 60, M decides to put his personal trading company into voluntary liquidation. He holds all the share capital and has been a full-time working officer for 20 years. In November 2001, the company sold off machinery for £7,000. The company ceases to trade in February 2002, and in November 2002 the liquidator pays M a cash distribution of £12,000 and transfers to him the lease of its premises, then worth £24,000.

M's chargeable gain for 2002/03 (after indexation to April 1998) on the consequent disposal of his shares is £27,000.

At cessation, the company's assets (at market value) were

	Assets £	Chargeable Business £	Chargeable Non-business £
Lease of premises	25,000	25,000	
Flat over premises (let)	5,000		5,000
Plant, fixtures	13,000	13,000	
Motor cars	8,000		
Stock, debtors, cash	19,000		

M elects under *TCGA 1992, Sch 6 para 12(5)* to substitute the machinery sold in November 2001 for the proceeds of its sale held at cessation in order to increase the proportion of chargeable business assets.

The chargeable gain is calculated as follows

	£
Gain on disposal	27,000

Restricted to cash portion of distribution   (note (*b*))

$$\frac{12,000}{12,000 + 24,000} \times £27,000 = \underline{£9,000}$$

Allowable for retirement relief (at 100%)

$$\frac{25,000 + 13,000 + 7,000}{25,000 + 13,000 + 7,000 + 5,000} \times £9,000 \qquad 8,100$$

Chargeable gain 2002/03 subject to TAPER RELIEF (227)   £18,900

Notes

(*a*) The liquidator's distribution must be within one year of the date of cessation of business or such longer period as the Board allows. (See definition of 'permitted period' in *TCGA 1992, Sch 6 para 1(2)*.)

(*b*) No retirement relief is available on that part of the gain attributable to the proportion of the capital distribution consisting of chargeable business assets. [*TCGA 1992, Sch 6 para 11*].

(*c*) It is assumed that no item of the plant and fixtures is covered by the £6,000 chattel exemption.

Retirement Relief 222.3

222.3 AMOUNT OF RELIEF

(A) Aggregation of earlier business periods [*TCGA 1992, Sch 6 para 14; FA 1996, Sch 39 para 7*]

A sold the hotel he had owned and run for ten years in July 1994. In January 1995 he reinvested £65,000 in a similar business, rolling over the earlier chargeable gain of £50,000. When he was 51, in January 2003, the hotel was severely damaged by fire and A decided to retire. He received £200,000 from the insurance company and £45,000 for the sale of the land. The indexation factor for the period January 1995 to April 1998 (note (*b*)) is 0.114.

	£	£
Disposal proceeds — sale of land	45,000	
— insurance monies	200,000	
		245,000
Cost	65,000	
Less rolled over gain	50,000	
		15,000
		230,000
Indexation allowance £15,000 × 0.114		1,710
		228,290

Maximum retirement relief available at 100% £50,000
Restricted by qualifying period

$$\frac{8 + 1\frac{1}{2}}{10} \times £50,000 \times 100\% \quad \text{(note } (a)\text{)} \qquad\qquad 47,500$$

	180,790

Maximum retirement relief available at 50%

$$£200,000 \times \frac{9\frac{1}{2}}{10} = £190,000 - £47,500 = £142,500$$

£228,290 − £47,500 = £180,790 but restricted to £142,500 × 50%   71,250

Chargeable gain 2002/03 (subject to TAPER RELIEF (227))   £109,540

Notes

(*a*) The two business periods falling within the ten-year qualifying period are aggregated but the qualifying period is restricted by the gap between the ownership of the two businesses.

(*b*) Other than for the purposes of corporation tax on chargeable gains, indexation allowance is frozen at its April 1998 level. Therefore, the indexation factor for April 1998 is used in respect of disposals in a later month (and expenditure incurred in April 1998 or later does not attract indexation allowance at all). See 210 INDEXATION.

222.3 Retirement Relief

(B) Relief given on earlier disposal [*TCGA 1992, Sch 6 para 15*]

P, who was born in May 1941, carried on the following businesses, and made gains qualifying for retirement relief on disposals of them at cessation, as follows

| Business A | 1.4.84 – 30.6.96 | £100,000 |
| Business B | 1.4.98 – 30.6.02 | £125,000 |

His entitlement to retirement relief is calculated as follows

Business A

| Gains qualifying for relief | £100,000 |
| Qualifying period | 10 years |

Maximum available for 100% relief

$10/10 \times £250,000 \times 100\% = £250,000$

	£
Relief given £100,000 × 100%	£100,000
Chargeable gain 1996/97	Nil
Underlying gains	£100,000

Business B

(1) Before restriction applied

| Gains qualifying for relief | £125,000 |

Qualifying period (extended under *TCGA 1992, Sch 6 para 14* as gap between businesses less than 2 years — 10 years (maximum) less 1.75 years from 1.7.96 to 31.3.98)   8.25 years

Maximum available for 100% relief

| | £ |
| $8.25/10 \times 50,000 \times 100\%$ | 41,250 |

Maximum available for 50% relief		
$8.25/10 \times £150,000$	£123,750	
Excess of gains £125,000 – 41,250	£83,750	

| £83,750 × 50% | 41,875 |
| Relief due subject to (2) below | £83,125 |

Retirement Relief 222.3

(2) Applying *TCGA 1992, Sch 15 para 15* restriction

		£
Gains qualifying for relief		125,000
Add Underlying gains on earlier disposal		100,000
		£225,000

Qualifying period for later disposal (as above)	8.25 years	
Extended by qualifying period for earlier disposal up to a maximum of 10 years	1.75 years	10 years

Maximum available for 100% relief

		£
10/10 × £50,000 × 100%		50,000

Maximum available for 50% relief 10/10 × £150,000	£150,000	
Excess of gains £225,000 − 50,000	£175,000	

£150,000 × 50%		75,000
		125,000
Less Relief given on disposal of Business A		100,000
Relief due (as less than £83,125 in (1) above)		£25,000
Chargeable gain 2002/03 (£125,000 − £25,000)		£200,000

Note

(*a*) The 2002/03 chargeable gain of £100,000 is subject to TAPER RELIEF (227).

222.3 Retirement Relief

(C) Married persons — aggregation of spouses' qualifying periods — transfer on death [*TCGA 1992, Sch 6 para 16; FA 1996, Sch 21 para 44(5)*]

R acquired her late husband's 30% shareholding in X Ltd on his death in June 1998. She took over the office he had held for 15 years as a full-time working officer until, at the age of 63, she sold her shares in June 2002, realising an otherwise chargeable gain of £66,000 (after indexation and before taper relief).

The chargeable gain is calculated as follows

	£
Gain eligible for relief	66,000
Maximum available for 100% relief	
$\dfrac{4+6}{10} \times £50,000 \times 100\%$	(50,000)
Maximum available for 50% relief	
$\dfrac{4+6}{10} \times £200,000 = £200,000 - £50,000 = £150,000$	
£66,000 − £50,000 = £16,000 × 50%	(8,000)
Chargeable gain 2002/03 (subject to TAPER RELIEF (227))	£8,000

Note
(a) Written election must be made, by the first anniversary of 31 January following the tax year in which the disposal occurs, for the qualifying period to be extended by the spouse's qualifying period.

(D) Married persons — aggregation of spouses' qualifying periods — lifetime transfer [*TCGA 1992, Sch 6 para 16; FA 1996, Sch 21 para 44(5)*]

In May 1995, J, who was 65 that month, gave 40% of the shares in Y Ltd, a trading company, to his son realising an otherwise chargeable gain of £20,000. He had been a full-time working officer for 12 years. His wife G, aged 54, already held 20% of the share capital and both she and the son became full-time directors. Later that year, J's health failed and he transferred his remaining 40% holding to G who continued as a full-time working officer until November 2002 when she gave her shares to her son realising an otherwise chargeable gain of £120,000 (after indexation and before taper relief). All the company's chargeable assets are chargeable business assets.

Gift by J to son	£
Gain eligible for relief	20,000
Retirement relief available (£20,000 × 100%)	20,000
Chargeable gain 1995/96	Nil

Retirement Relief 222.3

Disposal by G

| | £ | £ |

No election to aggregate qualifying periods
Gain eligible for relief   120,000
Maximum available for 100% relief

$\dfrac{7\frac{1}{2}}{10} \times £50,000$ (37,500)

Ceiling for 50% relief

$\dfrac{7\frac{1}{2}}{10} \times £200,000 = £150,000 - £37,500 = £112,500$

£120,000 − £37,500 = £82,500 × 50%   (41,250)

Chargeable gain 2002/03 (subject to TAPER RELIEF (227))   £41,250

Election made to aggregate qualifying periods   £
Gain eligible for relief   120,000
Maximum available for 100% relief

$\dfrac{10}{10} \times £50,000 =$ 50,000

Deduct Relief at 100% previously given   20,000   (30,000)

Ceiling for 50% relief

$\dfrac{10}{10} \times £200,000 = £200,000 - £50,000 = £150,000$

£120,000 − £30,000 = £90,000 × 50%   (45,000)

Chargeable gain 2002/03 (subject to TAPER RELIEF (227))   £45,000

The election is not beneficial.

Notes

(*a*)   Where, following a lifetime gift, the election is made for aggregation, retirement relief on the later disposal is restricted to that available if that disposal had been made by the transferor spouse. [*TCGA 1992, Sch 6 para 16(3)(4)*]. Thus, in this example, the relief must take into account retirement relief already given to the transferor spouse on an earlier disposal (see (B) above). [*TCGA 1992, Sch 6 para 15*].

(*b*)   G and her son could make a joint claim for the gain on her gift to be held-over under *TCGA 1992, s 165*, but retirement relief takes priority. See 209.2 HOLD-OVER RELIEFS for examples including the interaction between the two.

223.1 Rollover Relief — Replacement of Business Assets

223 Rollover Relief — Replacement of Business Assets

Cross-reference. See also 204.2 ASSETS HELD ON 31 MARCH 1982 for relief under *TCGA 1992, s 36, Sch 4* for certain gains accruing before 31 March 1982.

[*TCGA 1992, ss 152–158*]

223.1 NATURE OF RELIEF [*TCGA 1992, s 152*]

(A)

N Ltd carries on a manufacturing business. It makes the following disposals and acquisitions of assets during the company's accounting periods ended 31 December 2000, 31 December 2001 and 31 December 2002.

	Asset	Bought/ (sold) £	Chargeable gains £
1.10.2000	Freehold depot	18,000	—
12.12.2000	Leasehold warehouse	(50,000)	28,000
19.6.01	Business formerly carried on by another (unrelated) company:		
	Goodwill	20,000	—
	Freehold factory unit	90,000	—
1.2.02	Land adjacent to main factory, now surplus to requirements	(40,000)	19,000
8.9.02	Industrial mincer (fixed plant)	(30,000)	5,000
1.11.02	Extension to new factory	35,000	—

(i) The gain on the leasehold warehouse may be rolled over against the following

	Cost £		Gain £
Freehold depot	18,000	$\dfrac{18,000}{50,000} \times £28,000$	10,080
Goodwill	20,000	$\dfrac{20,000}{50,000} \times £28,000$	11,200
Freehold factory (part)	12,000	$\dfrac{12,000}{50,000} \times £28,000$	6,720
	£50,000		£28,000

See note (*b*)

(ii) The gain on the surplus land may then be rolled over as follows

Freehold factory (part)	£40,000	Gain rolled over	£19,000

(iii) The gain on the industrial mincer may be rolled over as follows

Extension to new factory (part)	£30,000	Gain rolled over	£5,000

Rollover Relief — Replacement of Business Assets

The position at 31 December 2002 is then as follows

	£
Freehold depot	
Cost	18,000
Deduct gains rolled over	10,080
Allowable cost	£7,920
Goodwill	
Cost	20,000
Deduct gains rolled over	11,200
Allowable cost	£8,800
Freehold factory	
Cost	90,000
Deduct gains rolled over (£6,720 + £19,000)	25,720
Allowable cost	£64,280
Extension to new factory	
Cost	35,000
Deduct gains rolled over	5,000
Allowable cost	£30,000

Notes

(a) The expenditure still available to match against disposal proceeds is

　　Extension to factory (£35,000 − £30,000)　　　£5,000

The expenditure is available only against disposals up to 31 October 2003.

(b) There is no statutory rule prescribing the way in which the gain on an asset must be rolled over against a number of different assets. The taxpayer's allocation of the rolled over gain against the cost of the new assets should be accepted by the Revenue, providing specified amounts of consideration are positively earmarked and set against the cost of specified new assets (Revenue Capital Gains Manual, CG60775). In (i) the chargeable gain has been rolled over rateably to the costs of the items, but bringing in only part (i.e. the balance of proceeds) of the cost of the freehold factory.

(c) If the acquisition of goodwill from an unrelated party had taken place a year later (i.e. after 31 March 2002), the goodwill would have fallen within the corporation tax intangible assets regime at *FA 2002, Sch 29* and would *not* have been a qualifying asset for chargeable gains rollover relief purposes. [*FA 2002, s 84, Sch 29 paras 132(5), 137*].

223.1 Rollover Relief — Replacement of Business Assets

(B)

L Ltd carries on a vehicle repair business. In December 2000 it sells a workshop for £90,000 net of costs. The workshop had cost £45,000 inclusive in April 1993. A new workshop is purchased for £144,000 (including incidental costs of acquisition) on 11 January 2001 and sold for £168,000 on 14 January 2003.

Indexation factors April 1993 to December 2000	0.225
January 2001 to January 2003 (estimated)	0.050

L Ltd claims rollover of the chargeable gain.

	£
Allowable cost of original workshop	45,000
Indexation allowance £45,000 × 0.225	10,125
	55,125
Actual disposal consideration	90,000
Chargeable gain rolled over	£34,875
Cost of new workshop	144,000
Deduct Amount rolled over	34,875
Deemed allowable cost	£109,125
Disposal consideration, replacement workshop	168,000
Allowable cost	109,125
Unindexed gain	58,875
Indexation allowance £109,125 × 0.050	5,456
Chargeable gain (January 2003)	£53,419

(C)

The facts are as in (B) above except that the business is carried on by M, an individual. M makes no disposals in 2002/03 other than that of the replacement workshop. The indexation factor for the period April 1993 to April 1998 is 0.156.

	£
Allowable cost of original workshop	45,000
Indexation allowance £45,000 × 0.156	7,020
	52,020
Actual disposal consideration	90,000
Chargeable gain rolled over (note (*a*))	£37,980
Cost of new workshop	144,000
Deduct Amount rolled over	37,980
Deemed allowable cost	£106,020
Disposal consideration, replacement workshop	168,000
Allowable cost	106,020
Gain subject to taper relief	£61,980
Business asset taper relief: £61,980 @ 75% (note (*b*))	46,485
Chargeable gain 2002/03 (note (*b*))	£15,495

Rollover Relief — Replacement of Business Assets 223.1

Notes

(a) No taper relief is available on a rolled over gain (see Tolley's Capital Gains Tax 2002/03 at 61.17 TAPER RELIEF).

(b) The qualifying holding period of the replacement workshop for taper relief purposes runs from 11 January 2001 to 14 January 2003, comprising two complete years. [*TCGA 1992, s 2A; FA 1998, s 121(1); FA 2000, s 66*]. The period of ownership of the original workshop is not taken into account. In fact, two years is sufficient (for disposals after 5 April 2002) to attract the maximum 75% taper relief on assets that have been business assets throughout the period of ownership.

(c) Other than for the purposes of corporation tax on chargeable gains, indexation allowance is frozen at its April 1998 level. Therefore, the indexation factor for April 1998 is used in respect of disposals in a later month (and expenditure incurred in April 1998 or later does not attract indexation allowance at all). See 210 INDEXATION.

(D) Companies: transition from chargeable gains rollover relief to intangible assets rollover relief [*FA 2002, s 84, Sch 29 paras 130, 132, 137(1)*]

On 30 October 2002, Farming Company Ltd sells an area of land with attached milk quota for £1.25m. Under the contract for sale, the proceeds allocated to the quota are £150,000, equivalent to their current market value. Immediately before the sale, the 'pool' of milk quota held by the company, all acquired before 1 April 2002, had a total current value of £600,000, a historical cost of £250,000 and an indexed cost to date of £400,000. The land sold has an acquisition cost for chargeable gains purposes of £450,000 (inclusive of indexation allowance to date).

On 1 February 2002, the company had acquired some other land (with no quota attached) for £800,000.

On 1 June 2003, Farming Company Ltd acquires an existing business from a non-related party (see *FA 2002, Sch 29 para 95*) for £340,000. The purchase price comprises land at £200,000, goodwill at £100,000 and net current assets (not available for rollover relief of any kind) at £40,000.

The company's gains on the 30.10.02 disposal are as follows

	Land £	Quota £
Proceeds	1,100,000	150,000
Cost (including indexation allowance):		
Land	450,000	
Quota £400,000 × $\dfrac{150,000}{150,000 + 600,000}$		80,000
Gains	£650,000	£70,000

Note that the milk quota and the land to which it attaches are separate assets for chargeable gains purposes (*Cottle v Coldicott (Sp C 40), [1995] SSCD 239*).

The company's rollover options are as follows

Land. The gain of £650,000 on the sale of the land for £1.1m can be rolled over partially against the £800,000 cost of land acquired on 1.2.02 and partially against the £200,000 cost of land acquired on 1.6.03, leaving £100,000 of the gain chargeable — equal to the proceeds not reinvested (see 223.2(A) below as regards partial relief where not all

223.1 Rollover Relief — Replacement of Business Assets

proceeds reinvested). It would not be possible to rollover the gain only against the 1.6.03 acquisition — the proceeds not reinvested (£900,000) would be more than the gain (£650,000).

No part of the gain can be rolled over against the goodwill acquired on 1.6.03 as the goodwill is a chargeable intangible asset, i.e. it is within the intangible assets regime for companies set out in *FA 2002, Sch 29* (see *FA 2002, Sch 29 para 137(1)*), having been acquired after 31 March 2002 other than from a related party; thus, it is not a qualifying asset for the purposes of chargeable gains rollover relief under *TCGA 1992, s 152* (see *FA 2002, Sch 29 para 132(5)*).

Milk quota. These are intangible fixed assets. They are excluded from the intangible assets regime as they were acquired before 1 April 2002 (see *FA 2002, Sch 29 paras 118, 126*). Nevertheless, the gains are eligible only for intangible assets rollover relief and, subject to transitional rules, not for chargeable gains rollover relief. Under the transitional rules, the gain may, however, be rolled over against acquisitions of qualifying assets (within *TCGA 1992, s 155*) made before 1 April 2002 (and within the 12 months immediately preceding the disposal).

Thus, under *intangible assets rollover relief*, the gain of £70,000 on the sale of quota for £150,000 could be set partially against the £100,000 cost of goodwill on 1.6.03. Alternatively (or in addition), under *chargeable gains rollover relief*, the gain could be rolled over against the 1.2.02 acquisition of land. (A company has the option of claiming relief under either set of provisions or partly under one and partly under the other.) [*FA 2002, Sch 29 paras 37–45, 132(1)(2)*]. To the extent though that the gain on quota is rolled over against the 1.2.02 acquisition, the company could not then roll over the gain on the 30.10.02 disposal of land against the same acquisition.

Revised computation. The revised computation below assumes, as regards the land, that chargeable gains rollover relief is claimed as far as possible (and in priority) and, as regards the milk quota, that intangible assets rollover relief is claimed as far as possible.

The amount available for intangible assets rollover relief is £20,000, i.e. (where not all proceeds are reinvested) it is the excess of qualifying expenditure (£100,000) over the cost of the old asset (£80,000 — per *FA 2002, Sch 29 para 130(5)*). [*FA 2002, Sch 29 para 41(3)*].

The chargeable gains computation on the 30.10.02 disposal is revised as follows.

	Land £	Quota £
Proceeds	1,100,000	150,000
Deduct Amount available for intangible assets relief [*FA 2002, Sch 29 para 130(7)*].		20,000
		130,000
Cost (as above):		80,000
	1,100,000	50,000
Deduct Proceeds reinvested	1,000,000	
Chargeable gains not rolled over	£100,000	£50,000

Rollover Relief — Replacement of Business Assets 223.2

223.2 PARTIAL RELIEF

(A) Assets only partly replaced [TCGA 1992, s 153]

G carries on an accountancy practice. In March 2002, he agrees to acquire the practice of another sole practitioner, who is about to retire. As part of the acquisition, G pays £20,000 for goodwill. In January 2003, G moves to new premises, acquiring the remaining 70 years of a 99-year lease for £50,000. The sale of his former office on 25 February 2003 realises £80,000, and a chargeable gain (after indexation to April 1998) of £59,000 arises. (The former office had been owned since 1992.)

	£	£
Amount of proceeds of disposal of old office		80,000
Costs against which gains can be rolled over		
Goodwill	20,000	
Lease	50,000	
		70,000
Chargeable gain not rolled over		10,000
Business asset taper relief @ 75% (note (c))		7,500
Chargeable gain		£2,500
Chargeable gain rolled over (£59,000 − £10,000)		£49,000
Allowable cost of assets (see note (a))		
Goodwill	20,000	
Gain rolled over $\frac{20,000}{70,000} \times £49,000$	14,000	
		£6,000
Lease	50,000	
Gain rolled over $\frac{50,000}{70,000} \times £49,000$	35,000	
		£15,000

Notes

(a) There is no statutory rule prescribing the way in which a gain is to be rolled over against more than one acquisition. See note (b) to 223.1(A) above.

(b) It would not have been possible to roll over the gain only against the acquisition of the goodwill. The consideration not reinvested (£60,000) would be more than the gain (£59,000).

(c) The qualifying holding period for taper relief purposes runs from 6 April 1998 to 25 February 2003, comprising four complete years. [TCGA 1992, s 2A; FA 1998, s 121(1); FA 2000, s 66].

(d) A gain does not qualify for taper relief to the extent that it is rolled over (see Tolley's Capital Gains Tax 2002/03 at 61.17 TAPER RELIEF).

223.2 Rollover Relief — Replacement of Business Assets

(B) Partial business use [*TCGA 1992, s 152(7)*]

N carries on a consultancy business from commercial premises formerly used as a shop. N has owned the property since 1 July 1980, but it was let until 1 March 1992 when N moved in, following the expiry of the lease held by the former tenant. On 1 February 2003, N sells the property for £100,000, moving to a new office with a long lease which he acquires for £60,000 and which is wholly used for his business. The value at 31 March 1982 of the property sold was £40,000 and N has made the global re-basing election under *TCGA 1992, s 35(5)*. The indexation factor for March 1982 to April 1998 (note (*d*)) is 1.047.

For rollover relief purposes, N is treated as having disposed of two separate assets, one representing his occupation and professional use of the property, the other his ownership of it as an investment. In practice, the proceeds and chargeable gain may be allocated by a simple time apportionment.

Proceeds attributable to business use

Proceeds £100,000 $\times \dfrac{10y\ 11m}{20y\ 10m}$ (note (*c*))   £52,398

Chargeable gain attributable to business use

[£100,000 − £40,000 − (£40,000 × 1.047)] = £18,120 $\times \dfrac{10y\ 11m}{20y\ 10m}$ £9,494

Notes

(*a*) The proceeds attributable to business use are less than the cost of the new office, so that the whole of the chargeable gain attributable to business use can be rolled over. The allowable cost of the new office is then £50,506 (£60,000 − £9,494).

(*b*) The balance of the chargeable gain, £8,626 (£18,120 − £9,494) is not eligible for rollover. It *is* fully eligible for business asset taper relief by reference solely to the use of the property after 5 April 1998 (see 227.2 TAPER RELIEF).

(*c*) The time apportionment takes into account only the period of ownership after 30 March 1982. [*TCGA 1992, s 152(9)*].

(*d*) Other than for the purposes of corporation tax on chargeable gains, indexation allowance is frozen at its April 1998 level. Therefore, the indexation factor for April 1998 is used in respect of disposals in a later month (and expenditure incurred in April 1998 or later does not attract indexation allowance at all). See 210 INDEXATION.

* example of Round down £9494.88

Rollover Relief — Replacement of Business Assets   223.3

223.3 **WASTING ASSETS** [*TCGA 1992, s 154*]

(A) Crystallisation of held-over gain

In March 1998, a father and son partnership carrying on a car dealing trade sold a freehold showroom for £400,000 realising a chargeable gain (after indexation) of £190,000. On 30 June 1998, the firm purchased for £450,000 the remaining term of a lease due to expire on 30 June 2028 and used the premises as a new showroom. The whole of the gain on the old asset was held over under *TCGA 1992, s 154* on the acquisition of the new asset. In consequence of the father's decision to retire from the business and the resulting need to downsize the operation, the firm assigns the lease for £490,000 on 1 July 2002.

The chargeable gains to be apportioned between the two partners for 2002/03 are as follows

	£	£
Proceeds of assignment		490,000
Cost (see note (*a*))	450,000	
Deduct Wasted $\dfrac{87.330 - 82.496}{87.330} \times £450,000$	24,909	425,091
Chargeable gain 2002/03 (see also note (*b*))		£64,909
Held-over gain becoming chargeable under *TCGA 1992, s 154(2)(a)*		£190,000

Notes

(*a*) The gain of £190,000 is deferred as opposed to being rolled over and does not reduce the cost of the new asset.

(*b*) Each of the partners will be entitled to taper relief on their share of the gain of £64,909 to the extent that it is not reduced by the offset of capital losses (and the father's share may attract retirement relief). Taper relief on the deferred gain of £190,000 operates by reference to the date of disposal and period of ownership of the old asset, and none is due in this case as the disposal was before 6 April 1998. See 227.4 TAPER RELIEF. The deferred gain cannot be covered by retirement relief as the disposal giving rise to it did not take place on retirement.

(*c*) Expenditure incurred in April 1998 or later does not attract indexation allowance. See 210 INDEXATION.

(*d*) See also 213.3(D)–(G) LAND for further examples on the assignment of short leases.

223.3 Rollover Relief — Replacement of Business Assets

(B) Rollover of held-over gain

C Ltd, a manufacturing company, sells an item of fixed plant for £30,000 in February 1998. A chargeable gain of £7,200 arises. In 2000, the company buys storage facilities on a 20-year lease for £40,000. In 2002, an extension to the company's freehold factory is completed at a cost of £25,000.

The position is as follows

(i) The company may claim holdover of the £7,200 chargeable gain in 1998, against the cost of the lease.

(ii) In 2002, part of the chargeable gain can be rolled over against the cost of the factory extension, as follows

	£
Expenditure available for rollover	25,000
Maximum capable of rollover	
£7,200 – (£30,000 – £25,000)	2,200
Adjusted base cost of extension	£22,800

Notes

(a) The balance of the chargeable gain, £5,000 (£7,200 – £2,200) may continue to be held over against the cost of the lease, either until it crystallises or until further rollover is possible.

(b) Had the company not claimed holdover against the cost of the lease, a claim against the cost of the extension in 2002 would not have been possible, as the expenditure was incurred outside the normal three-year time limit.

224 Settlements

Cross-reference. See 217.1 OFFSHORE SETTLEMENTS as regards capital gains of non-resident settlements.

224.1 ANNUAL EXEMPTIONS AND RATES OF TAX [*TCGA 1992, ss 3, 4(1AA), Sch 1 para 2; FA 1998, s 120; FA 1999, s 26(3)*]

The trustees of the E settlement, created in 1974, realise net chargeable gains and allowable losses, all on disposals of non-business assets for taper relief purposes, as follows

	Chargeable gain/ (allowable loss) £
1998/99	(2,250)
1999/2000	3,100
2000/01	4,700
2001/02	3,200
2002/03	10,550

The settlor does not have an interest in the settlement (see note (*b*)).

The trustees' capital gains tax liability is computed as follows

	£
1998/99	
Taxable amount	Nil
Losses carried forward	£2,250
1999/2000	
Net chargeable gains	3,100
Losses brought forward	—
Taxable amount (covered by annual exemption of £3,550)	£3,100
CGT	Nil
Losses carried forward	£2,250
2000/01	
Net chargeable gains	4,700
Losses brought forward	1,100
Taxable amount (covered by annual exemption)	£3,600
CGT	Nil
Losses carried forward (£2,250 – £1,100)	£1,150
	£
2001/02	
Net chargeable gains	3,200
Losses brought forward	—
Taxable amount (covered by annual exemption of £3,750)	£3,200
CGT	Nil
Losses carried forward	£1,150

224.1 Settlements

2002/03

Net chargeable gains	10,550
Losses brought forward	1,150
Untapered gains	9,400
Deduct Taper relief @ 15% (note (*c*))	1,410
Taxable gains	£7,990
CGT at 34% on £4,140 (7,990 − 3,850)	£1,407.60
Losses carried forward	Nil

Notes

(*a*) For 1998/99 onwards, the rate of capital gains tax on gains accruing to the trustees of any settlement, whether it be an interest in possession trust or an accumulation and maintenance trust is equivalent to the 'rate applicable to trusts' under *ICTA 1988, s 686*. The rate is 34% for 2002/03. [*TCGA 1992, s 4(1AA); ICTA 1988, s 686(1A); FA 1993, Sch 6 para 8; FA 1998, s 120; FA 1999, s 26(3)*].

(*b*) If the settlor had an interest in the settlement (as defined by *TCGA 1992, s 77(2)–(5)*) at any time during 2002/03, the gain of £7,990 (after deducting losses and taper relief but before deducting the annual exemption) would be chargeable on the settlor and not on the trustees. His own annual exemption of £7,700 may be set against the gain (see also 201.2(B) ANNUAL RATES AND EXEMPTIONS and 214.2 LOSSES). Any tax payable could be recovered from the trustees. See also 224.2 below. [*TCGA 1992, ss 77–79; FA 1995, s 74, Sch 17 paras 27–29*].

(*c*) It is assumed that the 2002/03 chargeable gains all arose on disposals of assets acquired before 17 March 1998, thus giving a qualifying holding period for taper relief purposes of four years plus the bonus year for non-business assets so acquired.

(*d*) See *TCGA 1992, Sch 1 para 2(4)–(6)* for the annual exemption available to two or more settlements made by the same settlor after 6 June 1978.

Settlements 224.2

224.2 **SETTLEMENT IN WHICH SETTLOR HAS AN INTEREST** [*TCGA 1992, ss 77–79; FA 1995, s 74, Sch 17 paras 27–29; FA 2002, Sch 11 paras 3, 8*]

In May 2000 Henry, a UK resident, settled £25,000 on trust to his wife for her life with the remainder to his adult daughter absolutely. The trustees are resident in the UK. For 2001/02, the trustees make disposals on which they incur losses of £300. For 2002/03, they realise gains of £4,000 and losses of £700 (these figures being net of any available taper relief). Henry has personal gains of £5,400 for 2002/03 (again after any available taperrelief) with no losses brought forward. Henry's taxable income for 2002/03 is £50,000 and he is thus liable to tax at 40% on capital gains.

Henry's capital gains tax liability for 2002/03 is calculated as follows

	£	£
Personal gains		5,400
Settlement gains	4,000	
Deduct Losses	700	
	3,300	
Deduct Losses b/f	300	3,000
		8,400
Deduct Annual exemption		7,700
Gain liable to CGT		£700
CGT payable at 40%		£280.00
CGT recoverable from trustees (note (*a*))		£280.00

Notes

(*a*) For the purposes of recovery from the trustees, the settlement gains are regarded as forming the highest part of the total amount on which Henry is liable to CGT. His personal gains are therefore fully covered by his annual exemption and the whole of the liability relates to the settlement gains; it is thus fully recoverable from the trustees. [*TCGA 1992, s 78*].

(*b*) If either Henry or his wife died during 2002/03, or if they ceased to be married during that year, *TCGA 1992, ss 77–79* would not apply and the settlement gain of £3,300 (before deducting losses brought forward) would be covered by the trustees' annual exemption of £3,850, with losses of £300 carried forward to 2003/04. [*TCGA 1992, s 77(6); FA 1995, Sch 17 para 27*].

(*c*) For the offset of personal capital losses of the settlor against gains attributed to him under the rules illustrated in this example, see 214.2 LOSSES.

224.3 Settlements

224.3 CREATION OF A SETTLEMENT [*TCGA 1992, s 70*]

(A)
In December 2002, C transfers to trustees of a settlement for the benefit of his children 10,000 shares in W plc, a quoted company. The value of the gift is £85,000. C bought the shares in 1981 for £20,000 and their value at 31 March 1982 was £35,000. The indexation factor for March 1982 to April 1998 (note (*b*)) is 1.047.

	£	£
Deemed disposal consideration	85,000	85,000
Cost	20,000	
Market value 31.3.82		35,000
Unindexed gain	65,000	50,000
Indexation allowance £35,000 × 1.047	36,645	36,645
Gain after indexation	£28,355	£13,355
Chargeable gain (subject to TAPER RELIEF (227))		£13,355
Trustees' allowable cost		£85,000

Notes

(*a*) If the transfer had been a chargeable lifetime transfer for inheritance tax purposes, or would be one but for the annual inheritance tax exemption, C could have elected under *TCGA 1992, s 260* to roll the gain over against the trustees' base cost of the shares. The trustees do not join in any such election. This would normally cover only a transfer to a discretionary settlement. It is the *untapered* gain that is held over (see Tolley's Capital Gains Tax 2002/03 at 61.16 TAPER RELIEF).

(*b*) Other than for the purposes of corporation tax on chargeable gains, indexation allowance is frozen at its April 1998 level. See 210 INDEXATION.

Settlements 224.4

(B)
In late April 2002 H settles farmland on trust for himself for life, with interests in reversion to his children. The land cost £20,000 in 1975 and its agreed values are £60,000 at 31 March 1982 and £125,000 at the date of settlement. H's interest in possession in the settled property is valued at £90,000. The indexation factor from March 1982 to April 1998 (note (*c*)) is 1.047.

The chargeable gain is computed as follows

	£	£
Deemed disposal proceeds	125,000	125,000
Cost	20,000	
Market value 31.3.82		60,000
Unindexed gain	105,000	65,000
Indexation allowance £60,000 × 1.047	62,820	62,820
Gain after indexation	£42,180	£2,180
Chargeable gain (subject to TAPER RELIEF (227))		£2,180

Notes
(*a*) The value of H's interest in the settled property is ignored and the transfer is not treated as a part disposal.

(*b*) For as long as H has an interest in the settlement the provisions of *TCGA 1992, ss 77–79* will apply to any settlement gains, with the effect that they will be chargeable on the settlor and not on the trustees. See 224.2 above.

(*c*) Other than for the purposes of corporation tax on chargeable gains, indexation allowance is frozen at its April 1998 level. See 210 INDEXATION.

224.4 PERSON BECOMING ABSOLUTELY ENTITLED TO SETTLED PROPERTY
[*TCGA 1992, s 71*]

(A)
M is a beneficiary entitled to an interest in possession in settled property, under a settlement made by her mother. The trustees exercise a power of appointment to advance capital to M, and, in September 2002, transfer to her a house valued at £80,000. The house was acquired by the trustees by gift from the settlor in 1998, when its value was £45,000.

The trustees realise a gain of £35,000 (£80,000 – £45,000) (before any indexation allowance and taper relief) on the advancement of capital to M.

Notes
(*a*) Any indexation allowance (computed to April 1998 — see 210.1(B) INDEXATION) available to the trustees will be based on their deemed acquisition cost of £45,000. Taper relief is also available, by reference to the trustees' period of ownership after 5 April 1998 (including, where applicable, the bonus year for assets acquired before 17 March 1998).

(*b*) If, while it was settled property, the house had been occupied by M as her private residence with the permission of the trustees, then all or part of the gain would qualify for the private residence exemption under *TCGA 1992, s 225*.

224.4 Settlements

(B) Transfer of settlement losses [*TCGA 1992, s 71(2)–(2D); FA 1999, s 75*]

F is the sole remaining beneficiary of an accumulation and maintenance settlement established under his late uncle's will and in which he became entitled to an interest in possession upon reaching the age of 18 in 1993. On 18 September 2000, his 25th birthday, he becomes absolutely entitled as against the trustees to the capital of the trust. At that date, the trust capital consists of the following

- cash of £12,000,
- 10,000 shares in ABC Ltd (purchased for £6,000 in May 1999 and currently valued at £11,000), and
- 15,000 shares in DEF Ltd (transferred into the trust at a CGT value of £27,000 but now valued at only £13,000).

On 30 June 2000, the trustees had sold shares in GHK Ltd at a gain of £3,000 (after deducting indexation allowance to April 1998). On 7 July 2000, they sold shares in LMN Ltd at a loss of £500. None of the above-mentioned trust investments were business assets for taper relief purposes. At 6 April 2000, the trustees had allowable capital losses of £1,000 brought forward from earlier years.

In December 2000, F sells the ABC Ltd shares for £11,600. He also disposes of other assets in 2000/01 realising chargeable gains of £9,400 (with no taper relief due). In 2002/03, he sells the DEF Ltd shares for £15,700 and also disposes of other assets realising chargeable gains of £18,000 (all attracting 15% taper relief) and allowable losses of £1,500.

F takes over entitlement to trust losses as follows

	£	£
Loss on DEF Ltd shares transferred to F £(27,000 – 13,000)		14,000
Deduct Trustees' 'pre-entitlement gains'*:		
(i) gain on ABC Ltd shares transferred to F	5,000	
(ii) other gains in period 6.4.2000–18.9.2000	3,000	8,000
Loss treated as accruing to F (note (*a*))		£6,000

* See *TCGA 1992, s 71(2A)*

F's CGT position for 2000/01 and 2002/03 is as follows

2000/01

	£
Gain on sale of ABC Ltd shares £(11,600 – 11,000)	600
Other gains	9,400
	10,000
Deduct Annual exemption	7,200
Gains chargeable to tax	£2,800
Ex-trust losses carried forward	£6,000

Settlements 224.4

2002/03

	£	£
Gain on sale of DEF Ltd shares £(15,700 – 13,000)	2,700	
Deduct Ex-trust losses brought forward and treated as a loss for the year	2,700	—
Other gains	18,000	
Deduct Losses for the year	1,500	
	16,500	
Deduct Taper relief @ 15%	2,475	14,025
		14,025
Deduct Annual exemption		7,700
Gains chargeable to tax		£6,325

	£
Ex-trust losses brought forward	6,000
Utilised in 2002/03	2,500
Unused balance (note (*b*))	£3,500

Notes

(*a*) Trust losses of £1,000 brought forward and £500 accruing in 2000/01 cannot be transferred to F and in this case are wasted. The 'pre-entitlement gains' cannot be reduced by those losses before being set against the loss on DEF Ltd shares. If F had become absolutely entitled before 16 June *1999*, losses such as those would have been transferable in addition to the £6,000 transferred in this example.

(*b*) In F's hands, the loss can only be set against a gain on the DEF Ltd shares on which it arose. As all those shares are sold in 2002/03, the loss cannot be carried forward any further and the unused balance of £3,500 is written off. If F had become absolutely entitled before 16 June *1999*, losses transferred to him from the trust could have been used against his chargeable gains without restriction.

224.5 Settlements

224.5 **TERMINATION OF INTEREST IN POSSESSION ON DEATH** [*TCGA 1992, s 72; FA 1996, Sch 39 para 5*]

(A)
K is entitled to an interest in possession under a settlement. The settled property consists of shares and cash. On K's death, L is entitled to a life interest in succession to K. K dies on 1 December 2002, when the shares are valued at £200,000. The trustees' allowable cost in respect of the shares is £40,000.

On K's death, the trustees are deemed to have disposed of and immediately reacquired the shares for £200,000, thus uplifting the CGT base cost, but no chargeable gain then arises.

(B)
In 1976, E created a settlement for the benefit of his children M and N and his grandchildren, transferring an investment property valued at £10,000 to the trustees. The terms of the settlement were that M and N each have a life interest in half of the trust income, with the remainder passing to E's grandchildren. In 1990, N assigned his interest to P, an unrelated party, for £35,000, its then market value. In 2002, N dies. The value of a half share of the trust property is then £65,000.

On N's death, his life interest terminates. There is no effect on the trustees as N was no longer the person entitled to the life interest within the meaning of *TCGA 1992, s 72*.

Notes
(*a*) No chargeable gain arises on the disposal by N of his interest. [*TCGA 1992, s 76*].

(*b*) P may claim an allowable loss on extinction of the interest. For an example of the computation if the interest is a wasting asset, see 228.3 WASTING ASSETS.

225 Shares and Securities

Cross-references. See also 203 ASSETS HELD ON 6 APRIL 1965, 204 ASSETS HELD ON 31 MARCH 1982, 210 INDEXATION, 221 QUALIFYING CORPORATE BONDS and 226 SHARES AND SECURITIES — IDENTIFICATION RULES.

225.1 REORGANISATION OF SHARE CAPITAL — VALUATION OF DIFFERENT CLASSES OF SHARE ON SUBSEQUENT DISPOSAL [*TCGA 1992, ss 126–131*]

(A) Unquoted shares

V acquired 10,000 ordinary shares in X Ltd, an unquoted trading company, in April 1997 at a cost of £15,000. In April 2000, as part of a reorganisation of share capital, V was additionally allotted 3,000 new 9% preference shares in X Ltd for which he paid £3,900. In June 2002, V sold his ordinary shareholding, in an arm's length transaction, for £20,000, but retained his preference shares, then valued at £4,000. The indexation factor for the period April 1997 to April 1998 (see note (*b*)) is 0.040.

The chargeable gain on the disposal of the ordinary shares is calculated as follows

	£
Disposal consideration	20,000
Cost (£15,000 + £3,900) × $\dfrac{20{,}000}{20{,}000 + 4{,}000}$	15,750
Unindexed gain	4,250
Indexation allowance $\dfrac{15{,}000}{18{,}900} \times £15{,}750 \times 0.040$	500
Chargeable gain 2002/03 (subject to TAPER RELIEF (227))	£3,750
Allowable cost of 3,000 preference shares (£15,000 + £3,900 − £15,750)	3,150
Indexation allowance to April 1998 $\dfrac{15{,}000}{18{,}900} \times £3{,}150 \times 0.040$	100
Indexed cost	£3,250

Notes

(*a*) The ordinary shares and preference shares held after the reorganisation (the 'new holding') constitute a single asset. [*TCGA 1992, s 127*]. A disposal of part of the new holding is thus a part disposal. If neither class of shares comprising the new holding is quoted on a recognised stock exchange at any time not later than three months after the reorganisation, acquisition cost on a part disposal is apportioned by reference to market values at the date of disposal. [*TCGA 1992, s 129*].

(*b*) Other than for the purposes of corporation tax on chargeable gains, indexation allowance is frozen at its April 1998 level. Therefore, the indexation factor for April 1998 is used in respect of disposals in a later month (and expenditure incurred in April 1998 or later does not attract indexation allowance at all). See 210 INDEXATION.

225.1 Shares and Securities

(B) Quoted shares
Assume the facts to be as in (A) above except that both the ordinary and preference shares are quoted on a recognised stock exchange. On the first day of dealing after the reorganisation took effect, the ordinary shares were quoted at £1.85 and the preference shares at £1.35. V's holdings were therefore valued at £18,500 and £4,050 respectively.

The chargeable gain on the disposal of the ordinary shares is calculated as follows

	£
Disposal consideration	20,000
Cost (£15,000 + £3,900) × $\dfrac{18,500}{18,500 + 4,050}$	15,506
Unindexed gain	4,494
Indexation allowance $\dfrac{15,000}{18,900}$ × £15,506 × 0.040	492
Chargeable gain 2002/03 (subject to TAPER RELIEF (227))	£4,002
Allowable cost of 3,000 preference shares (£15,000 + £3,900 − £15,506)	3,394
Indexation allowance to April 1998 $\dfrac{15,000}{18,900}$ × £3,394 × 0.040	108
Indexed cost	£3,502

Note
(a) Where one or more of the classes of shares or debentures comprising the new holding is quoted on a recognised stock exchange at any time not later than three months after the reorganisation, acquisition cost on a part disposal is apportioned by reference to market values on the first day of dealing on which the prices quoted reflect the reorganisation. [TCGA 1992, s 130].

Shares and Securities 225.1

(C) Quoted shares — reorganisation after 31 March 1982, original holding acquired on or before that date

In 1980, W subscribed for 5,000 £1 ordinary shares at par in L plc, a quoted company. The value of his holding at 31 March 1982 was £8,000. In November 1990, L plc offered ordinary shareholders two 7% preference shares at £1 per share in respect of each five ordinary shares held. W took up his entitlement of 2,000 preference shares. On the first day of dealing after the reorganisation, the ordinary shares were quoted at £3.00 (making W's holding worth £15,000) and the preference shares at £1.02 (valuing W's holding at £2,040). In June 2002, W sells his preference shares on the market at £1.40 (total proceeds £2,800). (For simplicity, costs of acquisition and disposal are ignored in this example.) The indexation factor from March 1982 to April 1998 (see note (*b*)) is 1.047 and from November 1990 to April 1998 it is 0.251.

The gain on the disposal of the preference shares is computed as follows

The calculation, without re-basing to 1982, is

	£
Disposal consideration	2,800
Cost (£5,000 + £2,000) × $\dfrac{2,040}{2,040 + 15,000}$	838
Unindexed gain	1,962
Indexation allowance (see below)	1,063
Gain after indexation	£899

The calculation, with re-basing to 1982, is

	£
Disposal consideration	2,800
(31.3.82 value £8,000 + cost £2,000) × $\dfrac{2,040}{2,040 + 15,000}$	1,197
Unindexed gain	1,603
Indexation allowance $\dfrac{8,000}{10,000} \times £1,197 \times 1.047 = £1,003$	
$\dfrac{2,000}{10,000} \times £1,197 \times 0.251 = 60$	
	1,063
Gain after indexation	£540
Chargeable gain 2002/03 (subject to TAPER RELIEF (227))	£540

Notes

(*a*) On a subsequent disposal of the ordinary shares, their cost would be £6,162 (£5,000 + £2,000 − £838) or, if re-basing applied, £8,803 (£8,000 + £2,000 − £1,197). In either case, indexation would be based on £8,803.

(*b*) Other than for the purposes of corporation tax on chargeable gains, indexation allowance is frozen at its April 1998 level. Therefore, the indexation factor for April 1998 is used in respect of disposals in a later month (and expenditure incurred in April 1998 or later does not attract indexation allowance at all). See 210 INDEXATION.

225.2 Shares and Securities

225.2 BONUS ISSUES [TCGA 1992, ss 126–128, 130]

(A) Bonus of same class

In October 1993, Y plc made a scrip issue of one ordinary share for every 10 held. L held 5,000 ordinary shares, which he acquired in May 1986 for £5,500, and therefore received 500 shares in the bonus issue. In October 2002, L sells 3,000 of his shares for £7,000. The indexation factor for the period May 1986 to April 1998 (see note (*a*)) is 0.662.

Section 104 holding	Shares	Qualifying expenditure £	Indexed pool £
May 1986 acquisition	5,000	5,500	5,500
October 1993 bonus issue	500		
Indexed rise: May 1986 – April 1998			
£5,500 × 0.662			3,641
	5,500	5,500	9,141
October 2002 disposal	(3,000)	(3,000)	(4,986)
Pool carried forward	2,500	£2,500	£4,155

Calculation of chargeable gain	£
Disposal consideration	7,000
Allowable cost $\dfrac{3,000}{5,500} \times £5,500$	3,000
Unindexed gain	4,000
Indexation allowance	
$\dfrac{3,000}{5,500} \times £9,141 = £4,986$	
£4,986 – £3,000	1,986
Chargeable gain 2002/03 (subject to TAPER RELIEF (227))	£2,014

Note

(*a*) Other than for the purposes of corporation tax on chargeable gains, indexation allowance is frozen at its April 1998 level. Therefore, the indexation factor for April 1998 is used in respect of disposals in a later month (and expenditure incurred in April 1998 or later does not attract indexation allowance at all). See 210 INDEXATION.

The indexed pool is upgraded as if the entire holding had been disposed of at the end of 5 April 1998 but is not adjusted for any subsequent indexed rise in expenditure. [TCGA 1992, s 110A; FA 1998, s 125(2)(4)(5)].

Shares and Securities 225.2

(B) Bonus of different class
At various dates after 5 April 1982 and before 6 April 1985, R bought a total of 2,000 'A' shares in T plc for £3,800. The value of the indexed pool immediately before 6 April 1985 was £4,460. In June 1989, R bought a further 500 'A' shares for £800. In October 1993 T plc made a bonus issue of 2 'B' shares for each 5 'A' shares held, and R received 1,000 'B' shares, valued at £1.20 each (total value £1,200) on the first dealing day after the issue. On the same day, the 'A' shares were quoted at £2 each (total value £5,000). In December 2002 R sells his 1,000 'B' shares for £2,000.

Indexation factors		
April 1985 to June 1989		0.218
June 1989 to October 1993		0.229
October 1993 to April 1998 (note (c))		0.147

Section 104 holding – 'A' shares	Shares	Qualifying expenditure £	Indexed pool £
Pool at 6.4.85	2,000	3,800	4,460
Indexed rise: April 1985 to June 1989 £4,460 × 0.218			972
June 1989 acquisition	500	800	800
	2,500	4,600	6,232
Indexed rise: June 1989 to October 1993 £6,232 × 0.229			1,427
	2,500	4,600	7,659
October 1993 bonus issue of 'B' shares: transfer proportion of expenditure and indexed pool to 'B' shares (see note (a))		(890)	(1,482)
	2,500	3,710	6,177
Indexed rise: October 1993 to April 1998 £6,177 × 0.147			908
Pool of 'A' shares carried forward	2,500	£3,710	£7,085

Section 104 holding — 'B' shares			
October 1993 bonus issue: proportion of pools transferred from 'A' shares holding	1,000	890	1,482
Indexed rise: October 1993 to April 1998 £1,482 × 0.147			218
	1,000	890	1,700
December 2002 disposal	1,000	890	1,700
	—	—	—

Calculation of chargeable gain on disposal of 'B' shares	£
Disposal consideration	2,000
Allowable cost (as allocated)	890
Unindexed gain	1,110
Indexation allowance £1,700 – £890	810
Chargeable gain 2002/03 (subject to TAPER RELIEF (227))	£300

225.2 Shares and Securities

Notes

(a) The cost of the 'A' shares is apportioned between 'A' and 'B' shares by reference to market values on the first day of dealing after the reorganisation. The indexed pool is apportioned in the same way.

Proportion of qualifying expenditure $£4,600 \times \dfrac{1,200}{1,200 + 5,000}$ £890

Proportion of indexed pool $£7,659 \times \dfrac{1,200}{1,200 + 5,000}$ £1,482

(Revenue Capital Gains Manual CG 51965 et seq.).

(b) A different basis of apportionment applies to unquoted shares (see Revenue Capital Gains Manual CG 51919 et seq.).

(c) Other than for the purposes of corporation tax on chargeable gains, indexation allowance is frozen at its April 1998 level. Therefore, the indexation factor for April 1998 is used in respect of disposals in a later month (and expenditure incurred in April 1998 or later does not attract indexation allowance at all). See 210 INDEXATION.

The indexed pool is upgraded as if the entire holding had been disposed of at the end of 5 April 1998 but is not adjusted for any subsequent indexed rise in expenditure. [*TCGA 1992, s 110A; FA 1998, s 125(2)(4)(5)*].

Shares and Securities 225.3

225.3 **RIGHTS ISSUES** [*TCGA 1992, s 42, s 123(1), s 128(4)*]

Cross-reference. See 225.8(B) below as regards sale of rights.

(A) Rights issue of same class
W plc is a quoted company which in June 1992 made a rights issue of one £1 ordinary share for every eight £1 ordinary shares held, at £1.35 payable on allotment. V, who held 16,000 £1 ordinary shares purchased in May 1984 for £15,000, took up his entitlement in full, and was allotted 2,000 shares. In December 2002, he sells 6,000 of his shares for £12,000.

Indexation factors	May 1984 to April 1985	0.065
	April 1985 to June 1992	0.470
	June 1992 to April 1998 (note (*a*))	0.167

Section 104 holding	Shares	Qualifying expenditure £	Indexed pool £
May 1984 acquisition	16,000	15,000	15,000
Indexed rise: May 1984 – April 1985			
£15,000 × 0.065			975
Pool at 6.4.85	16,000	15,000	15,975
Indexed rise: April 1985 – June 1992			
£15,975 × 0.470			7,508
June 1992 rights issue	2,000	2,700	2,700
	18,000	17,700	26,183
Indexed rise: June 1992 – April 1998			
£26,183 × 0.167			4,373
			30,556
December 2002 disposal	(6,000)	(5,900)	(10,185)
Pool carried forward	12,000	£11,800	£20,371

Calculation of chargeable gain	£
Disposal consideration	12,000
Allowable cost $\frac{6,000}{18,000} \times £17,700$	5,900
Unindexed gain	6,100
Indexation allowance	
$\frac{6,000}{18,000} \times £30,556 = £10,185$	
£10,185 − £5,900	4,285
Chargeable gain 2002/03 (subject to TAPER RELIEF (227))	£1,815

Note
(*a*) Other than for the purposes of corporation tax on chargeable gains, indexation allowance is frozen at its April 1998 level. Therefore, the indexation factor for April 1998 is used in respect of disposals in a later month (and expenditure incurred in April 1998 or later does not attract indexation allowance at all). See 210 INDEXATION.

225.3 Shares and Securities

The indexed pool is upgraded as if the entire holding had been disposed of at the end of 5 April 1998 but is not adjusted for any subsequent indexed rise in expenditure. [*TCGA 1992, s 110A; FA 1998, s 125(2)(4)(5)*].

(B) Rights issue of different class
On 1 March 1992, A acquired 6,000 quoted £1 ordinary shares in S plc at a cost of £7,800. In October 1995, S plc made a rights issue of one 50p 'B' share for every five £1 ordinary shares held, at 60p payable in full on application. A took up his entitlement in full, acquiring 1,200 'B' shares. On the first dealing day after issue, the 'B' shares were quoted at 65p and the £1 ordinary shares at £1.50. A sells his 'B' shares in December 2002 for £2,000.

Indexation factors	March 1992 to October 1995		0.096	
	October 1995 to April 1998 (note (*c*))		0.085	

Section 104 holding — ordinary shares	Shares	Qualifying expenditure £	Indexed pool £
Acquisition 1.3.92	6,000	7,800	7,800
Indexed rise: March 1992 to October 1995 £7,800 × 0.096			749
October 1995 rights issue of 'B' shares	—	720	720
	6,000	8,520	9,269
Transfer proportion of expenditure and indexed pool to 'B' shares (note (*a*))		(680)	(739)
	6,000	7,840	8,530
Indexed rise: October 1995 to April 1998 £8,530 × 0.085			725
Pool of ordinary shares carried forward	6,000	£7,840	£9,255

Section 104 holding — 'B' shares			
October 1995 rights issue: proportion of pools transferred from ordinary shares holding	1,200	680	739
Indexed rise: October 1995 to April 1998 £739 × 0.085			63
	1,200	680	802
December 2002 disposal	(1,200)	(680)	(802)
	—	—	—

Calculation of chargeable gain on disposal of 'B' shares	£
Disposal consideration	2,000
Allowable cost (as allocated)	680
Unindexed gain	1,320
Indexation allowance £802 − £680	122
Chargeable gain 2002/03 (subject to TAPER RELIEF (227))	£1,198

Notes

(a) The cost of the original shares is apportioned between the original shares and the 'B' shares by reference to market values on the first day of dealing after the reorganisation. The indexed pool is apportioned in the same way.

Proportion of qualifying expenditure

$$£8,520 \times \frac{1,200 \times 0.65}{(1,200 \times 0.65) + (6,000 \times 1.50)} \qquad £680$$

Proportion of indexed pool

$$£9,269 \times \frac{1,200 \times 0.65}{(1,200 \times 0.65) + (6,000 \times 1.50)} \qquad £739$$

(Revenue Capital Gains Manual CG 51965 et seq.).

(b) A different basis of apportionment applies to unquoted shares (see Revenue Capital Gains Manual CG 51919 et seq.).

(c) Other than for the purposes of corporation tax on chargeable gains, indexation allowance is frozen at its April 1998 level. Therefore, the indexation factor for April 1998 is used in respect of disposals in a later month (and expenditure incurred in April 1998 or later does not attract indexation allowance at all). See 210 INDEXATION.

The indexed pool is upgraded as if the entire holding had been disposed of at the end of 5 April 1998 but is not adjusted for any subsequent indexed rise in expenditure. [*TCGA 1992, s 110A; FA 1998, s 125(2)(4)(5)*].

(C) Rights issue of same class: disposal out of *section 104* holding and 1982 holding

G has purchased 100,000 25p ordinary shares in C plc as follows

Date	Number of shares acquired	Cost £
22.5.80	20,000	0.78
5.11.83	15,000	1.10
14.9.84	40,000	1.00
30.4.2000	25,000	2.30

In May 1992, C made a rights issue of one ordinary share for every five held, at £1.50 payable in full on application. G took up his rights in full (15,000 ordinary shares). He sells 105,000 shares in August 2002 for £2.50 per share. The shares were quoted at 90p on 31 March 1982. They are a non-business asset for taper relief purposes. Incidental costs of acquisition and disposal are disregarded for the purposes of this example.

Indexation factors		
	March 1982 to April 1998 (note (*c*))	1.047
	November 1983 to April 1985	0.094
	September 1984 to April 1985	0.052
	April 1985 to May 1992	0.470
	May 1992 to April 1998 (note (*c*))	0.167

225.3 Shares and Securities

Section 104 holding

	Shares	Qualifying expenditure £	Indexed pool £
5.11.83 acquisition	15,000	16,500	16,500
Indexed rise: November 1983 to April 1985 £16,500 × 0.094			1,551
14.9.84 acquisition	40,000	40,000	40,000
Indexed rise: September 1984 to April 1985 £40,000 × 0.052			2,080
Pool at 6.4.85	55,000	56,500	60,131
Indexed rise: April 1985 to May 1992 £60,131 × 0.470			28,262
May 1992 rights issue	11,000	16,500	16,500
	66,000	73,000	104,893
Indexed rise: May 1992 to April 1998 £104,893 × 0.167			17,517
	66,000	73,000	122,410
August 2002 disposal	(66,000)	(73,000)	(122,410)
	—	—	—

1982 holding

	Shares	Cost £	Market value 31.3.82 £
22.5.80 acquisition	20,000	15,600	18,000
May 1992 rights issue (note (*a*))	4,000	6,000	6,000
	24,000	21,600	24,000
August 2002 disposal	(14,000)	(12,600)	(14,000)
Pool carried forward	10,000	£9,000	£10,000

Calculation of chargeable gain

(i) Identify 25,000 shares sold with shares acquired on 30 April 2000.

	£
Disposal consideration 25,000 × £2.50	62,500
Allowable cost 25,000 × £2.30	57,500
Chargeable gain (no taper relief as held less than 3 years)	£5,000

(ii) Identify 66,000 shares sold with *section 104* holding	£
Disposal consideration 66,000 × £2.50	165,000
Allowable cost	73,000
Unindexed gain	92,000
Indexation allowance £122,410 − £73,000	49,410
Chargeable gain (subject to TAPER RELIEF (227))	£42,590

Shares and Securities 225.3

(iii) Identify 14,000 shares with 1982 holding

Without re-basing to 1982

	£
Disposal consideration 14,000 × £2.50	35,000
Cost $\dfrac{14,000}{24,000} \times £21,600$	12,600
Unindexed gain	22,400
Indexation allowance (see below)	11,579
Gain after indexation	£10,821

With re-basing to 1982

	£	£
Disposal consideration		35,000
Allowable expenditure $\dfrac{14,000}{24,000} \times £24,000$		14,000
Unindexed gain		21,000
Indexation allowance		
£14,000 × $\dfrac{18,000}{24,000}$ × 1.047	10,994	
£14,000 × $\dfrac{6,000}{24,000}$ × 0.167	585	
		11,579
Gain after indexation		£9,421
Chargeable gain (subject to TAPER RELIEF (227))		£9,421
Total pre-tapered gain 2002/03 £5,000 + £42,590 + £9,421		£57,011

Notes

(a) The 1982 holding cannot be increased by an 'acquisition', but can be increased by a rights issue as this is not treated as involving an acquisition. [*TCGA 1992, s 109(2), ss 127, 128*].

(b) Other than for the purposes of corporation tax on chargeable gains, disposals after 5 April 1998 are identified firstly with shares acquired on the same day, next with acquisitions in the following 30 days, then on a LIFO basis with post-5 April 1998 acquisitions as in (i) above, then with the '*section 104* holding' at 5 April 1998 as in (ii) above, then with the '1982 holding' as in (iii) above, and then on a LIFO basis with acquisitions on or before 6 April 1965. [*TCGA 1992, ss 105, 106A; FA 1998, s 124(1)(2)(7)*].

(c) Other than for the purposes of corporation tax on chargeable gains, indexation allowance is frozen at its April 1998 level. Therefore, the indexation factor for April 1998 is used in respect of disposals in a later month (and expenditure incurred in April 1998 or later does not attract indexation allowance at all). See 210 INDEXATION.

225.4 Shares and Securities

The indexed pool is upgraded as if the entire holding had been disposed of at the end of 5 April 1998 but is not adjusted for any subsequent indexed rise in expenditure. [*TCGA 1992, s 110A; FA 1998, s 125(2)(4)(5)*].

225.4 **EXCHANGE OF SECURITIES FOR THOSE IN ANOTHER COMPANY** [*TCGA 1992, ss 135, 137, 138; FA 2002, s 45, Sch 9 paras 1, 7*]

(A) Takeover by quoted company
S was a shareholder in N Ltd, an unquoted company. He subscribed for his 20,000 50p ordinary shares at 60p per share in 1979 and the shares were valued at £3 each at 31 March 1982. In July 1987, the shareholders accepted an offer by a public company, M plc, for their shares. Each ordinary shareholder received one £1 ordinary M plc share plus 45p cash for every two N Ltd shares held. S acquired 10,000 M plc shares and received cash of £4,500. The M plc shares were valued at £7.50 each at the time of the acquisition. On 25 April 2002, S sells 4,000 of his 10,000 M plc shares for £54,000.

Indexation factors	March 1982 to July 1987	0.281
	March 1982 to April 1998	1.047

(i) On the merger in 1987/88, S makes a disposal only to the extent that he receives cash

	£
Disposal consideration	4,500
Allowable cost $\dfrac{4,500}{4,500 + (10,000 \times £7.50 = £75,000)} \times £12,000$	679
Unindexed gain	3,821
Indexation allowance £679 × 0.281	191
Chargeable gain	£3,630

Note
(*a*) The fraction applied to allowable cost corresponds to 5.66%. If the percentage had not exceeded 5% the cash distribution of £4,500 would have been regarded as 'small' and could have been deducted from allowable cost (Revenue Tax Bulletin November 1992 p 46). [*TCGA 1992, s 122*]. No gain would then have arisen in 1987/88, but the allowable cost would have been reduced by £4,500. See also 225.8(B) below. (A distribution made after 23 February 1997 can additionally be regarded as 'small' if it does not exceed £3,000 — Revenue Tax Bulletin February 1997 p 397.)

(ii) The chargeable gain on disposal in 2002/03 is

Without re-basing to 1982

	£
Consideration for disposal of M plc shares	54,000
Allowable cost (12,000 − 679) × $\dfrac{4,000}{10,000}$	4,528
Unindexed gain	49,472
Indexation allowance (see below)	23,706
Gain after indexation	£25,766

With re-basing to 1982

	£
Disposal consideration (as above)	54,000
Market value 31.3.82	
$£(20,000 \times £3) \times \dfrac{75,000}{75,000 + 4,500} \times \dfrac{4,000}{10,000}$ (note (*b*))	22,642
Unindexed gain	31,358
Indexation allowance £22,642 × 1.047	23,706
Gain after indexation	£7,652
Chargeable gain (subject to TAPER RELIEF (227))	£7,652

Notes

(*a*) The M plc shares are regarded as the same asset as the original N Ltd shares. [*TCGA 1992, ss 127, 135*]. Re-basing to 31 March 1982 can thus apply, as the original shares were held on that date.

(*b*) Where there has been a part disposal after 31 March 1982 and before 6 April 1988 of an asset held on the earlier of those dates, and this is followed by a disposal after 5 April 1988 to which re-basing applies, the re-basing rules are deemed to have applied to the part disposal. [*TCGA 1992, Sch 3 para 4(1)*].

(B) Takeover by unquoted company

Y Ltd, a small unquoted company, is taken over in June 1996 by another unquoted company, C Ltd. The terms of the acquisition are that holders of £1 ordinary shares in Y Ltd receive two £1 ordinary shares and one £1 deferred share in C Ltd in exchange for every two ordinary shares held.

B acquired his holding of 500 Y Ltd shares on the death of his wife in May 1992, at probate value of £10,000. In May 2002, B sells his 250 C Ltd deferred shares for £4,500. The value of his 500 C Ltd ordinary shares is then £25,000. The indexation factor for May 1992 to April 1998 (note (*a*)) is 0.167.

There is no CGT disposal in 1996/97. The chargeable gain on the 2002/03 disposal is calculated as follows

	£
Disposal consideration	4,500
Allowable cost $\dfrac{4,500}{4,500 + 25,000} \times £10,000$	1,525
Unindexed gain	2,975
Indexation allowance £1,525 × 0.167	255
Chargeable gain (subject to TAPER RELIEF (227))	£2,720
The allowable cost carried forward of the 500 C Ltd ordinary shares is (£10,000 − £1,525)	£8,475

225.4 Shares and Securities

Note
(a) Other than for the purposes of corporation tax on chargeable gains, indexation allowance is frozen at its April 1998 level. Therefore, the indexation factor for April 1998 is used in respect of disposals in a later month (and expenditure incurred in April 1998 or later does not attract indexation allowance at all). See 210 INDEXATION.

(C) Earn-outs

K owns 10,000 ordinary shares in M Ltd, which he acquired for £12,000 in December 1997. In July 2002, the whole of the issued share capital of M Ltd was acquired by P plc. Under the terms of the takeover, K receives £2 per share plus the right to further consideration up to a maximum of £1.50 per share depending on future profit performance. The initial consideration is receivable in cash, but the deferred consideration is to be satisfied by the issue of shares in P plc. In December 2003, K duly receives 2,000 ordinary shares valued at £6 per share in full settlement of his entitlement. The right to future consideration is valued at £1.40 per share in July 2002. The indexation factor for the period December 1997 to April 1998 (note (c)) is 0.016.

Without an election by K under *TCGA 1992, s 138A* the position would be

2002/03

	£	£
Disposal proceeds 10,000 × £2	20,000	
Value of rights 10,000 × £1.40	14,000	34,000
Cost	12,000	
Indexation allowance £12,000 × 0.016	192	12,192
Chargeable gain (subject to TAPER RELIEF (227))		£21,808

2003/04

	£
Disposal of rights to deferred consideration:	
Proceeds — 2,000 P plc shares @ £6	12,000
Deemed cost of acquiring rights	14,000
Allowable loss	£2,000
Cost for CGT purposes of 2,000 P plc shares	£12,000

With an election, the position would be

2002/03

	£
Proceeds (cash) (as above)	20,000
Cost £12,000 × $\dfrac{20{,}000}{20{,}000 + 14{,}000}$	7,059
Unindexed gain	12,941
Indexation allowance £7,059 × 0.016	113
Chargeable gain (subject to TAPER RELIEF (227))	£12,828
Cost of earn-out right for CGT purposes (£12,000 − £7,059)	£4,941

2003/04

The shares in P plc stand in the place of the right to deferred consideration and will be regarded as having been acquired in December 1997 for £4,941. No further gain or loss arises until a disposal of the shares takes place.

Notes

(a) Under *TCGA 1992, s 138A*, on an election by the vendor, the right to deferred consideration (the 'earn-out right') is treated as a security within *TCGA 1992, s 132*. The gain on the original shares (to the extent that it does not derive from cash consideration) can then be held over against the value of the new shares. [*TCGA 1992, s 138A; FA 1997, s 89*].

(b) Various conditions must be satisfied for an election under *section 138A* to be possible. In particular, the value or quantity of the securities to be received as deferred consideration must be 'unascertainable' (as defined). Any right to receive cash and/or an ascertainable amount of securities as part of the deferred consideration does not fall within these provisions and must be distinguished from the earn-out right, though this does not prevent these provisions from applying to the earn-out right.

(c) Other than for the purposes of corporation tax on chargeable gains, indexation allowance is frozen at its April 1998 level. Therefore, the indexation factor for April 1998 is used in respect of disposals in a later month (and expenditure incurred in April 1998 or later does not attract indexation allowance at all). See 210 INDEXATION.

(d) See 206.3(B)(C) DISPOSAL above for deferred consideration generally.

225.5 Shares and Securities

225.5 **SCHEMES OF RECONSTRUCTION** [*TCGA 1992, s 136; FA 2002, s 45, Sch 9 paras 2, 7*]

N Ltd carries on a manufacturing and wholesaling business. In 1994, it was decided that the wholesaling business should be carried on by a separate company. Revenue clearance under *TCGA 1992, s 138* was obtained, and a company, R Ltd, was formed which, in consideration for the transfer to it by N Ltd of the latter's wholesaling undertaking, issued shares to the shareholders of N Ltd. Each holder of ordinary shares in N Ltd additionally received one ordinary share in R Ltd for each N Ltd share he held. W, who purchased his 2,500 N shares for £10,000 in December 1991, received 2,500 R shares. None of the shares involved is quoted. In August 2002, W sells 1,500 of his N shares for £6 each, a total of £9,000, agreed to be their market value. The value of W's remaining 1,000 N shares is also £6 per share, and the value of his R shares is £4.50 per share. The indexation factor for the period December 1991 to April 1998 (note (*a*)) is 0.198.

	£
Disposal consideration	9,000
Allowable cost £10,000 × $\dfrac{9{,}000}{9{,}000 + (1{,}000 \times £6) + (2{,}500 \times £4.50)}$	3,429
Unindexed gain	5,571
Indexation allowance £3,429 × 0.198	679
Chargeable gain 2002/03 (subject to TAPER RELIEF (227))	£4,892

Note
(*a*) Other than for the purposes of corporation tax on chargeable gains, indexation allowance is frozen at its April 1998 level. Therefore, the indexation factor for April 1998 is used in respect of disposals in a later month (and expenditure incurred in April 1998 or later does not attract indexation allowance at all). See 210 INDEXATION.

225.6 **CONVERSION OF SECURITIES** [*TCGA 1992, s 132; FA 1997, s 88*]

N bought £10,000 8% convertible loan stock in S plc, a quoted company, in June 1991. The cost was £9,800. In August 1995, N exercised his right to convert the loan stock into 'B' ordinary shares of the company, on the basis of 50 shares for £100 loan stock, and acquired 5,000 shares. In June 2002, N sells 3,000 of the shares for £5.00 each. The indexation factor for June 1991 to April 1998 (note (*c*)) is 0.213.

	£
Disposal consideration	15,000
Cost $\dfrac{3{,}000}{5{,}000}$ × £9,800	5,880
Unindexed gain	9,120
Indexation allowance £5,880 × 0.213	1,252
Chargeable gain 2002/03 (subject to TAPER RELIEF (227))	£7,868

Notes
(*a*) The shares acquired on the conversion in 1995 stand in the shoes of the original loan stock. [*TCGA 1992, s 132*].

(*b*) The loan stock cannot be a corporate bond (and thus cannot be a qualifying corporate bond) as it is convertible into securities other than corporate bonds, i.e. into ordinary shares. [*ICTA 1988, Sch 18 para 1(5); TCGA 1992, s 117(1)*].

(c) Other than for the purposes of corporation tax on chargeable gains, indexation allowance is frozen at its April 1998 level. Therefore, the indexation factor for April 1998 is used in respect of disposals in a later month (and expenditure incurred in April 1998 or later does not attract indexation allowance at all). See 210 INDEXATION.

225.7 SCRIP DIVIDENDS [*TCGA 1992, ss 141, 142; ICTA 1988, ss 249, 251(2)–(4); FA 1998, s 126*]

D holds ordinary 20p shares in PLC, a quoted company. The company operates a scrip dividend (also known as a stock dividend) policy whereby shareholders are given the option to take dividends in cash or in new fully-paid ordinary 20p shares, the option being exercisable separately in relation to each dividend. D purchased 2,000 shares for £1,500 in March 1980 and a further 3,000 shares for £8,100 in May 1992 and up until the end of 1997 he has always taken cash dividends. In January 1998, he opts for a scrip dividend and receives 25 shares instead of a cash dividend of £100. On 20 April 1998, he purchases a further 1,000 shares for £3,950. In July 1998, he opts for a scrip dividend of 44 shares instead of a cash dividend of £180. He opts for cash dividends thereafter. In May 2002, he sells 2,069 shares for £8,550 (ex div), leaving himself with a holding of 4,000.

In the case of both scrip dividends taken by D, the market value of the new shares is equivalent to the cash dividend forgone. The 'appropriate amount in cash' (see *TCGA 1992, s 142*) is thus the amount of that dividend. [*ICTA 1988, s 251(2)*]. Relevant indexation factors are as follows.

May 1992 to January 1998	0.145
January 1998 to April 1998 (note (*b*))	0.019

The gain on the disposal in May 2002 is calculated as follows

(i) Identify 44 shares sold with those received by way of scrip dividend in July 1998 (LIFO) (note (*a*))

	£
Proceeds £8,550 × 44/2069	182
Cost (equal to 'appropriate amount in cash')	180
Chargeable gain	£2

(ii) Identify 1,000 shares sold with those acquired on 20 April 1998

	£
Proceeds £8,550 × 1,000/2,069	4,132
Cost	3,950
Chargeable gain	£182

225.7 Shares and Securities

(iii) Identify remaining 1,025 shares sold with *'section 104* holding' at 5 April 1998

Section 104 holding	Shares	Qualifying expenditure £	Indexed pool £
May 1992 acquisition	3,000	8,100	8,100
Indexed rise: May 1992 to January 1998 £8,100 × 0.145			1,175
	3,000	8,100	9,275
January 1998 scrip dividend 25 × 3,000/5,000 (note (*a*))	15	60	60
	3,015	8,160	9,335
Indexed rise: January 1998 to April 1998 £9,335 × 0.019			177
Pool at 5.4.98	3,015	8,160	9,512
May 2002 disposal	(1,025)	(2,775)	(3,234)
Pool carried forward	1,990	£5,385	£6,278

	£
Proceeds £8,550 × 1,025/2,069	4,236
Cost £8,160 × 1,025/3,015	2,775
Unindexed gain	1,461
Indexation allowance £9,512 × 1,025/3,015 = £3,234	
£3,234 − £2,775	459
Chargeable gain (subject to TAPER RELIEF (227))	£1,002

Total pre-tapered gain 2002/03 (£2 + £182 + £1,002) £1,186

The remaining holding of 4,000 shares consists of a *'section 104* holding' of 1,990 as illustrated above and a '1982 holding' of 2,010 (which was irrelevant to the May 2002 disposal) consisting of 2,000 purchased in March 1980 and 10 scrip dividend shares acquired in January 1998 and equated with the said purchase (see note (*a*)).

Notes

(*a*) Scrip dividends after 5 April 1998 are treated as free-standing acquisitions. Previously, a scrip dividend received by an individual was treated as a reorganisation within *TCGA 1992, s 128* so that the new shares equated with those already held. Thus, in this example, the January 1998 scrip dividend is split pro rata between the '1982 holding' and the *'section 104* holding'.

(*b*) Other than for the purposes of corporation tax on chargeable gains, indexation allowance is frozen at its April 1998 level. Therefore, the indexation factor for April 1998 is used in respect of disposals in a later month (and expenditure incurred in April 1998 or later does not attract indexation allowance at all). See 210 INDEXATION.

The indexed pool is upgraded as if the entire holding had been disposed of at the end of 5 April 1998 but is not adjusted for any subsequent indexed rise in expenditure. [*TCGA 1992, s 110A; FA 1998, s 125(2)(4)(5)*].

(*c*) See also 226.1 SHARES AND SECURITIES — IDENTIFICATION RULES.

225.8 CAPITAL DISTRIBUTIONS

(A) [*TCGA 1992, s 122*]
T holds 10,000 ordinary shares in a foreign company M SA. The shares were bought in April 1996 for £80,000. In February 2003, M SA has a capital reconstruction involving the cancellation of one-fifth of the existing ordinary shares in consideration of the repayment of £10 to each shareholder per share cancelled. T's holding is reduced to 8,000 shares, valued at £96,000. The indexation factor for the period April 1996 to April 1998 (note (*a*)) is 0.066.

	£
Disposal consideration (2,000 × £10)	20,000
Allowable cost $\dfrac{20,000}{20,000 + 96,000} \times £80,000$	13,793
Unindexed gain	6,207
Indexation allowance £13,793 × 0.066	910
Chargeable gain 2002/03 (subject to TAPER RELIEF (227))	£5,297
The allowable cost of the remaining shares is £80,000 − £13,793	£66,207

Note

(*a*) Other than for the purposes of corporation tax on chargeable gains, indexation allowance is frozen at its April 1998 level. Therefore, the indexation factor for April 1998 is used in respect of disposals in a later month (and expenditure incurred in April 1998 or later does not attract indexation allowance at all). See 210 INDEXATION.

(B) Sale of rights [*TCGA 1992, ss 122, 123; FA 1996, Sch 20 para 52*]
X is a shareholder in K Ltd, owning 2,500 £1 ordinary shares which were purchased for £7,000 in October 1996. K Ltd makes a rights issue, but X sells his rights, without taking them up, for £700 in August 2002. The ex-rights value of X's 2,500 shares at the date of sale was £14,500. The indexation factor for the period October 1996 to April 1998 (note (*a*)) is 0.057.

'Section 104 holding' of K £1 ordinary shares	Shares	Qualifying expenditure £	Indexed pool £
October 1996 acquisition	2,500	7,000	7,000
Indexed rise to April 1998 £7,000 × 0.057			399
	2,500	£7,000	£7,399

The Revenue cannot require the capital distribution to be treated as a disposal, as the £700 received for the rights does not exceed 5% of (£700 + £14,500) and in any case does not exceed £3,000 (see Revenue Tax Bulletin February 1997 p 397). [*TCGA 1992, s 122(2); FA 1996, Sch 20 para 52*]. If the transaction is not treated as a disposal, the £700 is deducted from both the acquisition cost of the shares and the indexed pool, leaving balances of, respectively, £6,300 and £6,699. If the transaction is treated as a disposal (possibly because X wishes to utilise part of his annual exemption), the computation is as follows.

225.9 Shares and Securities

	£
Disposal proceeds	700
Allowable cost $\dfrac{700}{700 + 14{,}500} \times £7{,}000$	322
Unindexed gain	378
Indexation allowance $£7{,}399 \times \dfrac{700}{700 + 14{,}500} = £341$	
£341 − £322	19
Chargeable gain 2002/03 (subject to TAPER RELIEF (227))	£359

The allowable cost of the shares is then reduced to £6,678 (£7,000 − £322) and the balance on the indexed pool to £7,058 (£7,399 − £341).

Note
(a) Other than for the purposes of corporation tax on chargeable gains, indexation allowance is frozen at its April 1998 level. Therefore, the indexation factor for April 1998 is used in respect of disposals in a later month (and expenditure incurred in April 1998 or later does not attract indexation allowance at all). See 210 INDEXATION.

225.9 BUILDING SOCIETY TAKEOVERS AND CONVERSIONS

(A) Cash received by investor on a takeover or conversion

Mr C Bagger opened a share account with the Toytown Building Society in August 1993. The society was taken over by High Street Bank plc in December 1997 and Mr Bagger received in that month a cash distribution of £13,000 which comprised a fixed payment of £500 and a percentage payment based on the higher of the balances on the account at two stated dates but restricted to $12\frac{1}{2}\%$ of £100,000. Mr Bagger's passbook showed the following account details.

Date		Debit £	Credit £	Balance £
4.8.93	Deposit		50,000	50,000
31.3.94	Net interest		1,500	51,500
16.6.94	Deposit		75,000	126,000
31.3.95	Net interest		5,000	131,500
1.5.95	Withdrawal	25,000		106,500
31.3.96	Net interest		4,800	111,300
31.3.97	Net interest		5,300	116,600
1.6.97	Withdrawal	8,000		108,600
12.12.97	Cash bonus on takeover		13,000	121,600
12.12.97	Closing interest		2,800	124,400
12.12.97	Balance transferred to deposit account at High Street Bank plc	124,400		Nil

Shares and Securities 225.9

Relevant indexation factors are as follows

August 1993 to March 1994	0.008
March 1994 to June 1994	0.015
June 1994 to March 1995	0.019
March 1995 to May 1995	0.014
May 1995 to March 1996	0.013
March 1996 to March 1997	0.026
March 1997 to June 1997	0.014
June 1997 to December 1997	0.016

The chargeable gain on the cash bonus is computed as follows

	Qualifying expenditure £	Indexed pool £
4.8.93 acquisition	50,000	50,000
Indexed rise: August 1993 – March 1994		
£50,000 × 0.008		400
31.3.94 acquisition	1,500	1,500
	51,500	51,900
Indexed rise: March 1994 – June 1994		
£51,900 × 0.015		779
16.6.94 acquisition	75,000	75,000
	126,500	127,679
Indexed rise: June 1994 – March 1995		
£127,679 × 0.019		2,426
31.3.95 acquisition	5,000	5,000
	131,500	135,105
Indexed rise: March 1995 – May 1995		
£135,105 × 0.014		1,890
	131,500	136,995
Disposal (no gain/no loss)	(25,000)	(26,045)*
	106,500	110,950
Indexed rise: May 1995 – March 1996		
£110,950 × 0.013		1,442
31.3.96 acquisition	4,800	4,800
	111,300	117,192
Indexed rise: March 1996 – March 1997		
£117,192 × 0.026		3,047
31.3.97 acquisition	5,300	5,300
	c/f 116,600	125,539

225.9 Shares and Securities

	£ b/f 116,600	£ 125,539
Indexed rise: March 1997 – June 1997		
£125,539 × 0.014		1,758
	116,600	127,297
1.6.97 disposal (no gain/no loss)	(8,000)	(8,734)**
	108,600	118,563
Indexed rise: June 1997 – December 1997		
£118,563 × 0.016		1,897
12.12.97 acquisition	2,800	2,800
	111,400	123,260
12.12.97 disposal	(111,400)	(123,260)

$$* \; £136,995 \times \frac{25,000}{131,500} = £26,045$$

$$** \; £127,297 \times \frac{8,000}{116,600} = £8,734$$

	£
Proceeds:	
Cash bonus	13,000
Balance of account	111,400
Total proceeds	124,400
Allowable cost	111,400
Unindexed gain	13,000
Indexation allowance, where available (see 210.1(B) INDEXATION), £123,260 – £111,400	11,860
Chargeable gain	£1,140

Notes

(a) A cash bonus received (in respect of a share account, but not a deposit account) on the takeover or conversion of a building society is within the charge to capital gains tax, but is reduced by indexation allowance, where available (see 210.1(B) INDEXATION), based on the evolving balance of the account. (Revenue Press Release 27 March 1997, Tax Bulletin April 1998 pp 517–523).

(b) For the purpose of calculating the indexation allowance, each £1 deposited (or withdrawn) is treated in the same way as an acquisition (or disposal) of a share in a company.

Shares and Securities 225.9

(B) Shares received by investor on a takeover or conversion
Mr C Bagger in (A) above also has a share account (opened in November 1989) with the Farthing Wood Building Society which converted to plc status in May 1997. The balance of the account as at conversion was £27,000. Mr Bagger received no cash bonus but received a bonus of 1,600 ordinary shares in the new plc. On the first day of trading in the new shares, they opened at £3.55 per share. Mr Bagger retains his shares until February 2003 when he sells them for £7,800 (net of disposal costs).

The chargeable gain on the sale of shares is computed as follows

	£
Net proceeds	7,800
Cost of acquisition	Nil
Unindexed gain	7,800
Indexation allowance (none, as nil cost)	—
Chargeable gain 2002/03 (subject to TAPER RELIEF (227))	£7,800

Note
(*a*)   No chargeable gain arises in respect of the distribution of shares to members on a takeover or conversion of a building society. The shares are regarded as acquired for nil cost (and thus no indexation allowance can be due on a subsequent disposal). [*TCGA 1992, s 217*]. (Revenue Press Releases 21 March 1996, 27 March 1997, Tax Bulletin April 1998 pp 517–523.)

226.1 Shares and Securities — Identification Rules

226 Shares and Securities — Identification Rules

Cross-reference. See 225 SHARES AND SECURITIES.

226.1 **IDENTIFICATION RULES AFTER 5 APRIL 1998 (OTHER THAN FOR CORPORATION TAX PURPOSES)**

A has the following acquisitions/disposals of ordinary 25p shares in QED plc. Throughout their period of ownership by A, these shares are non-business assets for the purposes of TAPER RELIEF (227). QED ordinary 25p shares were worth 210p per share at 31 March 1982, and A has not made a global re-basing election (see 204 ASSETS HELD ON 31 MARCH 1982). In 2002/03, A made no disposals of chargeable assets other than as shown below.

Date	No. of shares bought/(sold)	Cost/(proceeds) £
1 May 1980	1,000	2,000
1 October 1983	2,000	4,500
1 December 1996	500	1,800
1 May 1999	(1,000)	(3,900)
25 May 1999	2,000	7,600
	4,500	
2 January 2000	(2,000)	(9,000)
1 July 2002	(2,000)	(12,000)
Remaining holding	500	

Relevant indexation factors are

March 1982 to April 1998 (note (*b*))	1.047
October 1983 to April 1985	0.097
April 1985 to December 1996	0.629
December 1996 to April 1998	0.053

(i) **The disposal on 1 May 1999** is matched with 1,000 of the shares acquired on 25 May 1999 (under the 30-day rule — see note (*a*)). The resulting chargeable gain is as follows.

	£
Proceeds 1.5.99	3,900
Cost (£7,600 × 1,000/2,000)	3,800
Chargeable gain (no taper relief due)	£100

Shares and Securities — Identification Rules 226.1

(ii) **The disposal of 2,000 shares on 2 January 2000** is matched firstly with the remaining 1,000 acquired on 25 May 1999 (LIFO), and secondly with 1,000 of the 2,500 forming the '*section 104* holding' as follows.

	No. of shares	Qualifying expenditure £	Indexed pool £
Pool at 6.4.85	2,000	4,500	4,500
Indexation allowance to date: October 1983 – April 1985 £4,500 × 0.097			437
	2,000	4,500	4,937
Indexed rise to December 1996: April 1985 – December 1996 £4,937 × 0.629			3,105
Acquisition 1.12.96	500	1,800	1,800
	2,500	6,300	9,842
Indexed rise to April 1998: December 1996 – April 1998 £9,842 × 0.053			522
	2,500	6,300	10,364
Disposal 2.1.2000	(1,000)	(2,520)	(4,146)
Pool carried forward	1,500	£3,780	£6,218

Chargeable gains are as follows.

	£	£
Proceeds 2.1.2000	4,500	4,500
Cost (£7,600 × 1,000/2,000)	3,800	
Cost (as above)		2,520
Unindexed gains	700	1,980
Indexation (£4,146 – £2,520)	—	1,626
Chargeable gains	£700	£354

Neither gain qualifies for taper relief. In each case, the shares acquired have been held for less than the requisite three complete years (for non-business asset taper relief) after 5 April 1998.

226.1 Shares and Securities — Identification Rules

(iii) **The disposal of 2,000 shares on 1 July 2002** is matched firstly with the remaining 1,500 in the '*section 104* holding', and secondly with 500 of the 1,000 shares forming the '1982 holding'.

Chargeable gains are as follows.

	£
Proceeds of 1,500 shares on 1.7.02	9,000
Cost (as per pool above)	3,780
Unindexed gain	5,220
Indexation (£6,218 − £3,780)	2,438
Chargeable gain subject to taper relief	2,782
Taper relief £2,782 × 15% (see below)	417
Chargeable gain	£2,365

	£		
Proceeds of 500 shares on 1.7.02	3,000	3,000
Cost (£2,000 × 500/1,000)	1,000	
Market value 31.3.82 500 × £2.10		1,050
Unindexed gain	2,000	1,950
Indexation to April 1998:		
£1,050 × 1.047	1,099	1,099
Gain after indexation	£901	£851
Chargeable gain subject to taper relief		851
Taper relief £851 × 15% (see below)		128
Chargeable gain		£723

Taper relief is at 15% as the shares are non-business assets and have been held for four plus one years since 5 April 1998, the one-year addition being by virtue of the fact that both the '*section 104* holding' and the '1982 holding' were acquired before 17 March 1998. [*TCGA 1992, s 2A(8)(9); FA 1998, s 121(1); FA 2000, s 66*].

Notes

(*a*) Other than for the purposes of corporation tax on chargeable gains, disposals after 5 April 1998 are identified (1) with shares acquired on the same day (with certain limited exceptions by election); (2) with acquisitions in the following 30 days; (3) on a LIFO basis with post-5 April 1998 acquisitions; (4) with the 'section 104 holding' at 5 April 1998; (5) with the '1982 holding'; (6) on a LIFO basis with acquisitions on or before 6 April 1965; (7) with shares acquired after the disposal (and after the expiry of the 30-day period in (2) above) taken in the order in which such acquisitions occur. [*TCGA 1992, ss 105, 105A, 105B, 106A; FA 1998, s 124(1)(2)(7); FA 2002, s 50(1)(2)*].

(*b*) Other than for the purposes of corporation tax on chargeable gains, indexation allowance is frozen at its April 1998 level. See 210 INDEXATION.

The indexed pool is upgraded as if the entire holding had been disposed of at the end of 5 April 1998 but is not adjusted for any subsequent indexed rise in expenditure. [*TCGA 1992, s 110A; FA 1998, s 125(2)(4)(5)*].

Shares and Securities — Identification Rules 226.2

226.2 SHARE IDENTIFICATION RULES BEFORE 6 APRIL 1998 (AND CONTINUING FOR COMPANIES) [*TCGA 1992, ss 104, 105, 107–110; FA 1994, s 93(6); FA 1998, s 123*]

(A) General

B has the following transactions in 25p ordinary shares of H plc, a quoted company.

		Cost/(proceeds) £
6.6.78	Purchased 500 at £0.85	425
3.11.81	Purchased 1,300 at £0.80	1,040
15.5.82	Purchased 1,000 at £1.02	1,020
8.9.82	Purchased 400 at £1.08	432
1.2.86	Purchased 1,200 at £1.14	1,368
29.7.87	Sold 2,000 at £1.30	(2,600)
8.6.90	Purchased 1,500 at £1.26	1,890
21.12.93	Received 1,000 from wife (cost £1,250, indexation to date £250)	1,500
10.5.97	Sold 3,900 at £2.10	(8,190)

The shares stood at £1.00 at 31.3.82.

Indexation factors		
	March 1982 to May 1997	0.975
	May 1982 to April 1985	0.161
	September 1982 to April 1985	0.158
	April 1985 to February 1986	0.019
	February 1986 to July 1987	0.054
	July 1987 to June 1990	0.245
	June 1990 to December 1993	0.120
	December 1993 to May 1997	0.106

Disposal on 10 May 1997

The 'section 104 holding' pool immediately prior to the disposal should be as follows

	Shares	Qualifying expenditure £	Indexed pool £
15.5.82 acquisition	1,000	1,020	1,020
Indexation to April 1985			
£1,020 × 0.161			164
8.9.82 acquisition	400	432	432
Indexation to April 1985			
£432 × 0.158			68
Pool at 6.4.85	1,400	1,452	1,684
Indexed rise: April 1985 – Feb. 1986			
£1,684 × 0.019			32
1.2.86 acquisition	1,200	1,368	1,368
	2,600	2,820	3,084
Indexed rise: February 1986 – July 1987			
£3,084 × 0.054			167
	2,600	2,820	3,251
29.7.87 disposal	(2,000)	(2,169)	(2,501)
c/f	£600	£651	£750

226.2 Shares and Securities — Identification Rules

	Shares	Qualifying expenditure £	Indexed pool £
b/f	600	651	750
Indexed rise: July 1987 – June 1990 £750 × 0.245			184
8.6.90 acquisition	1,500	1,890	1,890
	2,100	2,541	2,824
Indexed rise: June 1990 – December 1993 £2,824 × 0.120			339
21.12.93 acquisition	1,000	1,250	1,500
	3,100	3,791	4,663
Indexed rise: December 1993 – May 1997 £4,663 × 0.106			494
	3,100	3,791	5,157

The '1982 holding' is as follows

	Shares	Allowable expenditure £
6.6.78 acquisition	500	425
3.11.81 acquisition	1,300	1,040
	1,800	1,465

(i) Identify 3,100 shares sold with '*section 104* holding'

	£
Disposal consideration 3,100 × £2.10	6,510
Allowable cost	3,791
Unindexed gain	2,719
Indexation allowance £5,157 – £3,791	1,366
Chargeable gain	£1,353

(ii) Identify 800 shares sold with '1982 holding'

	£	£
Disposal consideration 800 × £2.10	1,680	1,680
Cost $\frac{800}{1,800} \times £1,465$	651	
Market value 31.3.82 $\frac{800}{1,800} \times £1,800$		800
Unindexed gain	1,029	880
Indexation allowance £800 × 0.975	780	780
Gain after indexation	£249	£100
Chargeable gain		£100
Total chargeable gain (1997/98) (£1,353 + £100)		£1,453

Shares and Securities — Identification Rules 226.2

Notes

(*a*) Share disposals after 5.4.85 (31.3.85 for companies) and before 6 April 1998 (continuing after that date for companies) are identified firstly with the '*section 104* holding' and secondly with the '1982 holding', both of which are regarded as single assets.

(*b*) On share disposals after 5.4.88 identified with shares held at 31.3.82, the re-basing provisions have effect, and indexation is based on the higher of cost and 31.3.82 value. If an irrevocable election is made under *TCGA 1992, s 35(5)* for all assets to be treated as disposed of and re-acquired at their market value on 31.3.82, indexation must be based on the 31.3.82 value even if this is less than cost. [*TCGA 1992, s 55(1)(2)*].

226.2 Shares and Securities — Identification Rules

(B) Special rules — 'same day' transactions, 'ten day' rule and 'bed and breakfasting' [*TCGA 1992, ss 105, 107(3)–(6); FA 1998, s 124(8)*].
C has the following transactions in 25p ordinary shares of J plc.

		Cost/(proceeds) £
16.12.84	Purchased 20,000 at £1.92	38,400
5.8.87	Purchased 12,000 at £2.40	28,800
3.4.88	Sold 4,000 at £2.00	(8,000)
4.4.88	Purchased 4,000 at £2.02	8,080
14.9.91	Purchased 5,000 at £2.20	11,000
14.9.91	Sold 1,000 at £2.19	(2,190)
30.4.97	Purchased 2,000 at £2.55	5,100
3.5.97	Purchased 2,000 at £2.58	5,160
8.5.97	Sold 6,000 at £2.80	(16,800)
20.3.98	Sold 7,500 at £3.00	(22,500)
23.3.98	Purchased 7,500 at £2.98	22,350

Holding at 5.4.98 – 34,000

Indexation factors	December 1984 to August 1987	0.124
	August 1987 to April 1988	0.036
	April 1988 to September 1991	0.271
	September 1991 to May 1997	0.166

1987/88
Disposal on 3.4.88
Establish '*section 104* holding' pool

	Shares	Qualifying expenditure £	Indexed pool £
16.12.84 acquisition	20,000	38,400	38,400
Indexed rise: December 1984 – August 1987 £38,400 × 0.124			4,762
5.8.87 acquisition	12,000	28,800	28,800
	32,000	67,200	71,962
Indexed rise: August 1987 – April 1988 £71,962 × 0.036			2,591
	32,000	67,200	74,553
3.4.88 disposal	(4,000)	(8,400)	(9,319)
4.4.88 acquisition	4,000	8,080	8,080
Pool carried forward	32,000	£66,880	£73,314

Disposal consideration	£8,000
Cost $\dfrac{4,000}{32,000} \times £67,200$	8,400
Unindexed loss	400
Indexation allowance	
$\dfrac{4,000}{32,000} \times £74,553 = £9,319$	
£9,319 – £8,400	919
Allowable loss	£1,319

Shares and Securities — Identification Rules 226.2

1991/92
Disposal on 14.9.91
Match with acquisitions on the same day (note (a))

Disposal consideration	£2,190
Cost $\dfrac{1,000}{5,000} \times £11,000$	2,200
Allowable loss	£10

Add balance of 14.9.91 acquisition to pool

	Shares	Qualifying expenditure £	Indexed pool £
Pool at 4.4.88	32,000	66,880	73,314
Indexed rise: April 1988 – September 1991 £73,314 × 0.271			19,868
Balance of 14.9.91 acquisition	4,000	8,800	8,800
Pool carried forward	36,000	£75,680	£101,982

1997/98
Disposal on 8.5.97
Match first with acquisition on 30.4.97 (note (b))

Disposal consideration 2,000 × £2.80	£5,600
Cost 30.4.97	5,100
Chargeable gain	£500

Match next with 3.5.97 acquisition (note (b))

Disposal consideration 2,000 × £2.80	£5,600
Cost 3.5.97	5,160
Chargeable gain	£440

Match finally with 'section 104 holding' pool

	Shares	Qualifying expenditure £	Indexed pool £
Pool at 14.9.91	36,000	75,680	101,982
Indexed rise: September 1991 – May 1997 £101,982 × 0.166			16,929
	36,000	75,680	118,911
Balance of 8.5.97 disposal	(2,000)	(4,204)	(6,606)
Pool carried forward	34,000	£71,476	£112,305

226.2 Shares and Securities — Identification Rules

Disposal consideration 2,000 × £2.80	£5,600
Cost $\dfrac{2{,}000}{36{,}000} \times £75{,}680$	4,204
Unindexed gain	1,396
Indexation allowance	
$\dfrac{2{,}000}{36{,}000} \times £115{,}546 = £6{,}606$	
£6,606 − £4,204 = £2,402 but restricted to	1,396
Chargeable gain	Nil

Disposal on 20.3.98
Match with acquisition on 23.3.98 (note (c))

Disposal consideration 7,500 × £3.00	£22,500
Cost 23.3.98	22,350
Chargeable gain	£150

Total chargeable gain 1997/98 (£500 + £440 + £150)	£1,090

Notes

(a) Under *TCGA 1992, s 105*, a disposal of securities is matched as far as possible with an acquisition on the same day. It follows that no indexation can be available.

(b) Subject to the overriding rule described in (a) above, and for disposals after 5.4.85 (31.3.85 for companies) and before 6.4.98 (continuing for companies), a disposal of securities is first matched with preceding acquisitions within a ten-day period on a first in/first out basis, and to the extent that they can be so matched, the securities are not pooled and no indexation allowance is due. [*TCGA 1992, s 107(3)–(6)*].

(c) No special rules applied before 17 March 1998 where an acquisition *followed* a disposal, so the above did not affect a 'bed and breakfast' transaction. Disposals on or after that date (other than by companies) must first be matched with any acquisitions of securities of the same class within the next 30 days, taking earlier acquisitions before later ones. The advantages of 'bed and breakfasting' are thereby negated. [*TCGA 1992, s 106A(5); FA 1998, s 124(1)(8)*].

227 Taper Relief

Cross-reference. See 226.1 SHARES AND SECURITIES — IDENTIFICATION RULES.

227.1 **THE BASIC RULES** [*TCGA 1992, s 2A, Sch A1; FA 1998, s 121, Sch 20; FA 2000, s 66; FA 2001, s 78, Sch 26; FA 2002, s 46*]

(A) Computing the tapered gain

Brett acquired an asset in 1996 for £20,000 and sells it in September 2002 for £35,000. He makes no other disposals in 2002/03. At no time after 5 April 1998 was the asset a business asset. The indexation factor from date of acquisition to April 1998 (see note (*a*)) is, say, 0.060.

The taxable gain is computed as follows

At the time of disposal, the asset has been held for four complete years after 5 April 1998. Because it was acquired before 17 March 1998 and it is a non-business asset, a further one year is added. Using the table at *TCGA 1992, s 2A(5)*, the taper relief for a non-business asset held for five complete years after 5 April 1998 is 15%.

	£
Proceeds	35,000
Less Cost of acquisition	20,000
Unindexed gain	15,000
Indexation to April 1998 £20,000 × 0.060	1,200
Chargeable gain	13,800
Less Taper relief £13,800 × 15%	2,070
Taxable gain subject to annual exemption	£11,730

Note

(*a*) Other than for the purposes of corporation tax on chargeable gains, indexation allowance is frozen at its April 1998 level. Therefore, the indexation factor for April 1998 is used in respect of disposals in a later month (and expenditure incurred in April 1998 or later does not attract indexation allowance at all). See 210 INDEXATION.

(B) Set-off of losses

Hannah made four disposals in 2005/06, as follows.

On Asset A, she realised a chargeable gain of £13,000 (after indexation to April 1998). This asset was acquired in 1995 and sold in May 2005 and was a non-business asset throughout its ownership.

On Asset B, she realised a chargeable gain of £2,000. This asset was acquired in December 2002 and sold in October 2005 and was a non-business asset throughout its ownership.

On Asset C, she realised a chargeable gain of £7,500. This asset was acquired in August 2002 and sold in December 2005 and was a business asset throughout its ownership.

On Asset D, she realised an allowable loss of £6,000.

227.1 Taper Relief

The gains qualify for taper relief as follows

Asset A was held for seven complete years after 5 April 1998 and qualifies for a one-year addition as it was acquired before 17 March 1998. The gain thus qualifies for 30% taper relief.

Asset B was held for less than the minimum period of ownership necessary for a gain on a non-business asset to qualify for taper relief (three complete years).

Asset C was held for three complete years. It thus qualifies for 75% taper relief.

The optimum set-off of losses is as follows

It is beneficial to offset the loss on Asset D firstly against the gain attracting no taper relief, i.e. the gain on Asset B, with the balance against the gain attracting the lower rate of taper relief, i.e. the gain on Asset A.

	£
Asset A	
Chargeable gain	13,000
Less Allowable loss (balance)	4,000
	9,000
Less Taper relief £9,000 × 30%	2,700
Tapered gain	£6,300
Asset B	
Chargeable gain	2,000
Less Allowable loss	2,000
Asset C	
Chargeable gain	7,500
Less Taper relief £7,500 × 75%	5,625
Tapered gain	£1,875
Total taxable gains subject to annual exemption	£8,175

Note

(*a*) Both current year and brought forward losses are set against gains in such a way as to maximise the taper relief due. [*TCGA 1992, s 2A(6); FA 1998, s 121(1)*].

Taper Relief 227.2

227.2 ASSETS WHICH ARE BUSINESS ASSETS FOR PART ONLY OF PERIOD OF OWNERSHIP [*TCGA 1992, Sch A1 para 3; FA 1998, s 121(2)(4), Sch 20*]

(A) General

Penny acquired a freehold property in March 1991 and sold it on 30 September 2007, realising a chargeable gain (after indexation to April 1998) of £95,000. Between March 1991 and September 2001 inclusive, the property was used as business premises and qualifies as a business asset for taper relief purposes. From October 2001 to September 2007 inclusive, it was let to a private tenant and was not a business asset. Penny made one other disposal in 2007/08, realising a loss of £10,000.

The gain is divided into two separate gains, which qualify for taper relief as follows

The relevant period of ownership for the purposes of taper relief is the 9.5 years from 6 April 1998 to 30 September 2007. During that period, the asset was a business asset for 3.5 years (April 1998 to September 2001) and a non-business asset for the remaining six years. Therefore, 3.5/9.5 of the gain (£35,000) qualifies for the business assets taper and 6/9.5 of the gain (£60,000) qualifies for the non-business assets taper.

The number of complete years in the qualifying holding period is nine. However, there is a one-year addition in the case of the non-business asset portion of the gain as the asset was acquired before 17 March 1998. [*TCGA 1992, s 2A(8)(9); FA 1998, s 121(1); FA 2000, s 66(3)(4)*].

The net taxable gains are computed as follows

	Business asset £	Non-business asset £	Total £
Chargeable gains	35,000	60,000	95,000
Deduct Allowable loss		10,000	10,000
Net chargeable gains	35,000	50,000	85,000
Deduct Taper relief @ 75%/40%	26,250	20,000	46,250
Taxable gains (subject to annual exemption)	£8,750	£30,000	£38,750

Notes

(*a*) The gain on the freehold property, a mixed use asset, is treated for taper relief purposes as if it were two separate gains accruing on separate disposals of separate assets, one business and one non-business. [*TCGA 1992, Sch A1 para 3(5)*]. Of the two gains, the available loss is set against the one attracting the lower rate of taper relief (see 227.1(B) above and Revenue Capital Gains Manual CG 17976).

(*b*) For a further example on change of use of an asset, see 227.3(A) below.

227.2 Taper Relief

(B) Shares becoming a business asset on 6 April 2000 by virtue of FA 2000 [*TCGA 1992, Sch A1 paras 4, 6; FA 2000, s 67; FA 2001, s 78, Sch 26 para 3*]

In September 1995, Bob acquired by gift from his father 100 £1 ordinary shares in an unlisted family trading company, YOY Ltd, with an issued ordinary share capital of £1,000, each share carrying one vote. Bob's acquisition cost for CGT purposes, as reduced by a claim for business asset gifts hold-over relief, is £100.

On 12 June 1999, the company capitalises some of its reserves by means of a two for one bonus issue, increasing Bob's holding to 300 out of 3,000 shares.

On 6 April 2002, following a family dispute, Bob sells all his YOY shares to a cousin at their agreed market value of £18.36 per share, receiving £5,508. He makes one other disposal in 2002/03, realising a gain after taper relief of £20,000. The indexation factor for the period September 1995 to April 1998 (note (*c*)) is 0.080.

Throughout his ownership of the shares, Bob, who is otherwise self-employed, was on the company payroll but put in only a few hours per week.

The pre-tapered gain is computed as follows

	£
Proceeds	5,508
Deemed acquisition cost (September 1995)	100
Unindexed gain	5,408
Indexation allowance £100 × 0.080	8
Chargeable gain subject to taper relief	£5,400

The gain qualifies for taper relief as follows

The relevant period of ownership is the 4 years from 6 April 1998 to 6 April 2002. The bonus shares acquired in June 1999 are treated, by virtue of *TCGA 1992, s 127*, as the same asset as, and as acquired at the same time as, the original shares.

Throughout the period 6 April 1998 to 5 April 2000 (2 years), the shares are a non-business asset for taper relief purposes. YOY Ltd is not a qualifying company in relation to Bob; he can exercise at least 5% of the voting rights but less than 25% and he is not a 'full-time working officer or employee'. [*TCGA 1992, Sch A1 para 4(2), para 6(2)(3) as originally enacted*].

Throughout the period 6 April 2000 to 6 April 2002 (2 years), the shares are a business asset for taper relief purposes. YOY Ltd is a qualifying company in relation to Bob on any of the following counts (only one of which need be satisfied):

(i) it is an unlisted company;
(ii) Bob is an employee of the company, albeit part-time;
(iii) he can exercise at least 5% of the voting rights.

[*TCGA 1992, Sch A1 para 4(2), para 6(1), para 22(1); FA 2000, s 67(4)(5)(7)*].

Therefore, $\frac{1}{2}$ of the gain (£2,700) qualifies for taper relief at the non-business asset rate and $\frac{1}{2}$ (£2,700) at the business asset rate.

The number of complete years in the qualifying holding period (6.4.98–6.4.02) is four. However, there is a one-year addition in the case of the non-business asset portion of the gain, as the shares were acquired before 17 March 1998. [*TCGA 1992, s 2A(8)(9); FA 1998, s 121(1); FA 2000, s 66(3)(4)*].

Taper Relief 227.3

The taxable gain is computed as follows

	Business asset £	Non-business asset £	Total £
Chargeable gain	2,700	2,700	5,400
Less Taper relief @ 75%/15%	2,025	405	2,430
Taxable gain	£675	£2,295	£2,970

Notes

(*a*) Amendments were made by *FA 2000, s 67* and by *FA 2001, Sch 26* to the definition of a business asset for taper relief purposes. These have effect for determining the status of an asset at any time after 5 April 2000. They do not affect the status of an asset at any time before 6 April 2000 even if that status falls to be determined as a result of a disposal on or after that date. [*FA 2000, s 67(7)*]. On the disposal of an asset which became a business asset on 6 April 2000 by virtue of the *FA 2000* or *FA 2001* changes, the gain must be apportioned using the rules illustrated in (A) above.

(*b*) As the disposal took place after 5 April 2002 and the qualifying holding period consisted of at least two complete years, the whole of the business asset portion of the gain qualifies for taper relief at the maximum rate of 75%. [*TCGA 1992, s 2A(5); FA 2002, s 46*].

(*c*) Other than for the purposes of corporation tax on chargeable gains, indexation allowance is frozen at its April 1998 level. Therefore, the indexation factor for April 1998 is used in respect of disposals in a later month (and expenditure incurred in April 1998 or later does not attract indexation allowance at all).

227.3 **INTER-SPOUSE TRANSFERS** [*TCGA 1992, Sch A1 para 15; FA 1998, s 121(2)(4), Sch 20*]

Note. See 215.1 MARRIED PERSONS as regards inter-spouse transfers generally.

(A) Assets other than shares and securities

Jack and Jill are a married couple living together. Jack owns a property which he acquired for residential letting in May 1996 for £60,000. On 7 April 2000, he gives the property to Jill who thereafter uses it as offices in her profession as a solicitor. Three years later, Jill decides to rent larger office premises and sells the property on 8 April 2003 for £110,000. She makes no other disposals in 2003/04. The indexation factor for the period May 1996 to April 1998 (note (*d*)) is 0.063.

Jack's disposal in 2000/01 is at no gain/no loss as follows

	£	£
Deemed consideration		63,780
Less: Cost of acquisition	60,000	
Indexation allowance £60,000 × 0.063	3,780	63,780
Gain/loss		Nil

227.3 Taper Relief

The gain on Jill's disposal in 2003/04 is computed as follows

	£
Proceeds	110,000
Less Cost of acquisition (as above)	63,780
Chargeable gain subject to taper relief	46,220
Less Taper relief (see below)	24,497
Taxable gain subject to annual exemption	£21,723

The relevant period of ownership for taper relief purposes is the five years from 6 April 1998 to 8 April 2003. During that period, the asset was a non-business asset for two years (6 April 1998 to 6 April 2000) and a business asset for three years (7 April 2000 to 8 April 2003). Therefore, two-fifths of the gain qualifies for non-business asset taper relief and three-fifths for business asset taper relief (see also 227.2 above) as follows.

The number of complete years in the qualifying holding period (6.4.98–8.4.03) is five. However, there is a one-year addition in the case of the non-business asset portion of the gain, as the property was acquired before 17 March 1998. [*TCGA 1992, s 2A(8)(9); FA 1998, s 121(1); FA 2000, s 66(3)(4)*].

	£
(£46,220 × $\frac{2}{5}$ = £18,488) @ 20%	3,698
(£46,220 × $\frac{3}{5}$ = £27,732) @ 75%(maximum)	20,799
Total taper relief	£24,497

Notes

(a) Taper relief applies as if the time when the transferee spouse acquired the asset was the time when the transferor spouse acquired it.

(b) The question of whether an asset (other than shares or securities) was a business asset at any specified time in the combined period of ownership after 5 April 1998 is determined by reference to the use to which it was put by the spouse holding it at that time.

(c) As regards that part of the combined period of ownership which falls *before* the inter-spouse transfer, the asset is also a business asset at any time if it then qualifies as such by reference to the spouse to whom it is eventually transferred, i.e. where an asset owned by one spouse is used in the other's business (not illustrated in this example).

(d) Other than for the purposes of corporation tax on chargeable gains, indexation allowance is frozen at its April 1998 level. Therefore, the indexation factor for April 1998 is used in respect of disposals in a later month (and expenditure incurred in April 1998 or later does not attract indexation allowance at all). See 210 INDEXATION.

(B) Shares and securities

George and Kelly are a married couple living together. They each subscribed for and received 2,500 £1 shares at par (representing $2\frac{1}{2}$% of the voting rights) in Getrichquick.com plc when that company was floated on the London Stock Exchange on 30 April 2000. On 29 April 2003, Kelly gives her shares to George. On 30 April 2004, George sells his 5,000 shares for £25,000.

Throughout his ownership of Getrichquick.com shares, George is an employee of that company, but his wife is not.

Kelly's disposal in 2003/04 is for a deemed consideration of £2,500 thus producing no gain and no loss.

The gain on George's disposal in 2004/05 is computed as follows

	£
Proceeds (5,000 shares)	25,000
Less Cost of acquisition (£1 per share)	5,000
Chargeable gain subject to taper relief	20,000
Less Taper relief (£20,000 @ 75% — see below)	15,000
Taxable gain subject to annual exemption	£5,000

The relevant period of ownership is the four years to 30 April 2004. During the whole of that period, the company was a qualifying company by reference to George, by virtue of his being its employee. Therefore, the whole of the gain qualifies for business asset taper relief. The qualifying holding period is those same four years. Therefore, the gain qualifies in full for 75% business asset taper relief.

Notes

(*a*) Taper relief applies as if the time when the transferee spouse acquired the asset was the time when the transferor spouse acquired it.

(*b*) As regards shares and securities, the question of whether the asset was a business asset at any specified time in the combined period of ownership is determined only by reference to the individual making the ultimate disposal.

(*c*) If, instead, George had given his shares to Kelly and she made the ultimate sale, the gain would have qualified for business asset taper relief only from the date of the gift as only from that date would the company be a qualifying company by reference to her (due to her share of the voting rights then being 5%). The gain would have required apportionment using the method in (A) above.

227.4 Taper Relief

227.4 POSTPONED GAINS [*TCGA 1992, Sch A1 para 16; FA 1998, s 121(2)(4), Sch 20*]

Gordon disposes of shares in A Ltd, his family trading company, in August 2002, realising a chargeable gain (after indexation to April 1998) of £50,000. He had held the shares since 1989 and they qualified as a business asset for the purposes of taper relief. He acquires shares in a Venture Capital Trust in March 2003 for £60,000 and makes a claim for deferral relief under *TCGA 1992, SC Sch* (see IT 28.3(B) VENTURE CAPITAL TRUSTS). He makes no other disposals in 2002/03 and wishes to leave sufficient gains in charge to cover his annual exemption.

The A Ltd shares were held for four complete years after 5 April 1998. The taper is therefore 75% (see the table at *TCGA 1992, s 2A(5) as amended by FA 2002, s 46*).

The gain is computed as follows

	£
Gain before taper relief	50,000
Less Deferred on reinvestment in VCT (optimum amount)	19,200*
	30,800
Less Taper relief £30,800 × 75%	23,100
Tapered gain for 2002/03 covered by annual exemption	£7,700

* £7,700 × $\dfrac{100}{100 - 75}$ = £30,800. £50,000 − £30,800 = £19,200.

In June 2005, Gordon sells his VCT shares. **The deferred gain becomes chargeable in 2005/06 and is computed as follows**

	£
Deferred gain before taper relief	19,200
Less Taper relief £19,200 × 75% (April 1998 to August 2002)	14,400
Taxable gain subject to annual exemption	£4,800

Notes

(*a*) Taper relief on the deferred gain becoming chargeable is given by reference to the time and circumstances of the original disposal, not the disposal which brings the gain into charge. This applies in a number of circumstances in which gains are deferred or postponed, as listed at *TCGA 1992, Sch A1 para 16*. For a further example, see 207.3(A) ENTERPRISE INVESTMENT SCHEME.

(*b*) A special rule applies in cases of serial EIS reinvestment. See 207.3(B) ENTERPRISE INVESTMENT SCHEME.

228 Wasting Assets

Cross-references. See also 213.3 LAND, 223.3 ROLLOVER RELIEF.

228.1 GENERAL [TCGA 1992, ss 44–47]

V bought an aircraft on 31 May 1997 at a cost of £90,000 for use in his air charter business. It has been agreed that V's non-business use of the aircraft amounts to one-tenth, on a flying hours basis, and capital allowances and running costs have accordingly been restricted for income tax purposes. On 1 February 2003, V sells the aircraft for £185,000. The aircraft is agreed as having a useful life of 20 years at the date it was acquired. The indexation factor for May 1997 to April 1998 (note (*b*)) is 0.036.

	£
Amount qualifying for capital allowances	
Relevant portion of disposal consideration $\frac{9}{10} \times £185,000$	166,500
Relevant portion of acquisition cost $\frac{9}{10} \times £90,000$	81,000
Unindexed gain	85,500
Indexation allowance £81,000 × 0.036	2,916
Chargeable gain 2002/03 (subject to TAPER RELIEF (227))	£82,584

		£
Amount not qualifying for capital allowances		
Relevant portion of disposal consideration $\frac{1}{10} \times £185,000$		18,500
Relevant portion of acquisition cost		
$\frac{1}{10} \times £90,000$	9,000	
Deduct Wasted £9,000 × $\dfrac{5y\ 8m}{20y}$	2,550	6,450
Gain		£12,050

The whole of the £12,050 is exempt.

The total chargeable gain (subject to taper relief) is therefore   £82,584

Notes

(*a*) Gains on tangible moveable property which are wasting assets not qualifying for capital allowances are exempt (and any losses would not be allowable). [*TCGA 1992, s 45*].

(*b*) Other than for the purposes of corporation tax on chargeable gains, indexation allowance is frozen at its April 1998 level. Therefore, the indexation factor for April 1998 is used in respect of disposals in a later month (and expenditure incurred in April 1998 or later does not attract indexation allowance at all). See 210 INDEXATION.

228.2 Wasting Assets

228.2 **OPTIONS** [*TCGA 1992, ss 44, 46, 146*]

Cross-reference. See also 206.5 DISPOSAL.

(A) Unquoted shares
On 1 July 2000, R grants C an option to purchase unquoted shares held by R. The cost of the option is £600 to purchase 10,000 shares at £5 per share, the option to be exercised by 31 December 2002. On 1 September 2002 C assigns the option to W for £500.

	£	£
Disposal consideration		500
Acquisition cost	600	
Deduct Wasted £600 × $\frac{26}{30}$	520	80
Chargeable gain		£420

Note
(*a*) Other than for the purposes of corporation tax on chargeable gains, expenditure incurred in April 1998 or later does not attract indexation allowance). See 210 INDEXATION.

(B) Traded options
On 1 December 2002, C purchases 6-month options on T plc shares for £1,000. Two weeks later, he sells the options, which are quoted on the Stock Exchange, for £1,200.

	£
Disposal consideration	1,200
Allowable cost	1,000
Chargeable gain	£200

Note
(*a*) The wasting asset rules do not apply to traded options. [*TCGA 1992, s 146*].

228.3 **LIFE INTERESTS** [*TCGA 1992, s 44(1)(d)*]

(A)
N is a beneficiary under a settlement. On 30 June 1988, when her actuarially estimated life expectancy was 40 years, she sold her life interest to an unrelated individual, R, for £50,000. N dies on 31 December 2002, and the life interest is extinguished.

R will have an allowable loss for 2002/03 as follows

	£	£
Disposal consideration on death of N		Nil
Allowable cost	50,000	
Deduct wasted		
$\dfrac{14\text{y } 6\text{m}}{40\text{y}} \times £50,000$	18,125	
		31,875
Allowable loss		£31,875

Note

(*a*) The amount of the cost wasted is computed by reference to the predictable life, not the actual life, of the wasting asset.

228.3 Wasting Assets

(B)

Assume the facts to be as in (A) above except that the sale of the life interest was on 30 June 1981 and N's life expectancy *at that date* was 40 years. The value of the life interest remained at £50,000 at 31 March 1982.

Calculation without re-basing

	£	£
Disposal consideration on death of N		Nil
Allowable cost	50,000	
Deduct wasted		
$\dfrac{21y\ 6m}{40} \times £50,000$	26,875	
		23,125
Loss		£23,125

Calculation with re-basing

	£	£
Disposal consideration		Nil
Market value 31.3.82	50,000	
Deduct wasted		
$£50,000 \times \dfrac{20y\ 9m\ (31.3.82 - 31.12.02)}{39y\ 3m\ \text{(life expectancy at 31.3.82)}}$	26,433	
		23,567
Loss		£23,567
Allowable loss 2002/03		£23,125

Note

(*a*) The second of the above calculations shows how the wasting assets provisions interact with the re-basing provisions of *TCGA 1992, s 35*. Where, by virtue of the re-basing rules, an asset is deemed to have been disposed of and re-acquired at its market value on 31 March 1982, that market value must be reduced in accordance with the period of ownership *after* that date and the predictable life of the wasting asset *at* that date.

Table of Statutes

1970 Taxes Management Act		s 2A(8)(9)	226.1; 227.2(B); 227.3(A)
s 59B(4)	212.1	s 3	201.2; 224.1
s 59C	212.1	s 4	215.1
s 86	212.1	(1AA)	224.1
s 88	212.1(B)	s 10	218.3
		ss 19, 20	202.4
1979 Capital Gains Tax Act		s 22	206.4
s 44	210.1(D)	(1)	206.3
		s 23	206.4; 206.4(B)(C)
1980 Finance Act		(1)	206.4(E)
s 79	204.2; 209.1(C)	(2)	206.4(D)
		s 25	218.1; 218.3
		(1)(3)(8)	218.3
1988 Income and Corporation Taxes Act		s 29	202.1
s 34	213.3(C)	s 30	202.2; 202.3
s 87	213.3(G)	s 31	202.3
s 122	216.1	s 35	204.1; 213.3(E); 219.5; 228.3(B)
s 247	202.3	(1)	204.1(A)
s 249	225.7	(2)	203.1(A); 203.3(B); 204.1(A); 213.3(E)
s 251(2)–(4)	225.7	(3)	203.3(C); 204.1(A); 206.2(A)
s 282A	215.2	(*a*)	203.3(A)(B)(C); 213.3(E)
s 282B	215.2	(*b*)	203.1(B); 203.3(D)
s 291	207.3(A)	(*c*)	203.1(B); 204.1(B)
s 291B	207.3(A)	(*d*)	204.2; 210.2(A)
s 312	207.3	(4)	203.3(B); 204.1(A)
(1A)(*a*)	207.1; 207.2(B)	(5)	203.1(A); 204.1(A)(B); 206.2(B); 218.1; 222.2(B)
s 575	214.3	(7)	219.1
s 576	214.8	s 38	206.1(A); 209.1(B)
(4)	214.3	s 39	206.1(A); 213.3(G)
(4A)(4B)	214.3	s 41	206.1(B); 218.2
s 686(1A)	224.1	s 42	203.3(E); 206.2; 213.3(B); 215.2; 225.3
s 740(6)	217.1(D)	(4)	206.2(A)
Sch 18 para 1(5)	225.6	s 44	206.5; 228.1; 228.2
		(1)(*d*)	228.3
1988 Finance Act		s 45	228.1; 228.1(A)
ss 130–132	218.1	s 46	206.5; 228.1; 228.2
		s 47	228.1
1991 Finance Act		s 53	207.1(B); 210.1; 213.4
s 72	201.1(A)	(1)	206.4(E)
1992 Taxation of Chargeable Gains Act			
s 2(2)	201.2		
(4)–(8)	201.2; 214.2; 217.1(B)		
s 2A	223.1(A)(C); 223.2(A); 227.1		
(1)(2)	203.3(A)(B)(C)		
(5)	227.2(B); 227.3		
(6)	227.1(B)		

Table of Statutes

1992 Taxation of Chargeable Gains Act

s 53(1)(*b*)	210.1(D)
(1A)	206.4(E); 207.1;
	209.1(C); 209.3(A); 210.1(B)
(2A)	210.1(D)
(3)	206.4(E); 213.2(B)
s 54	210.1
(1)	207.1
(1A)	207.1; 209.1(C);
	209.3(A); 210.1(B)
(4)(*b*)	213.3(F)
s 55	210.1
(1)(2)	203.1(A); 203.3(A)(C);
	204.1(A); 206.2(A);
	210.1(C); 213.3(E); 226.2(A)
(5)(6)	210.2(A)(C)
(7)–(9)	210.2(C)
s 56	210.1
(2)	210.2(A)–(D)
(3)	210.2(D)
(4)	210.2(D)
s 57	206.4(E); 213.2(B)
s 58	210.2(A); 215.1;
	215.1(B)
s 59	219.1
s 62	210.1(C)
s 67	209.1(C)
s 70	224.3
s 71	224.4
(2)–(2D)	224.4(B)
s 72	224.5
s 76	224.5(B)
s 77	201.2; 214.2; 224.1;
	224.2; 224.3(B)
(2)–(5)	224.1
(6)	224.2
ss 78, 79	224.1; 224.2; 224.3(B)
s 86	201.2; 214.2
s 87	201.2; 217
s 89(2)	201.2
s 91(3)–(5)	217
ss 91–93	217
s 97	217
s 104	226.2
s 105	205.2; 225.3(C);
	226.1; 226.2; 226.2(B)
ss 105A, 105B	226.1
s 106	205.2
s 106A	221.1; 225.3(C); 226.1
(5)	226.2(B)
s 107	226.2
(3)–(6)	226.2(B)
s 108	226.2
(1)	221.1
s 109	226.2
(2)	225.3(C)
(4)	203.1; 203.1(A)
(5)	203.1
s 110	226.2
s 110A	225.2(A)(B);
	225.3(A)(B)(C); 225.7; 226.1
s 115	221
s 116	221; 221.2
(10)	221.2
s 117	214.3;
	221; 221.1
(1)	221.1; 225.6
(7)(*b*)(8)	221.1
s 119	210.3
s 122	225.4(A); 225.8(A);
	225.8(B)
(2)	225.8(B)
s 123	225.8(B)
(1)	225.3
s 126	225.1; 225.2
s 127	221.2;
	224.1; 225.1(A); 225.2;
	225.3(C); 225.4(A); 227.2
s 128	221.2; 225.1;
	225.2; 225.3(C); 225.7
(4)	225.3
s 129	221.2; 225.1;
	225.1(A)
s 130	221.2; 225.1;
	225.1(B); 225.2
s 131	225.1
s 132	225.4(E); 225.6
s 135	225.4;
	225.4(A)
s 136	225.5
s 137	225.4
s 138	225.4; 225.5
s 138A	225.4(E)
s 140	218.4
s 141	225.7
s 142	225.7
s 144	206.5
s 145	206.5
s 146	228.2; 228.2(B)
s 150A(1)	207.2;
	207.3; 207.3(B)
(2)(2A)(3)	207.1; 207.2
s 150D	207.3(B)
s 152	205.2;
	223; 223.1
(7)(9)	223.2(B)
s 153	223; 223.2(A)
s 154	223; 223.3

Table of Statutes

s 155	223	Sch A1 para 13(3)	206.5
ss 156–158	223	15	227.3
s 162	209.2(B); 209.3(A)(B)	16	207.3(A);
s 162A	209.3(B)		220.2; 227.3
s 163	222	22(1)	227.2(B)
(1)(2)	222.1(B);	22A	209.2(C)
	222.2(F)	Sch 1 para 2	224.1
(3)	222.1(B)	Sch 2 para 1	203.1
(4)	222.2(F)	2	203.1
(5)(7)	222.1(C)	(1)	203.1(B)
(8)	222.2(E)	3	203.1
s 164	222	4	203.1;
(3)–(5)	222.2(C)		203.1(A)
s 164A	209.3	5	203.1
s 165	209.1(C); 209.2;	6	203.1
	222.3(D)	7, 8	203.1
(10)	209.1(C)	9–15	203.2
s 171	210.2(C)(D); 218.2	16	203.3;
s 172	218.2		203.3(D)
s 176	202.5	(3)–(5)(8)	203.3(E)
ss 185, 187	218.1	17, 18	203.3
ss 201–203	216.1	19	203.3
s 217	225.9	(1)	203.3(C)
s 222	220.1; 220.1(B)	(2)	203.3(D)
(5)	220.2	(3)	203.3(C)(D)
s 223	220.1	Sch 3 para 1	210.2(A)
(1)	220.1(A)(B)	4(1)	203.3(E);
(3)(a)(b)	220.1(B)		206.2(B); 225.4(A)
(4)(7)	220.1(A)(B)	(2)	206.4(D)
s 224(1)(2)	220.3	6	203.3(B)
s 225	224.4(A)	7	204.1(A)
s 242	206.2(D); 213.1	8, 9	204.1(A)
(2)	213.1	Sch 4	204.2;
s 243	213.2; 213.2(B)		209.2(B); 209.3(A)
ss 244–246	213.2	para 1(a)	204.2
s 247	213.2; 213.2(A)	2	204.2
s 248	213.2	4	220.2
s 260	209.1; 224.3(A)	5–9	204.2
(5)	209.1(B)	Sch 5B	207.3
(7)	209.1(C)	Sch 5BA	207.3; 207.3(B)
s 262	202.4	Sch 5C	227.3
(2)	208.1(A)	Sch 6	222
(3)	208.1(B)	para 1	222.1(C)
(4)	208.1(C)	(2)	222.2(F)
s 283	211.1	2	222.1(D)
Sch A1	227.1	3	222.1(B)
para 3	227.2;	5(2)(4)	222.1(B)
	227.2(A)	6	222.2(A)(B)
4	227.2(B)	7	222.2(A)
(2)	227.2(B)	8	222.2(B)
5(2)	220.3	10	222.2(D)(E)
6	227.2(B)	11	222.2(F)
(1)	227.2(B)	12	222.2(A)(B)
(2)(3)	227.2(B)	(5)(6)	222.2(F)

Table of Statutes

1992 Taxation of Chargeable Gains Act

Sch 6 para 13	222.1(B); 222.2(C)
14	222.3(A)(B)
15	222.3(B)(D)
16	222.3(C)(D)
(3)(4)	223.3(D)
Sch 7	209.2
para 5	209.2(B)
7	209.2(C)
8	209.2(B)
(3)	209.2(C)
Sch 8 para 1	213.3(A)(D)(E)(F)(G)
(2)	213.3(A)
(4)(*b*)	213.3(F)
2	213.3(B)(C)
4	213.3(H)(J)
5	213.3(C)(H)(J)
(2)	213.3(H)(J)
Sch 11 para 10(1)	202.2
(2)	202.3

1993 Finance Act

s 87	222; 222.1(C); 222.2(A)(B)(C)(F)
Sch 7 para 1	209.2
Pt I	222; 222.1(C); 222.2(A)(B)(C)(F)
Sch 23 Pt III(7)	222

1994 Finance Act

s 92	222; 222.1(B)
s 93(1)(2)	206.1(B); 206.2(D); 206.3(C); 207.1(B); 210.1; 210.1(D)
(3)	207.1(B); 210.1
(4)	210.1; 210.2(C)
(5)	210.1; 210.2(A)
(6)	226.2(B)
(11)	210.2(A)
s 193	212.1
s 194	212.1
s 196	212.1
s 199	212.1
s 210	214.3
Sch 12	214.4
Sch 15 paras 28–30	207.1; 207.2; 207.3
Sch 19 para 20	212.1
46	211.1
Sch 20 para 8	214.3
Sch 26 Pt V(23)	211.1

1995 Finance Act

s 50	221.1
ss 66, 67	207
s 74	224.1; 224.2
s 109	212.1
s 110	212.1
Sch 13	207
para 2(1)	207.1, 207.2
(2)	207.2
(3)	207.1
4(3)(4)	207.3
Sch 17 paras 27–29	224.1; 224.2

1996 Finance Act

ss 104, 105	221.1
s 141(4)(6)	213.2
s 176	222
Sch 14 para 61	221.1
Sch 20 para 46	202.2; 202.3
47(*a*)	202.2; 202.3
52	225.8(B)
57	202.4
59	220.2
60	220.3
66	222.1(B)
(4)	222.2(D)(E)
Sch 21 para 37	213.1
38	213.2
42(1)(2)	203.1
(3)	203.3
43	204.2
44(1)(2)	222.1(D)
(3)	222.1(B)
(4)	222.2(F)
(5)	222.3(C)(D)
Sch 38 para 6(1)(2)(9)	214.3
Sch 39 para 5	224.5
7	222.3(A)
Sch 41 Pt V	
(3)	221.1
(10)	220.2

1997 Finance Act

s 88	225.6
s 89	225.4(E)
s 90	107.3
s 92(5)(6)	211.1

1997 Finance (No 2) Act

s 34	201.1(A)
Sch 4 para 24	201.1(A)

Table of Statutes

1998 Finance Act

s 40	213.3(C)
s 74	207.2(B); 207.3
s 80	214.3
(3)(5)	214.3
s 120	224.1
s 121	206(E); 206.5; 207.3(A)
(1)	203.3(A)(B)(C); 207.1; 223.1(A)(C); 223.2(A); 226.1; 227.1(B); 227.2; 227.3; 227.2(B); 227.3(A)
(2)	207.1; 221.2; 226.1; 227.2; 227.3
(3)	201.2; 207.1; 217.1(B)
(4)	201.2; 203.3(A)(B)(C); 217.1(B); 221.2; 226.1; 227.2; 227.3; 227.4
s 122(1)	206.4(E); 209.1(C); 209.3(A); 210.1; 219.1
(2)	209.1(C); 209.3; 210.1
(3)	209.1(C); 209.3; 210.1
(4)	206.4(E); 219.1
(5)	206.5
(6)	210.1
(7)	206.4(E); 206.5
s 123	226.2(A)
s 124(1)	225.3(C); 226.1; 226.2(B)
(2)	225.3(C); 226.1
(7)	225.3(C); 226.1
(8)	226.2(B)
s 125(2)(4)(5)	225.2(A)(B); 225.3(A)(B)(C); 225.7; 226.1
s 126	225.7
s 130	217.1
s 144	206.5
Sch 5 para 15	213.3(C)
63	213.3(C)(H)(J)
Sch 13 para 6	207.3
12	207.2(B)
24(1)	207.1
paras 26–36	207.3; 206.5; 207.3; 220.2
Sch 20	207.3(A); 227.1; 227.2; 227.3; 227.4
Sch 21 para 2	201.2; 217.1(B)
3	201.2
Sch 27 Part III(31)	222

1999 Finance Act

s 26(3)	224.1
s 72	207.3; 207.3(B)
s 73	207.3
s 75	224.4(B)
Sch 7	207.3; 207.3(B)
Sch 8	207.3

2000 Finance Act

s 37	201.1
s 63(2)(3)	214.3
s 66	223.1(C); 223.2(A); 226.1; 227.1
(2)	227.4
(3)	227.2; 227.2(B); 227.3(A)
(4)	227.2; 227.2(B); 227.3(A); 227.4
s 67	227.2(B)
(4)	227.2(B); IT 27.5
(5)	227.2(B)
(7)	227.2(B)
Sch 16 para 3(3)	214.3
Sch 17 para 6(4)	207.1
7 (2)(3)	207.3
8	207.1; 207.3
Sch 29 para 3	218.2
12	206.2(B)
18	205.2

2001 Capital Allowances Act

Sch 2 para 78	206.2(B)

2001 Finance Act

s 78	227; 227.2(B)
Sch 15 para 10	207.3(A)
25–37	207.3
38	214.3
40	207.3; 207.3(A)
Sch 26	227
para 3	227.2(B)

2002 Finance Act

s 45	225.49
s 46	206.4(E); 227.1; 227.2(B)
s 49	209.3(B)
s 50(1)(2)	226.1
s 51	201.2; 214.2
s 84	209.2(B); 209.3(A); 223.1(A)(D)
Sch 9 para 1	225.4
2	225.5
7	225.4; 225.5
Sch 10 para 9	209.2(C)

Table of Statutes

2002 Finance Act

Sch 11 para 2	201.2; 214.2	Sch 29 para 95	209.2(B); 209.3(A); 223.1(D)
3	214.2; 224.2	paras 117, 118	209.2(B); 209.3(A)
7	201.2; 214.2	para 121	209.2(B); 209.3(A)
8	201.2; 214.2; 224.2	130	223.1(D)
Sch 29	209.2(B); 209.3(A); 223.1(A)	132	223.1(A)(D)
		137	223.1(A)(D)

Index

This index is referenced to chapter and paragraph number within the book. The entries in bold capitals are chapter headings in the text.

A

Accrued income scheme	
CGT effect	209.3; 221.1
Allowable and non-allowable	
expenditure	206.1
ANNUAL RATES AND	
EXEMPTIONS	**201**
losses, interaction with	201.2
—attributed settlement	
gains	201.2(B)
married persons	215.1
settlements	224.1
ANTI-AVOIDANCE	**202**
disposal to connected	
person	202.4
gains of offshore settlements	217.1
groups of companies	
—depreciatory transactions	202.5
value-shifting	202.1; 202.2; 202.3
Assets disposed of in series	
of transactions	202.4
ASSETS HELD ON 6 APRIL	
1965	**203**
buildings	203.3(B)
chattels	203.3(A)
land and buildings	203.3(B)
land reflecting development	
value	203.2
part disposals after	
5 April 1965	203.3(F)
quoted shares and securities	203.1
time apportionment	203.3
unquoted shares	203.3(C)(D)(E)
ASSETS HELD ON 31 MARCH	
1982	**204**
deferred gains, relief	
for	204.2
general computation of	
gains/losses	204.1
no gain/no loss	
disposals	210.2(A)(C)
part disposals before	
6 April 1988	206.2(B)
partnerships, held by	219.1
private residences	220.1(A)(B)
short leases	213.3(E)
wasting assets	228.3(B)

B

Bondwashing	
CGT effect	221.1
Building Societies	
conversions and takeovers	225.9
Business assets	
deferment of chargeable gain	
on replacement of assets	223
disposal on retirement	222
gift of	209.2
taper relief	227.2(A)(B)
transfer to a company	209.3

C

Capital allowances	
capital gains, effect on	206.1(B); 218.2; 227.1
Capital losses	
See Losses	
Chattels	**208.1**
held on 6.4.65	203.3(A)
COMPANIES	**205**
capital losses	205.1
exchange of securities	225.4
reconstruction schemes	225.5
shares — acquisitions and disposals	
within short period	205.2
transfer of assets to non-resident	
company	218.3
Companies (migration of)	**218.1**
Compensation	
CGT on receipt of	206.4; 213.2
—taper relief	206.4(E)
Compulsory acquisition of	
land	213.2

D

Deferment of chargeable gain	
See Hold-over reliefs and Rollover relief	
Deferred consideration	**206.3** (B)(C); **225.4(C)**
Depreciatory transactions	**202.5**
DISPOSAL	**206**

Index

allowable expenditure	206.1	**G**	
—effect of capital allowances	206.1(B)	**Gifts**	**209**
capital sums derived from assets	206.3	assets held on 31 March 1982	204.2
—deferred consideration	206.3(B)(C); 225.4(C)	business assets deferment of gain	209.2 209.1; 209.2; 223.3
compulsory acquisition of land	213.2	**H**	
connected persons	202.4		
options	206.5; 228.2	**HERD BASIS**	**7**
part disposal	206.2; 206.3(A); 212.1; 213.2; 215.2	**HOLD-OVER RELIEFS** *See also* Rollover Relief	**209**
—assets held on 6.4.65	203.3(E)	assets held on 31 March 1982	204.2
—small part disposals of land	213.1	chargeable lifetime transfers	209.1(A)
premiums payable under leases	213.3	disposal consideration gifts	209.1(B)
receipt of compensation	206.4; 213.2	—business assets —chargeable lifetime	209.2
—capital sum exceeding allowable expenditure	206.4(D)	transfers IHT relief	209.1 209.1(C)
—compulsory acquisition	213.2	transfer of business to	
—indexation allowance	206.4(E)	company	209.3
—part application of capital sum received	206.4(C)	—election to disapply relief	209.3(B)
—restoration using insurance moneys	206.4(B)	—incorporation relief **Husband and wife**	209.3(A)
sets, assets forming	202.4	*See* Married Persons	
value passing out of shares	202.1; 202.2; 202.3	**I**	
Dwelling house, gains on	**220**	**Incorporation relief**	**209.3; 209.3(A)**
E		election to disapply **INDEXATION**	209.3(B) **210**
Earn-outs	**225.4(C)**	allowance on receipt of compensation	206.4(E)
ENTERPRISE INVESTMENT SCHEME	**207**	assets held on 31.3.82 general rules	210.1(C) 210.1
capital gains and losses —disposal more than three		indexation factor, calculation of	
years after acquisition	207.1; 207.2	—companies —individuals, etc.	210.1(A) 210.1(B)
deferral relief	207.3	no gain/no loss	
—serial investors	207.3(B)	disposals	210.2(A)–(D)
EXEMPTIONS AND RELIEFS	**208**	—inter-spouse transfers	210.2(A)(B)
chattels	208.1	—intra-group transfers	210.2(C)(D)
dwelling house	220	restriction	210.1(D)
qualifying corporate bonds	221	shares and securities,	
tangible movable asset	208.1	identification rules	226.2

Index

Intangible assets
  rollover relief 112.3
  —interaction with
    CGT rollover relief 223.1(D)
Inter-spouse transfers 210.1(D);
  210.2(A); 215.1; 215.2;
  227.3
  taper relief 227.3
INTEREST ON OVERPAID
  TAX 211
INTEREST ON UNPAID TAX 212

L

LAND 213
  compulsory purchase 213.2
  development value, reflecting 203.2
  held on 6.4.65 203.2; 203.3(B)
  leases 213.3
  —assignment of short
    lease 213.3(D)–(G)
  —grant of long lease 213.3(B)
  —grant of short lease 213.3(C)
  —premiums on short
    leases 213.3(C)(G)(H)(J)
  —short leases which are not
    wasting assets 213.3(A)
  —sub-lease granted out of
    short lease 213.3(H)(J)
  small part disposals 213.1
Leases
  See Land
LOSSES 214
  capital losses 205.1; 214
  —indexation losses 210.1(D)
  —set-off against settlement
    gains 214.2
  —tangible movable assets 208.1(B)
  chattels 208.1(B)
  interaction with annual
    exempt amount 201.2
  unlisted companies 214.3
  unquoted shares, capital losses available
    for set-off against
    income 214.3

M

MARRIED PERSONS 215
  jointly owned assets 215.2
  no gain/no loss
    transfers 210.2(A)(B);
      215.1; 215.2
  retirement relief 222.3(C)(D)

taper relief 227.3
Migration of companies 218.1
MINERAL ROYALTIES 216

N

Non-resident, company
  becoming 218.1
Non-resident company, transfer
  of assets to 218.3
Non-residents trading through UK
  branch or agency 218.2

O

OFFSHORE SETTLEMENTS 217
  gains attributed to UK
    beneficiary 217.1
Options 206.5; 228.2
Overdue tax
  See Interest on Unpaid Tax
OVERSEAS MATTERS 218
  company migration 218.1
  non-residents trading through
    UK branch or agency 218.2
  overseas resident settlements 217
  transfer of assets to non-
    resident company 218.3
  UK beneficiary of an overseas
    resident settlement 217.1

P

Part disposals
  See Disposal
PARTNERSHIPS 219
  accounting adjustments 219.3
  assets 219.1
  —distribution in kind 219.6
  changes in partners 219.2–219.4
  changes in sharing ratios 219.2–219.5
  consideration outside
    accounts 219.4
  disposal of partnership
    asset to partner 219.6
  indexation 210.2(A)(C); 219.2
  retirement relief 222.2(E)
  revaluation of assets 219.3;
    219.5
  shares acquired in stages 219.5
Premiums on short
  leases 213.3(C)(G)(H)
PRIVATE RESIDENCES 220
  capital gains tax exemption 220
  —part business use 220.3

Index

Q

QUALIFYING CORPORATE BONDS   **221**
- conversion of securities   225.6
- definition   221.1
- reorganisation of share capital   221.2

R

Repayments of tax, interest on   **211.1**
Residence
See Private Residences
Residence and domicile
- non-resident company, transfer of assets to   218.2
- offshore settlements   217.1

RETIREMENT RELIEF   **222**
- amount of relief   222.3
- associated disposals   222.2(C)–(E)
- capital distribution   222.2(F)
- earlier business periods   222.3(A)
- extent of relief   222.1
- full-time working officer or employee   222.1(C)
- gains qualifying for relief   222.2
- gifts hold-over relief, interaction with   209.2
- ill-health grounds   222.1(B)
- married persons   222.3(C)(D)
- non-business chargeable assets   222.2(A)(B)
- partnerships   222.2(E)
- personal asset used by company business   222.2(D)
- qualifying period   222.1(B)
- separate disposals   222.3(B)
- share for share exchange   222.1(D)
- shares in holding company   222.2(B)
- trustees   222.2(C)

ROLLOVER RELIEF   **223**
- compulsory acquisition of land   213.2
- gifts   204.2; 209.1; 209.2; 224.3
- receipt of compensation not treated as disposal   206.4(B)–(E); 213.2
- replacement of business assets   223
  - —nature of relief   223.1
  - —partial relief   223.2
  - —taper relief   223.1(C)
  - —transition to intangible assets relief   223.1(D)
  - —wasting assets   223.3
- transfer of business to a company   209.3

Royalties and licences
- mineral royalties   216

S

Schedule A—property income
- premiums on leases   213.3

Securities
See Shares and Securities

Self-assessment
- interest on unpaid CGT   212.1

SETTLEMENTS   **224**
- annual exemptions   224.1
- attributed gains, set-off of personal losses against   214.2
- creation of   224.3
- death of life tenant   224.5; 228.3
- interest in possession   224.5
- offshore   217.1
- person becoming absolutely entitled to settled property   224.4
- rates of tax (CGT)   224.1
- settlor retaining an interest   224.2
- termination of an interest in possession   224.4; 224.5; 228.3

SETTLEMENTS WITH INTERESTS IN POSSESSION   **224.5**
- termination of an interest in possession   224.4; 224.5
- —losses   224.5(C)

SHARES AND SECURITIES   **225**
- acquisitions and disposals within short period   205.2
- bonus issues   225.2
- capital distributions   222.2(F); 225.8
- conversion of securities   225.6
- corporate bonds, qualifying   221
- deferred consideration   206.3(B)(C); 225.4(C)
- earn-outs   225.4(C)
- exchange of securities   225.4
- holdings at 6.4.65
  - —quoted   203.1

Index

—unquoted	203.3(C)(D)
qualifying corporate bonds	221
reconstruction schemes	225.5
reorganisation of share capital	221.2; 225.1
rights issues	225.1; 225.3
—sale of rights	225.8(B)
scrip dividends	225.7
time apportionment	
— unquoted shares	203.3(D)
transfer of business to a company for shares	209.3
unquoted shares	
—losses relieved against income	214.3
—time apportionment	203.3(D)
value passing out of	202.1; 202.2; 202.3

SHARES AND SECURITIES—
IDENTIFICATION RULES   **226**

after 5 April 1998	226.1
before 6 April 1998	226.2
companies	226.2
qualifying corporate bonds	221.1

T

Tangible movable property	**208.1**
TAPER RELIEF	**227**
basic rules	227.1(A)
business assets, part use as	227.2
compensation	206.4(E)
EIS deferral, interaction with	207.3(B)
FA 2000 changes	227.2(B)
inter-spouse transfers	227.3
losses	227.1(B)
postponed gains	227.3
rollover relief, interaction with	227.1(C)
Time apportionment	**203.3**
Transfer of business to a company	**209.3**
Trusts	
See Settlements	

V

Value-shifting	
anti-avoidance	202.1; 202.2; 202.3

W

WASTING ASSETS   **228**

eligible for capital allowances	228.1
leases	213.3
—assignment of short lease	213.3(D)–(G)
—grant of long lease	213.3(B)
—grant of short lease	213.3(C)
—short leases which are not wasting assets	213.3(A)
—sub-lease granted out of short lease	213.3(H)(J)
life interests	228.3
options	206.5; 228.2
rollover relief	223.3